W9-CLE-500

PAGE 162

The War Comes to Plum Street

The War Comes to

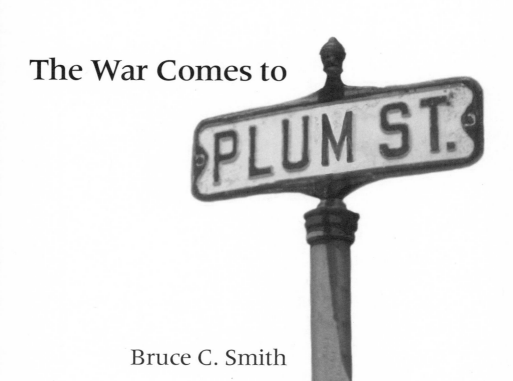

Bruce C. Smith

Indiana University Press
Bloomington & Indianapolis

This book is a publication of

Indiana University Press

601 North Morton Street

Bloomington, IN 47404-3797 USA

http://iupress.indiana.edu

Telephone orders	800-842-6796
Fax orders	812-855-7931
Orders by e-mail	iuporder@indiana.edu

© 2005 by Bruce C. Smith

All rights reserved

*No part of this book may be reproduced or utilized in
any form or by any means, electronic or mechanical,
including photocopying and recording, or by any
information storage and retrieval system, without
permission in writing from the publisher. The
Association of American University Presses'
Resolution on Permissions constitutes the
only exception to this prohibition.*

*The paper used in this publication meets the
minimum requirements of American National
Standard for Information Sciences—Permanence of
Paper for Printed Library Materials, ANSI Z39.48-1984.*

MANUFACTURED IN THE UNITED STATES OF AMERICA

Library of Congress Cataloging-in-Publication Data

The war comes to Plum Street / Bruce C. Smith.

p. cm.

Includes bibliographical references and index.

ISBN 0-253-34534-0 (alk. paper)

1. World War, 1939–1945—Indiana—New Castle.

2. New Castle (Ind.)—Biography. I. Title.

D769.85.I7N487 2005

977.2'64—dc22

2004016273

1 2 3 4 5 10 09 08 07 06 05

For the Moles daughters
Gemma, Maxine, Marie, and Wanda

Contents

Acknowledgments

Many people helped with the research for this project, which began in 1990. I would like to thank the staffs at the Henry County Library, Henry County Historical Society, and Indiana Basketball Hall of Fame, New Castle; Western Michigan University Library and staff, especially Natasha Alexander; Kalamazoo College; Sam Hyde of Hyde Brothers Books in Ft. Wayne, Indiana; and Dr. Barbara Allen for her patience in showing me how oral history ought to be done.

Many others contributed directly to my understanding of the war and its impact on the people who knew it, including

Harry Ridout
Fred and Charlotte Walker
Judy Capshaw VanMatre
Sarah Wright Madison
Charlie and Barbara Bunch Purvis
Phil and Martha Perry
Vernie Griffin
George and Esta Belle Woods
Chet and Mary Curry, who read the manuscript and made
    many valuable suggestions
Natasha A. Smith, who read the manuscript many times and
    provided expert proofreading
Cora Pope, who shared Keith's story and memory
Carolyn Nycum, a gal in wartime Kalamazoo, and Jim
    Nycum, B-17 waist gunner
Walter Dugan
Mabel Frogge Smith
Florence Smith Swann
Paul Borgman of the 448th AAA
Maj. Patrick Dugan, for information on the 448th AAA
Drs. Brad and Dedra Birzer, who never failed to encourage me
Dr. Kevin Smant, who read parts of the manuscript

Stewart and Connie Smith
Homer and Edith Smith
Betty Reece Smith
Jim and Karin Smith
Ethel Baltimore Moles
Julie Thompson Calhoun
William F. Dillon, 467th and 492nd Bomb Groups
Russell K. Bond, 467th and 492nd Bomb Groups
Maxine Moles Thompson
Marie Moles Hammond
Wanda Moles Grubbs
Gemma Moles Smith
Harold Rothrock
Jim and Delores Irwin
Barney Pfenninger
Jim and Sarah Bates

There are many no longer with us who contributed to this book over the years with memories they willingly shared, and with their love, including Edward M. Smith, Fred and Lillian Smith, Jess Moles, Fred Walker, Clay Grubbs, Phil Smith, and Orville Hammond.

If only I had known to ask all the unanticipated questions when they were still with us, this would have been a far better book, and more of their world would have been preserved to instruct those of us who came later.

Introduction

This is a different kind of book about World War II. Most of the many volumes on the epochal conflict are retrospective, examining events and people with hindsight unavailable to the participants at the time. They utilize books and traditional documentary materials such as military unit reports, letters, diaries, and other archival materials to put together a clear picture of what happened. Such a clear picture was not available to more than a very select few contemporaries during the war itself. Those at the very highest levels of civilian and military command often possessed a reasonably clear idea of the overall situation, but this view had to be very broad. Pulling back from the situation to get a wide-angle shot meant that individuals in the field gave way to unit designations, and even most of these give way above the divisional level to a few names of top commanders.

The War Comes to Plum Street looks at the war through the eyes of people who lived through it. The bulk of the day-to-day narrative of life on Plum Street and New Castle was written from extensive oral history interviews with many of the actual participants. Because it takes a close-up look at events, it does not attempt to explain the war using the voices of the participants. After all, they had no day-to-day narrator either, and wartime censorship prevented personal communications from containing anything much in the way of content. Radio provided headline coverage of the war, but the primary substantive source available to Americans at the time was the daily newspaper. Because newspapers printed information that had been cleared by military censors, it could be discussed and passed on to others without endangering military operations. For people living day to day through the war, the newspapers offered all the structure and understanding there was to be had so far as the big picture was concerned. So practically everyone concerned about the war devoured a daily newspaper if they could get it.

The broader narrative of contemporary national and world

events is just that, and makes little effort to interpret meaning or assign importance. For the most part, it is simply the irregular background of experience informing those who lived it in its own way, and the importance or meaning derived from it varied from individual to individual. The broader narrative in the book comes from contemporary newspapers, the *Order of Battle*, and from various secondary sources mined for factual information rather than interpretation or meaning.

On a personal level, the mail provided more immediate information on loved ones, although it was usually slow to arrive. Censorship in the field kept all substantive news out of the mail because of the danger posed if the letters were captured, say, from a torpedoed ship or from a captured soldier or airman. But because of the delay in transporting and delivering mail, the main solace provided by a letter was the knowledge that on the day it was written "somewhere in England" or "somewhere in the Pacific," the writer had been alive and well. What had happened in the days or weeks since the last letter was known to very few, and almost never to those back home.

Because the characters in the book could only see the war from a narrow personal view and from the papers, there is a danger of seeing the war through a lens distorted by personal fears, rumor, and incomplete official information. Nevertheless, this was the reality they faced and lived with every day of their lives during the war. If we are to attempt to experience the war as they did, insofar as it is possible, then we must understand that these are the very things that shaped their perception of everyday events. Then, as now, the future is an unknown, and the further into the future we look, the less knowable it is. Reliable prophets are only identifiable after some part of the future has become history.

To compensate for the difficulties of contemporary perspective, this work examines the lives of people who represent something very much like average Americans of their day. A large portion of them lived in smaller towns and villages all across the country when knowledge of the farm was common to most. Most of the direct participants in the war were in their late teens and early twenties, as were their friends and spouses back home. Their parents were in their forties and fifties. Most who served were not in frontline fighting forces, although many were. It took nearly a dozen people in support functions to keep a single man fighting in a combat unit on a distant front. Anyone in any kind of unit at home or abroad can be killed, however, and this danger was never far from the minds of every American. The closer the loved one at risk, the greater the fear. Emotional turmoil and hysteria might be checked at the national level by propaganda, but controlling it on an individual level required much self-control. Every notice in the paper that a local individual had been lost reopened the throbbing fear that your own loved one might be next. From hindsight we know that of the sixteen million American men and women in uniform during World War II, only about three hundred thousand were actually killed, a trifling number as a percentage of the total engaged. This is, of course, a big-picture perspective. Three hundred thousand anonymous people seems a pretty reasonable price to pay, almost sixty years later. At the time, however, no one knew what the total would be but, more important, no one knew whether the final total would include the one most sacred and important to them. The sixteen million were not anonymous. That special one was the only one who really mattered. It's elementary psychology. Random reinforcement, in this case of total and final terror, is the most effective. Everyone sweated and prayed for those who might be called upon to make the ultimate sacrifice.

So this is a contemporary perspective, made as real and immediate as it was possible to do. But to understand what it was like to experience the war firsthand as a member of what we now recognize as "The Greatest Generation," we must try to understand what it meant to be born in the 1920s and to grow up in the 1930s, for this was not a generation raised like the ones which have followed it.

The War Comes to Plum Street

1. Migration and a
New Start in the 1920s

THIS IS A STORY of how ordinary people create the mosaic of American life in a part of the country far removed from teeming cities and the seats of power. On the farms and in the small villages and middling towns of the vast heartland, generations live out the ebb and flow of their lives in localized obscurity. Theirs is the real world of birth and death, growing up, reaching for a place in life, finding the way, or leading a life to be counted lost. The accumulation of the lives of these individuals each decade makes up the columns and figures in the compendium of the U.S. census. In the census we see who and where we are, where we have been, and how we add up, but those statistics represent real people like the ones who are the central figures in this book.

In the 1920s, the census showed industrial America continued a growth begun over a hundred years before. For nearly that long, railroads fueled economic expansion everywhere the rails went. After the Civil War, limited opportunities in the rural South prompted many people there to seek work in other places, and some of the best of these were the scattered industrial towns of the Midwest north of the Ohio River. This interregional shift of population accelerated during the Great War of 1914–1918, and it was this migration which brought people to Plum Street, in New Castle, Indiana, to play out their lives. The railroads brought two particular families to New Castle as part of the great migration. Like many others who made similar journeys, they were optimistic they would find their places in life by going there. As it turned out, events far away shaped the story of their lives more than most generations as they lived, raised their own families, and faced a future far more dark and dangerous than they could have imagined.

Converging Trails:
The Smith Family Moves North

The Smiths arrived in New Castle first. James Fred Smith of Duvall Valley in rural Clinton County, Kentucky, answered his country's call to war and went to France in 1918 as a twenty-four-year-old private with the First Pioneer Infantry. While he was away at camp and overseas, he wrote to Lillian Frogge, a girl nearly ten years his junior who had grown up in the same small valley and attended the same school. When he returned in 1919 after three military campaigns in France and occupation duty on the Rhine, it did not take him long to decide that her father expected that any prospective husband needed to provide a better living than he could expect to make near the old home place in Duvall Valley. His oldest brother Walter and his wife Rena had moved to New Castle, Indiana, during the Great War and ran a boardinghouse, so Fred went there to look for work. At the same time, Lillian's father Lewis Frogge sent her to Texas to stay with relatives, hoping to cool her interest in Fred.

Fred arrived in New Castle in the middle of the economic slump which followed the end of the Great War, and jobs were not easy to find. He went to the Hoosier Kitchen Cabinet factory on hiring day several Mondays in a row but was always turned down along with the rest of the crowd. He decided to wear his army uniform the next time, hoping it might give him an advantage. That Monday the foreman came out on the dock and told everyone there were no jobs, as he had done the previous weeks, but as the disappointed men began to walk away he caught Fred's eye and waved him over. There was one job, the man said, and Fred could have it because he had been in the army. Fred took it without asking what it paid. Inside, he was given the task of attaching the wire spice jar rack to the inside of the lower door on each of the cabinets.

Fred, Lillian, and Kenny Smith in 1922, probably on G Avenue in New Castle. Fred is twenty-eight, Lillian nineteen, Kenny about eight months. Fred was working steady hours at Hoosier Cabinet by this time.

Fred settled into his new job at the Hoosier while Lillian pleaded with her father to allow her to follow Fred to New Castle. Finally, Lewis gave in and allowed his seventeen-year-old daughter to join Fred there. Lillian arrived in New Castle on the train on June 4, 1920, and she and Fred were married the next day. They stayed at Walter and Rena's boardinghouse until spring, then moved to a modest house on G Avenue. By the time they moved, Lillian had discovered she was pregnant. Their first child, a son, was born there on July 3, 1921, and they named him Edward McKendrick, using the first name of Fred's father and the middle name of Lillian's father. Everyone in the family called him Kenny.

As their son grew and passed his first birthday, Lillian became pregnant again. They moved to a better house on N Avenue where she gave birth on December 15, 1923, to a daughter they named Hazel May. As Fred worked steadily at the Hoosier, Lillian managed their home and their two small children, and all went well until a week before Hazel's first birthday. When Lillian discovered little Hazel on the floor that day, she was already choking. With time running out quickly, Lillian tried to find the object her baby had put in her mouth but could not see or reach anything in her throat, and pounding on her back failed to stop the choking. Hazel died in her arms that December 7, 1924. Although he was not yet four at the time, Kenny retained vague memories of the gravity of the doctor coming to the house to sign the death certificate. Something terribly random and mysterious had struck their world and taken his baby sister from them forever.

Paralyzed with grief so profound they never really recovered, Fred and Lillian took their baby to Clinton County for a funeral and burial in the cemetery at Central Union Church in Duvall Valley. Kenny stayed behind with Walter and Rena. As many family members as could make it gathered for the occasion, because a funeral was something that the Smiths did not miss. Every subsequent journey to the valley included a visit to the place where little Hazel slept, and there the tears and mute grief always came easily at the small red granite marker.

Hazel's death changed their lives. There were no more pregnancies, and perhaps no more attempts. Only their boy was left now, and every effort went into protecting and preserving him. The loss of a daughter awoke their gratitude that they still had their son. He became the center of their lives in a way that was sharpened by Hazel's loss. As a family of three, they carried on as best they could, always quietly harboring the lesson that death needed no invitation to visit.

Converging Trails: The Moles Family Moves North

Jess and Ethel Moles had already been married for two and a half years when they arrived in New Castle in April 1923. Jess met Ethel Baltimore at the post office in their little hometown of Wilder, Tennessee, soon after his return from a hitch in the navy where he served with the first crew of the battleship USS *Tennessee*. Jess fled an abusive home and lied about his age to join the navy at age sixteen, making him a worldly man of nearly nineteen when he returned in 1921. Ethel was fourteen and old enough to be married by the standards of the day as, after all, she had finished all eight grades of her schooling. Her mother and father were not convinced that an ex-sailor was the best match for their daughter, because the Baltimore family was well situated with good work in the local coal mines. Jess had worked in the mines, too, since his return, but in their eyes living with his uncle demonstrated that he was not well enough established to marry and support a family. The opposition of her family did not deter them for long once their attraction to each other became apparent. Just a few months after his return from the navy, Jess and Ethel married on December 18, 1921. Ethel's family remained unhappy about what she had done. On their own, the newlyweds rented a tiny house in the poorest area of Wilder known as "Dogtown." There Ethel became pregnant almost immediately. At only two inches over five feet tall, she weighed about a hundred pounds, and it soon became clear the baby would be a hefty one. Throughout the spring and summer of 1922, she carried her growing burden and set about making a home for her new husband. Jess's dream was to go to Bellingham, Washington, a city he had seen as a sailor. He immediately had liked its crisp air and distant mountain scenery and decided it would be the best place in the world to make a future home. But for now they settled into the workaday routine and saved what money they could against the day when they would follow Jess's dream of moving west to a new life.

Ethel began to have light contractions on Monday, September 18. On Wednesday the 20th she gradually slipped into heavy labor. That night and the next day she groaned and sweated when the contractions swept over her, but the baby did not come. Relatives assisted her as best they could, but the doctor said it was up to her, that she would have to do her necessary part, no matter how long it took. All the next day, Friday, she continued her effort, and it was becoming grim now. Her cries had been heard outside for almost two days, and the ordeal was taking its toll on her strength. Friday night was the same. Many babies were born in the wee hours of the morning, and there was hope that Ethel would end her struggle and deliver the baby before dawn, but it did not happen. She was just too tiny and the baby was large enough to make the delivery difficult at best. Everyone sensed that Saturday was crucial. If she could not deliver soon, she and the baby would both die, and the doctor advised the family that it was likely neither of them would make it anyway. Ethel was exhausted and beyond caring, and with her voice gone, there was little sound from the small house except for the whispers of those concerned for her life. When the doctor arrived early on the morning of September 23, he decided that he had to intervene in spite of the risks. Using his heavy forceps, he literally pulled the baby out. The baby girl weighed ten and a half pounds, but with her head bruised and swollen, some thought she would probably die. Ethel was nearly dead herself, and lay for days utterly spent while everyone waited to see who would survive the ordeal. Jess wanted to name her Gemma Juanita after a girl who had been his friend when he was in the navy. Ethel, now fifteen years old, was too worn-out to object. After a week, they both turned the corner. Ethel took more than a month to rebuild her strength to the point she could move around the house. The baby's color improved and she nursed fairly well considering her traumatic arrival. The bruised and misshapen head improved and mother and daughter were soon clearly on the road to recovery.

They stayed in Wilder during the winter of 1922–1923 while Ethel healed and little Gemma recovered and began to grow. Jess continued to work in the coal mines, but they decided they should leave as soon as possible. Ethel's family continued to be cool toward Jess, and there was no use sweating in the coal mines when there was a future in the golden West just waiting for them. Geographically speaking, they had to go north and west to get to Bellingham. Jess's sister Haley and her husband Jim Cowan had moved north with the boom that the war years had brought to a town called New Castle, in Indiana. Jess's older brother George and his wife Nina had done the same thing. They both had families and had been in Indiana for a few years. Jess had written to them and George and Nina agreed they could stay with them while he worked a little while and saved up enough money for the next leg of their journey west. They boarded the train in Wilder in April 1923, winding their way through Louisville to Indianapolis, then eastward to New Castle.

Jess immediately began looking for work and found it. George and Nina had three children of their own, so staying with them while taking care of their own baby was trying and soon became uncomfortable for everyone. Jess and Ethel found "light house-keeping" rooms on Walnut Street in New Castle, within sight of the passenger depot where they had arrived just a few days before. These were cheaper than staying in a boardinghouse because cooking could be done in the rooms on tiny hot plates or gas laundry stoves. It also was cheaper than an apartment because there was only one room and the toilet was down the hallway. Others in similar circumstances lived in the building, too. It was temporary quarters until they could move on west. Jess could walk to work or, if the weather was bad, take the streetcar. Here they settled into life for a while until a little more money could be accumulated.

Jess and Ethel did not exactly decide to stay in New Castle, but for the next couple of years there was never quite enough money to make the long trip to Washington and have enough left over for rent and hunting a job when they got there. Unlike in New Castle, they knew no one in Bellingham with whom they could stay or whom they could use to find immediate employment. For a stay of more than a few months, the light house-keeping rooms on Walnut Street were too cramped, so they eventually rented a house just south of the industrial district, on P Avenue, late in 1923 and it was probably there that Ethel became pregnant again. With Ethel expecting, it was no time to travel across the country, so they settled in, hoping that this baby might arrive a little less traumatically than had little Gemma. The house on P Avenue was also within easy walking distance of the major employers in New Castle, so Jess could work without the expense of operating an automobile.

Ethel's pregnancy proceeded without difficulty, and she gave birth at home to another daughter, this time without complications, on August 8, 1924. They named her Maxine. The house on P Avenue, with four rooms, was large enough to remain their base while they got their feet underneath them and waited for a day to move on. As each child reached her first birthday, she was weaned and Ethel easily became pregnant again. For the two and a half years they lived there, Ethel was either expecting or nursing an infant. It would just not do to drag everyone across the country just then, so they stayed. On May 26, 1926, nine months

Jess, Ethel, and Gemma Moles in 1924, soon after their arrival in New Castle. Jess is twenty-one, Ethel seventeen, and Gemma one, when they lived on P Avenue in New Castle.

after Maxine's first birthday, a third daughter, named Marie, was born. This addition to the family made the P Avenue house too crowded, so in the spring of 1927, when baby Marie began to gain mobility, they moved to 2028 Plum Street, just three blocks from the room they had shared on Walnut, and once again north of the railroad tracks. It was bigger than the house that they had left on P Avenue, but the house on Plum Street had never been large, in spite of the fact that small rooms had been attached to it in the back over the years. It was narrow, only one room wide on a narrow lot, with the furthest room back divided to make a kitchen and bathroom. Above the front room was only a half story used as a sleeping area for all of them. A small porch ran the width of the house in front, but there was only the tiniest of front yards. The house was close to the bend on Plum Street, a location which afforded a view in both directions up and down the street, which few houses had. It was an improvement, at least, in the sense that this area lacked the industrial dreariness which characterized the more southerly neighborhoods in town. Gemma was four when they moved this time, Maxine two, and Marie ten months. Ethel, with three children, was twenty, and Jess almost twenty-five.

New Castle Becomes Home for Both Families

New Castle had several major employers after the Great War, among them the Jesse French Piano Company, Hoosier Kitchen Cabinets, and the Maxwell Motor Car Company. When Walter Chrysler bought Maxwell and created the Chrysler Corporation, the New Castle plant became an important parts supplier for the cars Chrysler built. From the mid-1920s onward, Chrysler shaped New Castle's fortunes and mood. Fortunately for the local economy of New Castle, Walter Chrysler worked to reduce debts and expenses while allowing research and development free rein. While company after company folded in the 1930s, Chrysler prospered. Exceptionally good years in 1934 and 1935 helped make the company debt-free by 1937. There were layoffs and cutbacks at the New Castle plant at various times in the 1930s, but they never reached severe levels. Chrysler avoided the worst of the bitter strikes that plagued General Motors and Ford in those years. New Castle sat on a hill above Blue River and the large swampy area around it to the west. South and east of this lowland the land rolled slightly and made good farm ground, so the town grew in that direction. Two freight railroads formed a wedge shape as they approached the center of town, and within this wedge was the area which was the working core of town in the twentieth century. Working and living in this area meant that the mournful sound of train whistles was never far away. The Moles family lived in or within two blocks of this wedge from the first day they arrived in New Castle. On Plum Street it was only a couple of blocks to a line which carried daily freight up toward the crossing at Broad Street. Eighteenth Street and I Avenue, just a few blocks south of Plum Street, became the crossroads of industrial New Castle. On the southwest corner of this intersection lay the Jesse French Piano Company, and to the southeast stood the Chrysler, as it was called by residents of New Castle.

Four blocks to the north was the Hoosier Kitchen Cabinet complex. Rail spurs connected all three companies to the nearby main tracks as well as the coal yards and lumber companies which supplied materials and fuel.

Downtown New Castle showed its evolution from the horse-and-buggy town it had been in the 1800s. Back then, Broad Street was the sole commercial street with its variety of banks, dry goods stores, druggists, saloons, milliners, doctors, and dentists mostly in two- and three-story buildings made of brick and frame. Half a block south of Broad and parallel to it was Race Street. In the 1930s the buildings still stood which had served as livery stables, blacksmith shops, and funeral parlors before there were cars. By the 1930s, these structures had been converted to other uses such as garages, taxi stands, or apartments. As Broad became crowded and high-priced in the twentieth century, first Race Street, then Central Avenue also became significant commercial streets. The overflow of businesses spread down Main and 14th, then down 15th. Department and 5 & 10 stores, theaters, and clothing stores scattered along Broad past Penney's and Sears and Roebuck to the corner of 15th, where Shuffman's furniture store stood on the northeast corner. Within this block were the railroad tracks and taverns, and service stations could be found among other businesses. Southward from Broad on 18th, one came to railroad tracks and the Pennsylvania passenger station, then Indiana Avenue, Walnut Street, Plum Street, and Lincoln, then more tracks. At Grand Avenue were grocery stores, service stations, and the Redelman hardware store, then eight blocks of residential streets before coming to I Avenue, the industrial crossroads. On the south side of I were the Chrysler and the piano factory, and across from these, from 14th all the way to 21st, were drug stores, service stations, barber shops, grocery stores, cab stands, furniture stores, boardinghouses, garages, lunchrooms, and bars, all seeking a part of the industrial wage carried out of the doors across the street. When the shifts changed, traffic stopped as men streamed across the streets to the streetcars and parking lots, or walked home. The coming and going of delivery trucks, cars, and trolleys joined the hum and crash of machinery inside the big buildings.

Further east along I Avenue, between 21st and 22nd, stood Chrysler's tall metal-sided forge shop. Here, hammers large and small produced a constant thudding of steel against hot forgings as workmen made new parts. Outside, bins of these forgings sat in the weather to season before they were taken to the machining part of the plant to be finished. They were then sent on to Dodge Main in Hamtramck, Michigan, or to other assembly plants. Overhead cranes moved the heaviest loads, and a constant scurry of hand carts kept the hammer men busy. Growing deafness was widespread among the forge room employees, and it was common for them to speak at a near shout out on the street or at home the way they had to do to be heard in the shop. The different parts of town had their distinctive sounds and smells. At the Jersey Creamery stables on Indiana Avenue, horse manure and harness smells reminded passersby of the days when everyone in New Castle moved by horse or on foot. There were plenty of farm horses in the county, but the milk wagon horses still lived and worked in town. Downwind from the piano factory the smells of sawdust and varnish remained most noticeable, along with the whine of planers and saws. Sanding and fitting of parts inside made humming and hammering audible in the neighborhood. The Chrysler machine shop ran on motors and belts, so there was always the deep, steady hum of belting and the smell of hot oil and steel shavings. The Chrysler power plant ran on coal the year around, producing cinders on the ground and smoke that was sent high up into the air through the big stack. From the Hoosier came the odor of paint and varnish used on the cabinets. Railroads ran on coal, and everywhere the trains went the sharp bite of coal smoke from the locomotives was only sometimes offset by the pleasant scent of steam. In the winter the smell of coal smoke pervaded the town because most of New Castle's families burned coal in their furnaces and stoves. Even the snow did not stay pure white for long.

Life on Plum Street

Jess and Ethel did not know how long they would stay when they moved to Plum Street. It was a practical move into a better part of town and nothing more. As it turned out, it would be the stage for their domestic lives for over twenty years. Plum Street ran east from the freight tracks at 17th Street across 18th to 20th. There Plum turned toward the southeast, continuing to 21st Street and beyond. Twenty-first Street was busy, with cross traffic that did not stop. The three blocks between 18th and 21st constituted the home neighborhood for the Moles family during the decades of the 1930s and 1940s. For the Moles girls, Plum Street was the world they first knew well, and New Castle was the extent of their universe.

Jess had found a job at the Chrysler by the time they settled into their new quarters on Plum Street. There were many families nearby, but Ethel, twenty years old with her three children when they moved there, was easily the youngest mother. Gemma did not know that her mother had become pregnant again, and, of course, the younger girls also were unaware of her condition. Gemma and Maxine remembered that Ethel wore loose dresses but never said a word to them about it. They all sensed something was wrong, however, when Jess gathered up the three of them and got them ready to go out into a cold, pouring rain on a January afternoon just as the doctor pulled up to the house in his black car. Jess took the children to the home of his brother George and wife Nina, who had taken them in when they first arrived in town six years before. There was no explanation. The girls remembered Nina from this visit and later ones as mean and cross. Three more children were an imposition, and Nina made little effort to hide her feelings. They had bean soup for supper, and the girls asked for more when they finished their bowls but were told there wasn't any. One of them took the lid off the pot and discovered there was indeed, but they were not allowed to have any more. It was a bleak place, and they wanted to go home, but they had to stay the night. Jess took them home the next day, and only then did they learn they had a new sister. There was no explanation for this surprise, either. Gemma did not remember much about it and tried to put it out of her mind.

Back at the house on Plum Street, eight months after Marie turned one, Wanda's uncomplicated birth came on that cold January 28, 1929. At this point, Ethel made it clear that four children would have to be enough. The wear and tear on her small frame was taking its toll, and the burden of caring for them all was not helping matters. She knew many women back home who had given birth about every two years from the time they were fifteen or sixteen until they were forty-five or even older. She was not going to do that. In the way of the hill people of the upper South, where they had come from, she put a stop to any more pregnancies. This was fortuitous, as it turned out, because hard times were on the way for the people of this little town and many others across the land. Wanda's arrival completed their family, and much of that year they spent getting her through the dangerous infant stage of life. Ethel said many times that on Plum Street she and the girls grew up together.

The Moles Family Plunges into the Tunnel

Gemma started at Weir Elementary School in January 1929 and helped her mother with her sisters when she could. Her birthday the previous September fell eight days past the deadline for fall enrollment, so she had to start at the beginning of the next term. As the oldest, she soon grew accustomed to many of the chores that went along with raising children. Her sisters looked up to her then and later, and she accepted the extra duties as part of the way life was. Sisters also provided fun for games and play.

The stock market crash in October 1929 had little immediate effect on people in New Castle. No one was really sure what it meant, and, at any rate, things seemed to go on as usual the next day and the next. There were scary stories in the papers of big losses and suicides in New York, and near misses in which people had sold their stock for cash just before the crash or put their entire savings into the market the day before it all came down. A depression does not arrive all in one day. But during 1930 and 1931 the quiet despair which began in the big cities gradually spread outward to the towns and farms across the countryside. Layoffs became more frequent and sometimes plants simply closed up and stayed that way. In the papers, the word "depression" began to appear, but President Hoover made rousing speeches filled with confidence and optimism. Prosperity was just around the corner, he assured everyone.

For Jess, the beginning of economic decline across the country marked the family's entry into the tunnel. He had been in

New Castle, trapped really, for more than six years now and had come to accept the place. But when the downturn began, there was no way to tell when it would end, if ever. It was not a short tunnel, experienced in the way a tunnel can thrill passengers in a car with its sudden darkening, then approaching glow at the other end. This tunnel went on and on with sudden ups and downs and no light growing nearer at all. There was no choice about going on because turning back was not an option, but when would it end? How long could they keep going with little in the way of savings or steady income to keep them alive? In towns like New Castle, the changes were so subtle as to be barely noticeable from week to week. Those who were there scarcely noticed any change at all, and many children lived through the entire period without realizing there was a problem. For adults, reduced work hours or occasional layoffs and gradually falling wages began to affect debt payment and the standard of living, but only gradually. Many people tightened their belts, hoping it would get no worse. For others there was no substantial change at all: life went on much the same as before, with their wealth secure, or with perhaps only reduced incomes that were still better than most. Much of New Castle took on a tattered look, a little threadbare, as though it was neglected.

A high point in the town's history came in the depression winter of 1932. New Castle High School's strong basketball team that year won all of its sectional, regional, and semi-state games, earning the honor to be one of the final four teams that would battle for the state title in Indianapolis. This was Indiana basketball in the early days, but these winter games played in humid gyms were the delight of students, parents, and other fans like Jess throughout the state. Big schools from Indianapolis, Muncie, Fort Wayne, Terre Haute, and Evansville tended to dominate the tourney, but in that 1931–1932 season, New Castle, its team heavy with seniors, emerged as a major powerhouse in the east-central region of the state. Jess held a season ticket as usual and had followed the team with great hope through the early tourney battles. Traveling to Indianapolis was beyond his means that year, though, so he went to the cigar store on the corner of Race and 15th Street to join the crowd of local fans who listened together as the play-by-play came over the radio. Ethel stayed home with the children, as usual. That Saturday night he pulled into the driveway and burst into the house shouting that New Castle's Trojans had won the final game and become state champions! It was too wonderful to believe! Jess's euphoria could not be contained, nor could the celebration in the town be stopped. All night long the girls were awakened and reawakened by the explosion of firecrackers, the honking of horns, and the wail of sirens. A framed photograph of the fabled 1932 team went up in the Moles house and became a permanent fixture. Jess never tired of telling anyone who would listen about that season.

As winter faded that year, Maxine met with an accident which worsened their financial situation. Going to the park was an inexpensive treat for the girls, and they went soon after the new corkscrew slide (everyone called it the crooked slide) opened at Memorial Park. Maxine went down in front of a group of bigger boys who didn't wait for her to pick herself up and move away once she landed at the bottom. One of them came down just as Maxine was beginning to get up, landing on her outstretched arm, breaking it at the elbow. It was not a simple break that a cast and two months' recuperation would repair. Jess and Ethel had to take her to the Clinic repeatedly for attention and therapy in order to keep the joint from becoming unusable because of lack of movement. It was painful, and on some occasions the doctor administered gas to anesthetize her so the joint could be moved and evaluated. On some of these occasions Gemma went along, and she remembered the terror she felt when Maxine's eyes rolled back in her head as though she had died. After all, the little ones were part of her responsibility, too. They had little cash, so the charge for these visits added to the bills they owed, or were simply written off. Physicians in the depression did a great deal of charity work in struggling towns like New Castle.

For Christmas 1932, Jess did manage to scrape together enough money to buy a new bicycle for the girls at the Guarantee Tire and Rubber Company on Broad Street, and it instantly became an object lesson for them all. They could not ride it all at once, so methods had to be devised to allow each to ride in turn. Jess worked in the machine shop at the Chrysler now and was good with tools, so he made repairs on it when they were needed. They could not ride far, but they and the neighborhood children put countless miles on it every year when weather permitted. When it rained or was too cold to play outside, the sisters provided each other with plenty of opportunities for games inside or playing make-believe with dolls and the few toys they had.

But by the Christmas season of 1932, difficult times had come to New Castle. Jess, working a twelve-hour shift in the Chrysler machine shop, was one of hundreds of men working side by side who hoped that the depression would spare them. The newspaper brought news nearly every day of the spreading collapse that had only begun with the stock market crash in 1929. Starting in 1931 the country went into a tailspin that could end in riot and revolution, the way some people talked. Businesses failed in even greater numbers than they had been doing for the past two years. The times took hold of Jess and Ethel, and refused to let go. Toward the end of 1932 and during 1933, Jess was laid off for periods of time. Some of these layoffs were only for a few days, but on other occasions they stretched into a week, then several weeks. These spells of unemployment posed a serious problem for the family. Jess was the sole breadwinner and the family depended on a regular income, even if it was not spectacular. It paid the bills and put food on the table. Depending on the timing of a layoff, the impact could be manageable or very difficult. A few days here and there between the 5th and 20th of the month was tough but could be dealt with by cutting back on treats and putting off some purchases. Idleness toward the end of the month spelled trouble because his pay was down just when the rent came due or installment payments had to be made.

Jess was trapped, and he knew it. He had once dreamed of making a locomotive engineer's pay or of working in the shops and docks of the great naval base at Bellingham. He was known among his friends at the shop for his honesty, and it was not in him to abandon his family as some men began to do when their jobs and hopes disappeared. His integrity made him get up and face the uncertainty every day, but there was a toll that he paid in the strain on his nerves, and the sick feeling in the pit of his stomach. The shop foreman told the men each Friday who should come in the next week. The announced length of the layoff might be cut short and work could resume sooner than expected but, as the months went by, it was more often the case that the callback did not come when promised. Chrysler kept itself solvent, and many worked there, but the company could only build what could be sold, and in 1931, 1932, and 1933 there were not many people buying new cars. Jess did not have the money to go back to Tennessee, and there was nothing there at any rate. Family members did not have the means to help much because they had families, too, and were going through the same thing. He found extra work for a few days at a time in the summer detasseling seed corn for the new hybrids that a few farmers were beginning to use, but this did not last long. Even if he had the extra money to get them out of New Castle, there was no place that he knew about where he could go and expect to find work, so moving was not an option for him. Laid off at the Chrysler and working for less pay at the Hoosier, the pressure of desperation grew on him with every setback, and he began to lapse into despair.

The period 1933–1934 was the worst time the Moles family had ever known. Jess was laid off much of that time, with only occasional days of work to relieve long weeks of idleness. One jobless stretch went on for six months. Hope expired, and Jess began to show his dilemma by taking to bed in a state of melancholia which mirrored the country's mood. He ate infrequently and lost weight, and seemed to be able to do nothing to bring himself out of it. He eventually had a kind of emotional breakdown and refused to allow Ethel out of his sight for more than a few minutes at a time.

Ethel began to miss paying the weekly bill, sometimes for a month or more, at Craig's, the neighborhood grocery store they frequented at 22nd and Plum. Jess went to the doctor in the hope that there would be an explanation for his debility, but even that did not work. The doctor could find nothing wrong. People at church gave them food or cast-off clothing occasionally, or there were small loans offered with the uncertain hope that when things got better they might be repaid. Things did not get better. Jess stumbled about unable to cope with his failure as a provider, and Ethel could only stay at home and be a mother for the girls. The storeowner's wife asked Ethel to do the wash for them to help with the grocery bill. This was a humiliation for the girls as well as for their mother. Handling someone else's dirty laundry was worse than handling one's own. Ethel scrubbed the clothes on her washboard and hung them in the kitchen to dry in the winter, which fogged the windows and made for beautiful frost patterns when it was cold outside. Then she ironed. The girls felt the embarrassment acutely when Ethel gave them the task of carrying the clean laundry down to the store in baskets. It announced to everyone on Plum Street that their mother had to take in laundry to feed them. The neighbors noticed that Jess could not take care of his own children. Deep in his gloom, endless days went by as he sank further.

A near tragedy changed this situation for the family. One wall and a narrow, open staircase separated the tiny upstairs room where they all slept. It was during this time that Maxine woke up in the wee hours of the morning as she often did, wanting to go to the bathroom downstairs. She went in to wake Ethel, but stepped backward toward the edge of the open stairs and plunged downward into the darkness, all the way to the bottom. Jess, for months stricken to near immobility, reached her first. It was the first time in weeks he had done more than drag himself from the bed to the bathroom. Maxine's fall left her bruised and sore, and they took her to the doctor to make sure she had not broken anything. The visit brought Jess face to face with the doctor. Having pronounced him in good physical shape months before, he noticed the continuing problems Jess had coping with his daily situation. Frustrated, he told Jess to just snap out of it; he had a family he had to take care of better than he was doing. It was time to pick himself up and get back in the game. Somehow, it worked. Shamed, Jess began to feel sorry for himself less, and this put him on the road to recovery.

Jess would experience more layoffs in the next two years, but they would never be as frequent nor last as long as before. The mentality of failure and hardship remained, but he grimly began to fight back against the debts and despair. Ethel continued doing laundry to reduce the grocery bill, which she eventually paid off. She also cleaned house for a schoolteacher twice a month. When Jess was working, they could pay cash for the groceries they needed, while her work cut down the debt they owed. Jess did without luxuries like the occasional cigar and wore his work clothes longer before buying new ones. It was in these years that even on Plum Street he raised chickens in a little shed in the back yard three years in a row, which he fed on kitchen scraps and the cheap feeds that could be had a few blocks away at the elevator. They dressed the chickens in the back yard and had fried chicken meals.

Others on Plum Street felt the sting of hard times, too. One family whose father was a builder lived in a trim bungalow about a block away. But it seemed hardly anyone had the money to build or pay for a house in those days, so they fell behind in mortgage payments. In 1934 the bank repossessed the house, and they had to move out to a rented house in the country where there were no sidewalks and no electricity. Everyone in the neighborhood knew that the same thing could happen to them.

2. Coping with Hard Times in the 1930s

The Smith Family Pursues a Dream

By the 1930s, nearly every male member of the Smith family worked for Chrysler: Fred went to work there while it was still Maxwell, and stayed on during the transition to Chrysler. Brothers Walter and Tom, nephews, and cousins all worked there at one time or another. Fred started in timekeeping, then went to the new Forge Room where he began working in forge hammer repair. His quiet affability suited those he worked with and made him many friends. He had always been tall and lean, and his work there built bulging biceps and a strong back. The sound of the hammers pounded incessantly, and it was hot in the metal-sided building which never closed its doors in the warm months in order to allow the heat to escape. Fred learned the ins and outs of all of the big hammers which were used to give strength to the steel castings which went into so many of Chrysler's cars and trucks. Through the rest of the 1920s and even in the depression of the 1930s, Fred worked 6:00 A.M. to 6:00 P.M., with few layoffs, and on Fridays in the 1920s, he lined up with the other men at the paymaster's office after work to draw his weekly pay in gold. He combined this steady industrial wage with a natural frugality which downplayed display and encouraged savings and the avoidance of debt. Lillian worked steadily at home to cook, can and preserve food, and keep house. They lived in four different houses before 1933, not including the boardinghouse, renting at modest rates and building a savings account. They even tried to start a neighborhood grocery business, common at that time, but gave it up after only a year.

They moved to a one-story house on Grand Avenue in 1927. Kenny remembered this as the place where he and his mother both had the whooping cough, a common childhood affliction in those days before a vaccine. The gasping during a coughing bout became so bad that the rush of air through the throat took on the characteristic whooping sound. In 1930 they moved again, this time to a modest story-and-a-half house on South Main Street in New Castle adjacent to the Parker Elementary School. Kenny attended grade school there. While the Smiths lived on South Main, the depression hit New Castle with full force.

Fred Smith was never laid off for more than a few days at a time during the entire depression period. Although unemployment reached 25 percent in the nation at one point in 1931–1932, he remained among the 75 percent who did not lose their jobs. This fact made all the difference in the Smith household. The Smiths had been solid Republicans ever since the Civil War had tainted the Democrats with the odor of disloyalty and slavery. Their party loyalty did not change after 1928. Resentment of and opposition to the schemes of New Deal Democrats both on the national and state levels were a foregone conclusion in this home. These views were firmly, but quietly held. Fred was never what in those days was called "radical," meaning one who spoke up vigorously at any mention of a political subject. In the presence of someone he knew held opposing views, he simply did not bring up politics. In spite of the fact that Fred enjoyed dependable employment through these years, the desire to find a permanent place to live remained. Paying rent to a landlord made no sense in the long run, of course, because it was money lost, with only the immediate gain of a place to live. When it came time to move on, there would be no equity to take with them. There were houses for sale in New Castle, of course, but the Smiths had come from a small farm and rural background, and both Fred and Lillian yearned to live a life closer to the one they had known in their youths. In 1932, Fred learned of a parcel of land, 8⅓ acres, that was for sale south of New Castle on Rural Route 2, later known as Riley Road. It was no more than a mile out of town, but it was surrounded by farms and trees. There was an old two-room house and barn there, and little else. It was priced at $1,300, but their savings would not cover that much, so he paid $750 down, and in May 1932 signed a promissory note on the Citizens State Bank for $550 at 6 percent, payable to the owners. Fred bought the land while keeping an eye out for building materials for a house.

In the meantime, he decided to turn an old Model T Ford into a truck. The old Fords were plentiful and cheap, so he was able to find one for practically nothing. Out in the driveway he cut off the body behind the front seat with a hacksaw, built a wooden bed onto the frame, enclosed the "cab" with sheet metal, and cut a rear window into it. It wasn't much good for hauling gravel or stone, but they used it to haul the dirt from the new basement out near the driveway where it was dumped. When word got around that the "temporary" framed-on rooms at the Parker School would be torn down before building a new masonry addition, he arranged to buy all the useful lumber that he would need. An out-of-work acquaintance agreed to haul the lumber to the building site on Riley Road with his team of horses for a small fee. A friend, Tom Davis, then agreed to build the house for $100. It was built almost entirely of the old materials out of the school. The flue bricks and roofing were new, but the framing lumber, flooring, decking lumber, windows and doors, and even the siding came from the school. The main floor rooms were plastered over lath, but they cut costs wherever they could. The abundance of lapped siding from the school was used to side the house and also for the interior wall surface in the basement kitchen. The driveway he built up out of Chrysler power plant cinders which were normally hauled to the city dump. In March 1933, the Smiths sat around the radio in the house on South Main to hear the newly inaugurated President Roosevelt address the nation in troubled times. The house in the hollow was nearing completion, and this would be their last winter on South Main. They moved into their "new" house just at the time when the depression was giving the country its worst battering. Frugality, good fortune, steady work, and Walter Chrysler had helped them move up one rung on the ladder.

The Smith home in "the hollow," south of New Castle, where they
moved in 1933 to weather the economic storm.

They referred to the place on Riley Road as "the hollow." The
house sat in a tiny valley, with tree-covered hills sloping down
toward it on three sides: west, south, and east. The ground was
fairly level from the road to the house, which sat about fifty yards
back. A creek came down the hill from the south, ran along the
yard on the east side, crossed the front of the property, then went
under the road beneath a small bridge. The single-story side gable
house reminded them of a bungalow. A small gabled porch faced
north toward the road. Ample windows on each side of the house
sat in the white horizontal narrow lapped wood siding, accented
with dark vertical trim. On Armistice Day and the Fourth of July,
the American flag hung correctly from the front of the porch. The
house faced north, but it had been built into the hill which rose
behind it. Part way up that hill sat the original tiny house. Behind it a little further up the hill was the outhouse. Although a
kitchen had been planned for the back corner of the house, they
began using part of the new basement for a kitchen so that they
could move in. The basement kitchen became the heart of the
house. Attached to the brick flue was a Sears and Roebuck cook-

ing range, fed with wood and coal. Coal oil lamps provided light at night. The front of the house had a small porch which projected from the main floor, reached by steps in front of the basement. A lattice-enclosed area underneath the porch usually held coal or wood for the stove. Living quarters except the basement were up above the ground in front, at ground level in back. Half of the main floor was a living and sitting room divided by partial walls, which left a large door opening between the two. The other half of the floor consisted of two small bedrooms divided by a room which would, much later, become the bath, but which during the 1930s and early 1940s was empty. They washed and brushed their teeth in the kitchen sink. Lillian poured hot water from the reservoir on the range into a washtub for baths on Saturday. She did all the wash in the same tub on a zinc washboard, rinsed it in another, wrung it out by hand, and hung it in the kitchen to dry in the winter time. She hung her wash on the clothesline outside in warm weather. Fred or Kenny would dump the wash water outside in the afternoons. The area that was supposed to be the kitchen became a small porch in back.

Almost immediately upon their arrival, an incident occurred which introduced Fred to the neighbors and made them lifelong friends. The surveyor who came to lay out the boundaries for the sale of the place set the west line along the bottom of the hill rising toward neighbors named Burden atop the ridge. This alarmed George Burden because the well that they depended upon was on the Smith side of the line down in the valley bottom. It had been dug there originally because it was closer to the water table, and the owners weren't too sure where the line was supposed to be, but they had agreed that the well was on the Burden side. When the surveyor indicated otherwise, Fred insisted that the line appear on the survey in such a way that Burden's well was on Burden's side of the line. There was no compensation except a store of goodwill toward the Smiths. Fred and George later kept bees on a partnership basis, and remained the best of neighbors.

When they moved in there was the creek, but no well for their own use. They drove a sand point into the ground with sledgehammers, attached a pitcher pump, and filled buckets from there. Later, Fred trenched from the well to the basement and laid the water line below all danger of winter frost. This driven well served all their water needs for almost twenty years. A small pump pulled the water into a huge five-hundred-gallon pressure tank in the basement behind the kitchen. This tank, far larger than any typical home system of the day, had been obtained cheaply in town because it was used and unwanted. From there a line led to the kitchen faucet. In the summer the water was delightfully cool. In the winter the 56-degree temperature seemed icy on cold hands, but it did not freeze. The water from the sink went into a drain tile outside underground, where it ran north toward the road and emptied into the creek. Fred hired Wilford Stamper to wire the house, in spite of the fact that they were off the grid out on Riley Road. Stamper bought and sold power units as part of his electrician's business, and he sold the Smiths a used system he had salvaged from another job. The west side of the basement was a garage with a dirt floor. In one corner of the garage stood the 32-volt generator with its small gasoline engine, and in another stood an array of batteries used to store the power it produced. Fred ran the generator for about twenty minutes each day to charge the batteries. The 32-volt lights kept some of the dark away, and the 110-volt radio plugged into the system through a converter. One major advantage of the arrangement for Lillian was the electric iron. It pulled seventeen of the system's twenty amps when she used it, which meant that everything else had to be turned off, but it held temperature like no sadiron heated on the stove could. Most of their clothes, even for work, were cotton and had to be ironed. She washed on Monday, and ironed on Tuesday the year round.

Every house Lillian called home was soon blessed with flowers and vines, and this one was no exception. Her front porches always became home to thickly growing blue morning glories and golden honeysuckle. Planters appeared on the porch railings and some of the houseplants spent parts of the summers on the porch as well. Lilies, cosmos, sweet william, spiderflowers, and moss roses made the place colorful every year, and she carefully saved seeds from the annuals for planting the following year. She loved petunias and geraniums and these would be on the windowsills. Zinnias and nasturtiums showed their colors in the garden every summer. Fred took her picture one August standing beside the castor beans she had nurtured that summer near the new woven wire fence that separated the yard from the cow's pasture to the east and up the hill.

Always a picture of meekness, kindly, but capable of outbursts of anger, Lillian was a typical product of her rural, small-farm-and-neighbors background. Quick to laugh, she followed the time-honored rural tradition of beginning conversations with observations on the weather and activities in the home. She was shy among strangers or guests, looking down or away rather than directly at someone while speaking. She was raised in the school of the home arts. She performed all the household chores, including painting and decorating, but loved to sew on her treadle sewing machine and crochet as well. The house reflected her industry. The chair and sofa arms and backs were decorated with crocheted doilies. Dresser tops and pillowcases had handworked covers and edging. The decorative decals which the dime stores sold were her accent pieces, particularly in the kitchen. On all the beds, her piecework quilts kept away the winter chill. Summer and fall were busy times cooking and canning, but the quilting frame went up in the winter if she was not working just on quilt piecing.

Lillian set the tone inside and around the house, but Fred determined the way things were done outside. He had grown up around hardy people who rarely called on others when the task could be done alone. The old barn underwent a refitting, with quarters for a milk cow a priority. The barn was not large, but it was banked into the hill, and he soon made cozy quarters in the lower level. Upstairs was room for hay and straw. Fred began to accumulate farm equipment as spare cash and opportunity permitted. He bought a well-used Fordson tractor with steel wheels at Filson's on A Avenue. He found a spring harrow, a two-bottom plow, a mower, a dump rake for windrowing hay, and cultivators for weeding corn and other row crops. There was an old wagon with wood-spoke wheels for hauling hay in from the field. They forked the loose hay up onto the wagon, then forked it into the haymow in the barn before going back for another load. Later a disk replaced the harrow. He rented ground from the neighbors and traded work for the use of other tools or farmed on shares. Soon afterward Fred bought a Guernsey cow from John Keith's father for $35. Ollie produced more milk than they could use most of the year. They all drank the raw milk, of course, and Lillian churned butter from the cream, made buttermilk, and had skim milk and whey left over to feed to their pigs.

There were always feeder pigs available from nearby farmers, and these became a staple source of meat for the family. Garden scraps, vegetables, and sour milk never failed to make a hog feel very well cared for when mixed with ground feed and fed in a trough made from an old water heater tank. Purchased in early summer as 25-pound feeder pigs, they would be pushing 250 pounds by October. If well-fed and housed for another month, a fat hog weighing three hundred pounds meant hard work at butchering time, but there were wonderful rewards as well. Fred stunned the hog, bled it, scalded it by dipping it in boiling water, scraped it to remove the hair, and eviscerated it. The split carcass hung on a singletree in the unheated garage to age for two days. On the third day, the entire family, and sometimes other relatives, gathered to cut and preserve the meat. The big meat saw came off of its nail on the wall, and the knives were sharpened with a stone. As he removed cuts from the carcass, others would cut the meat off the bone for sausage making, saving the ample fat for making lard. Pork chops were wrapped for use in the next few days, and they cut the hind legs for curing into hams. The bellies were trimmed and made ready for curing into bacon. All of the cured meat would keep into warmer weather. Much of the meat went into sausage, because it would keep for many days if seasoned and kept cold. But some of the sausage was fried after it was made up. Kenny got the job of frying sausage on the cooking range and spooning the meat into canning jars. When the jars were full of browned meat, his mother filled them with hot grease, and sealed them with zinc caps. These would keep in the cool part of the basement until hot weather. Lillian and Kenny cut the firm fat into small pieces and added them to fat that was already boiling on the range. As the liquid fat came out of the pieces, it was poured into jars and small crocks for use in cooking and baking later. The pieces that were left went into the lard press while hot to extract all of the liquid lard. The cake of cracklings left in the bottom of the lard press was one of the delicacies of butchering time. They were delicious to just eat, but they also made cornbread even better when mixed in with the batter before baking. The lard would be used to fry everything from potatoes to corn cakes to apples, and, of course, it made the very best biscuits and pie crust. Fred cured the bacon and hams, and these and the sausage would be mainstays of their diet for the next several months. Fat and drippings left in the pan after meat had been fried or roasted, when combined with flour and milk, made fine gravy. In addition, Lillian used the lard to make lye soap for washing hands and laundry. Those who helped took fresh meat home with them. Left behind in the barn was as much as a ton of good manure which would go on the garden or on farm fields after it rotted.

Chickens had long been a mainstay of rural life and a source of income and trade for farm wives. The Smiths kept hens in part of the old barn at first, but in 1937 Fred and Kenny put up a new building, using new lumber this time at a site near the old barn toward the top of the hill behind the house. This building sat on cement corner pilings, with a foot of open space underneath. It looked like a miniature barn with gambrel roof, twenty feet square. The lower level became the chicken house and the upper loft area held straw for bedding. There were three hatcheries in New Castle, and baby chicks were cheap. Occasionally a broody hen would bring in a batch of her own chicks from out in the fencerow, but new chicks for frying chickens came from the hatchery every year. Every other year the old laying hens went into the soup pot, and they raised new birds for the laying flock. This gave them all the eggs and frying and stewing chicken they could use, and provided a surplus that they sold to the neighbors or to acquaintances at the forge shop. If Lillian needed a chicken for Sunday dinner, she might kill it herself if Fred was gone, but usually he got the job. He would grasp the victim by the neck with the head against the little finger and vigorously swing the bird as one would twirl a small lasso. About four or five such turns would leave the head in his hand, and the rest of the chicken flopping about the yard. Lillian was in charge of scalding, plucking, eviscerating, removing pinfeathers, cutting, and frying.

Soon after moving to the hollow, Fred took Kenny's picture with a pet rabbit in front of the chicken house. The chickens,

Kenny Smith in the hollow as a boy of about twelve with rabbits and chickens, signs of the family's growing security in the worst part of the depression.

Rhode Island Reds and White Rocks, scratched nearby. Kenny was obviously pleased, as was his father, that they could celebrate the success of their rural dream with the subsistence livestock which were the hallmark of the small-scale producer. The rabbit could remain a pet while the offspring went into the frying pan.

They always had a garden. Fred was equipped to plow, disk, and drag the soil smooth, and there was plenty of manure to keep it rich. They raised a typical American garden with sweet corn, cucumbers, tomatoes, green bell and red cayenne peppers, onions, cabbage, potatoes, and turnips. The red peppers Lillian dried for winter usage, and the onions were cured and kept in a dry place. Potatoes, cabbages, and turnips they buried in specially constructed pits insulated with straw and leaves and covered with dirt. During the winter, these could be opened carefully to remove a week's supply of one or the other vegetable, and carefully closed again to prevent freezing.

The Smiths lived frugally, but comfortably. Providing for their immediate needs and putting something back for a rainy day was the sum of their financial strategy. The land and the equity in the house and buildings was a major part of this, and the savings account grew slowly but steadily. They needed transportation, and for an employee of the Chrysler Corporation in New Castle, this meant driving the product he helped build. Fred, like many Americans, learned to drive horses while growing up, but when cars came along he began driving Model T Fords. This continued until after Maxwell became Chrysler. In 1926, Fred bought a used Chrysler 60 sedan, then traded it for a green 1928 Chrysler 72 with yellow wire wheels. He proudly took its picture in front of the unfinished new house in the summer of 1933. This car came with a fold-down luggage carrier across the back above a platform bumper. This allowed them to carry almost anything in the way of supplies and bulky items that were bagged or packaged. This was the family car until damaged in an accident in 1937, where-upon it was traded for a gray 1935 Chrysler sedan that had belonged to Sam Foust the lumberman. In 1939 he traded for a beige-over-maroon 1937 Chrysler Royal, which was the family car until after the war. Chryslers were not the most expensive cars of the day, but they were not the cheapest, either. Most of the family cars had been owned by prominent New Castle or area citizens. The impressive Chrysler Royal, for example, had belonged to a doctor in town. Fred's steady employment allowed him to keep low-mileage, well-cared-for used cars in the garage, but he could not afford new ones. Lillian never learned to drive, so Fred drove her everywhere until Kenny got his license.

On a typical weekday, Fred and Lillian and Kenny got up at 4:15 A.M. (in a cold house if it was cold outside). Fred took the scraps from last night's supper with him when he went to the barn to do chores. By the mid-1930s, Kenny went along and milked the cow. Lillian built a fire in the stove and put water on to heat, then fixed breakfast, usually biscuits and eggs with sausage or ham and gravy, and had it ready when they came back to the house with the bucket of milk. She fixed Fred's lunch from leftovers and packed it in the metal lunch pail. He left for work by 5:30 in order to be there by 6. She cleared the breakfast dishes while Kenny got ready for school. When he was washed up in the warm kitchen, she had biscuits she had kept in the warmer oven above the range, and eggs or oatmeal for him, with milk to drink. He went off to school with a packed lunch. She liked to sit down with a cup of coffee once they had gone, before she washed the dishes and started the second phase of her day. It took time and skill to keep a fire going in a cooking range. Lillian baked often, making bread, cakes, and pies. By noon, especially in the winter, there might be a kettle on with green beans nestling fat salt pork to cook during the afternoon. In the mornings, if it was not wash-day or Tuesday's ironing, she mended or sewed. There was cleaning to do because she believed in keeping a place spotless. There were beds to change and rugs to beat, and sweeping. For a treat, she did her handwork, delighting in the monthly arrival of the new Workbasket. She churned every second or third day, washed the butter, and made buttermilk because Fred loved it. She set the skim milk and scraps aside for the hogs and chickens. They kept Auntie and Uncle, Lillian's stepmother and stepfather who had moved to New Castle in the mid-1920s, supplied with milk and butter. They also accumulated regular butter and egg customers who came to the place in the hollow to pick up their orders. On the days she did not churn, she ran the cream separator with the last couple of days' milk, or got the milk ready for Kenny to run the separator when he got home. By three o'clock in the afternoon the beginnings of supper were on the range and she might be cutting cabbage for slaw or getting potatoes out of storage. Now that President Roosevelt had signed legislation making the eight-hour day the norm, Fred was usually home by three o'clock. He would go down to Riley School to pick up Kenny if he got home in time. Late afternoons were busy because it was the main opportunity to do things outside. There was wood or coal to bring in and ashes to haul outside. Kenny might carry water for livestock or haul out wash water his mother had used, and there was hay to throw down for the cow or straw for bedding in the barn and the chicken house, and eggs to gather. Fred started and ran the generator, put the car in the garage, and brought his empty lunch pail in for Lillian to fill the next morning. She had supper ready by five o'clock, and she washed and dried the dishes afterward as well, although Kenny helped sometimes. Homework had to be done in the early evening while Fred and Lillian read the afternoon New Castle *Courier-Times*. There was a little news on the radio in the evening around suppertime, and favorite programs that they might all enjoy, such as *Amos 'n Andy*. Kenny enjoyed the radio dramas created especially for children, with *Jack Armstrong the All American Boy* his particular favorite. *The Green Hornet, Gangbusters,* and *The Shadow* excited his imagination. By 8:30, everyone was in bed. The next morning, it started all over again. On Saturdays, the routine was different. Saturday evening was the time of the week set aside for going to town. When Fred and Kenny finished their activities for the day late in the afternoon, usually by 5 or 5:30, both would sit down to supper, then take baths in the washtub. Lillian would clean up the kitchen and then get herself ready for the fifteen-minute journey in the car into the heart of New Castle's business district by seven o'clock. In town, the electric lights, as they did on so many "white ways," lent an air of excitement and anticipation to the crowded sidewalks. Saturday was busy in New Castle and it was difficult to find a place to park on Broad Street, the main thoroughfare. They usually parked on 15th Street, a block or more from Broad, and walked from there. Typically they stayed together for most of the evening, and it was customary for all of them to go together to do the grocery shopping. Afterward, they might go to the department stores, particularly Sears and Roebuck. Lillian enjoyed this break from her routine and looked forward to it each week. Sale items merited special attention, but this was a place to look at linens, dresses, hosiery, kitchen hardware, and appliances like a wringer washer. Fred's work in the forge room called for layered clothing to insulate him from the intense heat of the red-hot forgings, so it was common to buy work pants or sweatshirts for him. These might be purchased at Rapp's Clothing Store. Fred had worked for Rapp as a clerk on Saturdays for a few months soon after his arrival in New Castle, and had maintained the acquaintance. Rapp, a Jew, did himself no economic harm by occasionally attending services at the First Baptist Church. There were five dime stores in New Castle where everything from toys to notions to hardware was to be found. Men's clothing, dress shops, jewelry stores, restaurants, shoe stores, and banks all crowded along Broad Street. On the side streets auto dealers, funeral homes, tire and variety stores, garages, and pool halls kept company with lumber and plumbing supply houses, the post office, and the junior high school. Near where the Smiths parked was the interurban depot and the *Courier-Times* office. On the way home, the Smiths stopped at Mensch's Drug Store at Grand Avenue, or the Cherrywood Drug Store to purchase the Sunday Chicago *Herald-American*, the New York *Daily Mirror*, and sometimes candy or nuts.

If they only needed to go to Gernstein's grocery on I Avenue near the Chrysler, they might not go downtown at all. They frequently stopped to visit brother Tom and his wife Erma. The Saturday trip to town was never very long in the winter because the fire in the stoves would not really keep the house warm for more than three or four hours. They went to town and looked for what they needed, then went home. Summer evenings were longer, and these allowed the leisure to window-shop or buy ice cream at Denton's or one of the other drugstore soda fountains. They frequently bought an extra sale item or two to take to Auntie and Uncle on their way home. In the summer there was no need to get home to keep the stove going, but morning chores came early, so by 9:00 they would be headed home. By the mid-1930s, Fred and Lillian had already lived in New Castle for fifteen years and it was common to see Fred's co-workers and their families in the stores or crossing the streets. Lillian's acquaintances were limited to family and neighbors and occasional egg or butter customers. Fred was an established and respected employee of the Chrysler, and a veteran of the world war, so they would on occasion see and greet people they knew. The Smiths fit into the American main street and rural culture of the 1930s and felt at home in it. Entertainment was scarce. There were the movies, of course, and New Castle had four theaters in the late 1920s and early 1930s: the Ideal, the Starrett, the Princess, and the Royal. Hollywood's version of history and life appeared on the silver screen in double features and matinees. On rare occasions, there might be a circus, but not every year, and there were picnics and outings to Memorial Park where the statue of the doughboy of the Great War stood up on the hill along the highway across from the interurban stop. The biggest public event of the year for children was the Easter egg hunt at Memorial Park. On Easter Sunday afternoon, over a thousand children came with their parents for the city-sponsored event. The little ones were released from the lines first, then a great wave of older children broke over the hills to look for eggs. These events were considered big enough at the time to be preserved on black-and-white movie film for later viewing. Even rarer was the visit of a barnstorming pilot to the area. South of New Castle on Highway 3 was a level farm where biplanes could land, and word of such an arrival spread quickly from the noise of the plane overhead and notices posted about, or from a newspaper ad. Kenny was taken down to see such a pilot when he was about nine, and even went for a ride. The heroes of such little boys were often the Spad and Nieuport pilots of the Great War such as Rickenbacker, Lufbery, Mannock, Bishop, and Fonck. They imitated these heroes in sound and appearance as best they could. Leather flying helmets and goggles were all the rage among Kenny and his friends, as a 1929 picture of the gang attests. These activities, and reading materials, toys, and friends, were the standard pastimes of the day. The typical Sunday was somewhat different. The Smiths attended the First Baptist Church occasionally on Sunday mornings but usually spent the day at home. They often had family for dinner Sunday noon, or went to a family member's home for dinner. If dinner was at the house in the hollow, they stayed home from church and Lillian spent the morning fixing the meal. If they went to Lillian's sister Mabel's home or visited Fred's sister or the brothers who lived in the area, she took a dish and helped upon arrival. Sunday dinner somewhere else was a welcome break from the work at home, especially for Lillian. After the dishes were done, there would be visiting in the afternoon, beans to snap, or peas to shell.

The Moles Family Continues Its Grim Struggle

The worst days of the depression came to an end for Jess and Ethel and their girls by mid-1934, but they didn't know the worst was behind them at the time. No one could know what might happen tomorrow. As it turned out, Jess's collapse and rebound coincided with the first year in Washington of the new president, Franklin Delano Roosevelt, and his New Deal for the American people. Jess voted for Herbert Hoover in 1928 less out of enthusiasm for the Republicans than out of disdain for the Catholic, old-line Democrat Al Smith. All in all, though, Hoover had been the energizing factor in every administration in the 1920s, with his tireless promotion of cooperation between business and government. His reputation as the brilliant and compassionate Food Administrator here during the Great War, and in Belgium after the Armistice, remained intact. Hoover could keep prosperity going if anyone could. But before the year ended following his inauguration, Hoover's world began to fall apart, and with it collapsed the dreams of millions of Americans who thought the false prosperity would never end. Inflation, disastrous new tariff restrictions, and an inept Federal Reserve wove a pattern of disaster for the nation, but most people were unaware of the causes. All they saw was the decline of manufacturing and the unemployment it brought, the appearance in the papers of pictures of soup lines in some of the large cities, and the sickening feeling that things would get much worse before they got better. After a couple of years of this, some began to believe that the condition was permanent and the depression was the future. Hoover tried to cajole and legislate a return to the good times, but his activity seemed to have no effect. By the time 1931 and 1932 arrived, gloom had become a fixture in the White House as it had in the rest of the country. Roosevelt preached a restrained, conservative message in his campaign of 1932, promising to balance the budget and act with caution in working to get the country moving. His message could have been almost anything, or nothing, so bitter were voter feelings toward Hoover and the Republicans. The worst features of the depression became associated with the luckless president, but the most damaging was the term "Hooverville," which was the name given to the collections of tin and tarpaper shanties which sprang up around the country to house people who had lost everything, including a place to stay. Pictures of these shantytowns appeared in the papers, magnifying their effect and soliciting sympathy especially when local officials tried to remove them or intervened to arrest a resident.

Millions of Americans, including Jess Moles, came to believe it was Hoover's fault that the country was collapsing, and that Hoover had failed to do what was necessary to stop it. It was no leap at all to the conclusion that Jess was out of work and his wife took in the grocery owner's laundry because Hoover was too interested in big business to care about the workingman. In this way Jess developed a bitterness toward all Republicans, but especially toward this particular one because, as he said himself, "Hoover made my little girls starve." Roosevelt, then, became the Great Deliverer, and he was regarded as just that in the house at 2028 Plum Street, much as many others on the same street and on other streets in New Castle adored him. This political doctrine of Democrat redemption became a given for Jess, and he brooked no dissent about it from his wife, his daughters, or his acquaintances. There was nothing to discuss, because it was self-evident that Roosevelt was in the process of saving the country every day. It said so in the papers. To Jess, FDR's critics were big-business types like Colonel McCormick of the Chicago *Tribune* and other malcontents who were not willing to allow a little of the pie for anyone else, especially workingmen like Jess. Roosevelt battled for the rights of the workingman everywhere, and his buoyant words over the radio gave many hope that finally something was being done, even if no one was quite sure what to do to fix the nation's problems. The new president promised bold experimentation in the hope that trying anything might result in the discovery of a solution, and that was more than Hoover had done. Roosevelt closed the banks and persuaded Congress to outlaw the ownership of gold, relaxed the antitrust laws, and hired thousands of "experts" to begin working on ways to get the nation out of the depression. Many of these experts had worked in the War Industries Board and other agencies during the Great War, and they knew firsthand how to handle big problems. They would find a way.

Hoover had been called the "human dynamo" in his Commerce Secretary days, but the activism of the New Deal made the Hoover era pale by comparison. Alphabet agencies sprang out of enabling legislation and dozens of appropriations bills in 1933 and 1934 as bureaucrats and secretaries and members of Congress commenced a flurry of work for themselves and some of the nation's unemployed. In his inaugural address, Roosevelt said that the first thing to be done was to put people to work, and the New Deal agencies began to do that. They raised taxes and borrowed money to pay for work on bridges and roads, for artwork in post offices, for raking leaves, for interviewing former slaves, and for copying cemetery records in most counties in the nation. Congress sent money to cities and to county governments to be handed out as relief, and promised there would be more soon. The administration was doing something, of that there could be no doubt. Four years into the depression, things began to look a little better, and this came in 1933 and 1934 just as New Deal programs began to go into effect. Jess drew hope from the trends he read about in the papers, and at the same time he began to get called back to the machine shop at the Chrysler more frequently. Roosevelt would lead the country back into the light again. FDR said in a ringing phrase in his inaugural address that "fear itself" was the only thing Americans had to fear. He won the battle to change the psychology of the nation and to tip the balance of feeling in the country toward the positive, and he continued to maintain this attitude personally and among his fellow citizens. Things might still be very bad, or getting worse, but many felt that, overall, a corner had been turned and it was only a question of time until prosperity would be back on every street. The country had fallen so very far that almost any improvement looked good, and the Moles family hung on and adapted to the unpleasant task of continuing to push through the long tunnel.

They accomplished this with Jess's more frequent work, with Ethel's help with the grocery bill, and with other means as well. There was enough yard behind the house to put in some garden, and this became a ritual with Jess. He turned the soil over with a spade and raked the clods smooth, then planted the seeds and set out tomato plants and onion sets from Redelman's hardware store. Much of this produce Ethel canned into quart jars in the late summer and stored in the kitchen because the house had no basement. From the two pear trees in the back yard they carefully picked and wrapped the fruit in newspaper to slowly ripen in the house after the cold weather began each year. This made for a free treat, and for pear preserves which made ordinary bread into dessert. Vegetables beyond Ethel's capacity to preserve were given to the girls with orders to take them door-to-door in the neighborhood to sell. This was another embarrassment, and they resented it, but they had to do it anyway. Nearly every other resident of their street was in a similar condition, with children to feed and uncertain work, but it was an opportunity to actually sell for cash something they had but could not use. Jess was a good gardener, and at least from those who did not have the room or did not take the time to grow things he got some small return this way when a dime or a nickel went a long way. But, like delivering the laundry, it was a public admission that the Moles family was still teetering on the edge financially, and had to rely on the goodwill of the neighbors to help them get by.

The girls thought about food often. There were evenings when the only thing to eat was fried potatoes, because potatoes were about as cheap as anything that could be bought. But potatoes fried in lard will fill up a man and stay with him and give him strength the next day. Jess sometimes went out in the country early on Saturday mornings and shot rabbits or squirrels and brought them back to fix for breakfast. There began a tradition of going out to the Villars place outside of town to buy chickens and eggs on occasions when there was a little money left over. Eggs cost very little on the farm, sometimes only ten or fifteen cents a dozen, and these, too, would satisfy hunger and make a good sandwich in the next day's lunch box. They gathered apples that fell from neglected trees and were not too proud to take handouts from neighbors and from people at the Nazarene church they attended. Marie's teacher at school regularly gave her clothes during an entire school year, and sent food home with her, too. Sometimes Gemma took the $10 monthly rent money to Mr. Garr, the kindly man who owned their house. When there was no money for rent, he allowed Jess to pay when he could, and never pressed him or threatened to evict them. They got by somehow.

Many of Jess's relatives from Tennessee came to stay with them in these years because of severe unemployment problems in the upper South. It was already crowded in the little house at 2028 Plum Street, but the visitors squeezed in anyhow, much as Jess and Ethel shared the limited space offered by Jim and Haley in 1923. Ethel's brother Beecher and wife Pauline, Uncle Porter, Grandma Baltimore, and Ethel's sister Hazel were all there at one time or another. These stays might go on for two or three months or even longer, with everyone feeling the discomfort of the inadequate space and the crowd around the table at meals. Sometimes they brought a little extra money for groceries, which helped, but they were in trouble financially or they would not have come north looking for work at such a time. If there were children, then there were additional faces to accommodate in the games, and more sharing of the bicycle. Everyone persevered, and the visitors would finally leave and life would return to normal.

Ethel kept the children clean, but they often dressed shabbily because there was not enough money to buy new clothes. As a result, hand-me-downs were the rule when they were younger. They wore dresses and shoes until they were worn out or until they no longer fit, and often beyond that. Other girls made fun of Gemma because she wore white shoes to school in the winter, but one school year it was the only pair she had. Gemma grew ashamed of their house and ashamed of the street where they lived. She noticed the ragged lifestyle they all lived, and she resented it secretly.

Their home on Plum Street was less than three blocks from three different railroads. As the depression wore on, thousands of men hopped freight trains in the hope of stumbling into a job or another meal somewhere down the track. As the trains slowed coming into New Castle, some of the men jumped off and looked for a handout or a dry place to call home for a few days. Seeing hoboes on trains became a commonplace event and sometimes they came into the neighborhood looking for something to eat. Hobo etiquette dictated that one always asked for food at the back door. Ethel responded to knocks on the back door with kindness. They did not have much, but if there was something left over from breakfast, a biscuit or two, or some bread that could be sopped in the frying pan to make a sandwich, or some green beans that had been simmered with a bit of fat, she gave it to them. There was little fear of these men, even though they might come from anywhere, and the doors were not locked at night or when they were away from the house. Hoboes reminded them they could be worse off, that they might have to beg at back doors because they had not eaten since the day before. The pity she showed them reminded them all that maybe things were not so bad after all, not that bad. The girls might answer the knock, but they were not afraid. The hopeless ones looked down and tipped hats, mumbled thanks, and shuffled off toward other back doors further along, perhaps grateful that there was no woodpile at this house (so they would not have to chop wood).

New Friends

The Moles family had lived on Plum Street for a little over four years when new neighbors moved in next door. Fred Wright bought an eighty-acre farm south of New Castle out of his father's estate in 1929, but Fred's wife Eva refused to move there. Fred decided to abandon the farm for a store building at 17th and G Avenue in 1930. The store was in a good location, about two blocks either way from the Chrysler and the Hoosier, and had rooms upstairs. Eva found them appalling, and refused to make a home there, either. Fred managed to find a family, the Browns, to rent the building, but the Browns failed in the grocery business in the early part of 1931, and this time Fred could find no one who would pay the rent. Fred Wright then rented the house near the Moleses at 2029 Plum Street in October 1931. The Wrights had two children, Sarah, born in 1924, and her younger brother George, born in 1929. Another brother, Paul, was born on Plum Street a year after they moved there. By the time Paul Wright and Wanda Moles came along, there were more than thirty children who lived on Plum between 18th and 21st Streets.

Sarah and Gemma became best friends almost immediately. It was Sarah who comforted Gemma after she had been teased about wearing white shoes in the winter. Sarah noted wisely that they were better than having no shoes at all. From that moment they were fast friends and confidantes, sharing their secrets and inner thoughts in the full confidence that not a word would be whispered or betrayed. They walked together to get away from annoying brothers and sisters and to feel the freedom of being out of earshot of everyone they knew. The Pennsylvania passenger depot was less than three blocks away, and it offered interesting scenes of travel to faraway places to the girls when they were a little older. In high school, Sarah and Gemma walked there countless times to watch the trains arrive and depart, pulled by the chuffing steam locomotives. Although Sarah was Maxine's age, Gemma was the friend she loved, and who loved her in return.

Both Gemma and Sarah were oldest children, so they shared the complaints that went with the position. Both mothers expected their oldest daughters to do whatever was demanded of them so far as babysitting, helping with dishes, cleaning house, and sewing and mending. Sarah's mother believed that idleness was a danger to be avoided at all costs. When finished with household duties, Sarah was expected to do embroidery work. Eva gave away the pillowcases and hankies Sarah made for Christmas gifts. Gemma spent much of her time at home helping her mother care for and entertain Maxine, Marie, and Wanda. These duties were in addition to homework and outside play.

Eva Wright grew up with family trauma. One of seven children, at age seven she and her little brother witnessed their father's suicide. Their mother gave away Eva's older sister as a child because she could not provide for all the children. Eva had been expected to earn her own keep from the age of ten, and always harbored the fear that she might be given away too. Eva Wright raised her family in the 1920s and 1930s as though she carried a grudge against the world. She was rough and unpleasant and often vented her considerable rage at anyone who happened to be nearby. The Moles girls could hear her swearing at Fred or her children from inside their house. She gave Sarah a difficult time and was the source of considerable embarrassment to all of them, as she did not hesitate to make a scene in public.

In spite of his domestic troubles, Fred worked hard at the Ingersoll Rolling Mill and began to make some headway. The house they rented at 2029 Plum Street, one of the largest on the street, cost them $32.50 per month, a considerable sum, in part because it had a coal furnace. Most of the houses in the area had only stoves, but the Wrights were better off. As the depression began in other cities, Fred bought a new wool rug for their living room and blue chinchilla coats for Sarah and her brother George one Christmas, and Sarah received a wicker doll carriage and doll. But, as the depression worsened, the Wrights fell on hard times like many others, and Fred decided to relocate to a smaller house at 2032 Plum Street. This move eliminated the high rent, but there was still a mortgage, and it was a severe blow to Eva. It was a much smaller house, and it had no furnace, so they had to haul ashes from the stoves like everyone else. Eva coped with the depression by seeing to it that no scrap of food, no idle moment, no item that had any value was wasted. The children wore clothes cut from the hand-me-down gifts of other people. When she got home from school, Sarah had to stay in while her only pair of stockings dried after she washed them. Even a seemingly trivial loss could shake their situation. Eva sent Sarah to the A&P with half a dollar for food that her mother needed. Walking along the railroad tracks near Broad Street, she dropped the two quarters, and could not find them. She ran home in tears to report the loss, and the whole family went back to help look for the coins. Sarah received no punishment, but they never found the money. The Wrights did without a car, and hunkered down for the duration of the storm that had struck them. Eva put meat on the table by working for the Householders, who farmed south of town. Every week for the whole year she washed, dried, and ironed their laundry. When the cold weather arrived early in the winter and it was time to butcher hogs, they gave the Wrights a hog to pay Eva for doing the laundry all year. The whole family helped to can the pork when it arrived so they could draw on the supply for the rest of the year without refrigeration.

Eva's anger with the situation life had given her never ended, and her fury often made their lives miserable. The scars of her earlier traumas stayed with her, even as the memories faded into the past. She fought those around her as if they had all played some part in forcing upon her the struggle she could not escape. Holidays were an ordeal. Eva refused to take the time to look for a Christmas tree, so when Fred showed up at the door with one, she started in on him, on the idea of a holiday, and on everyone who wanted to have one. The tree could not go up before Christmas Eve. She complained about it before it went up, while it was up, and when it came down. Having it in the living room for more than two or three days was intolerable, so the children's Christmas joy was short-lived.

Sarah did not understand why her mother behaved the way she did toward them all, and Eva's rages were just another fact of life on the street where they lived. So was the fact that she did not kiss her children or put her arms around them.

Playing in the 1930s

The neighborhood children played together harmoniously for the most part. Mothers with children did not work at outside jobs in those days, so when children were home, mothers were home, too. There were petty antagonisms, hurt feelings, an occasional fight, and scraped knees and elbows, but something as serious as a broken bone was relatively rare. Gemma found out that care was needed, however. She turned a corner on the bicycle soon after they got it and broke an arm in the crash. Having her arm in a sling for a month impressed upon her the need to watch for sharp turns. She fell on the steps, causing a gash in her shin that became infected. It took more than one trip to the doctor to get the area scraped and cleaned before it began to heal up. It left a scar the size of a quarter that could not be hidden. Seldom did neighborhood children except Gemma come to the Wright house to play. Mrs. Sherry and Mrs. Dudley lived near the streetlight corner and did not approve of children playing near their homes, but others like Mrs. Breckinridge loved all the children and enjoyed having them around. Some, like the Whites, seemed to always be outside working in their yards.

Most of them got along well. Gemma and Sarah liked to play with the Breckinridge kids, the Stigleman girls, and the Sterns. There were others who joined in occasionally, like the Filson kids, Roseanne Poston, and Dorothy Jean Zirkle, or Mrs. Davis's grandchildren when they visited. There were less frequent participants such as Eldon Ashabranner, or even Sarah's brother George. George could get carried away, like the time he drew the attention of his mother by chasing Maxine through their garden with a butcher knife, mock-threatening hellish harm. Eva brought the episode to an abrupt halt.

The corner of 20th and Plum Streets was the gathering place for the neighborhood children. In the daytime it was merely central and convenient, because it afforded a view in both directions

along Plum and allowed mothers to step onto their porches to see
if their children were playing within the territorial limits. In the
daytime there were dolls to play with, hopscotch, and jump rope
to join in, or jacks. At night, though, the corner was magical,
because it was the only place between 18th and 21st where there
was an overhead electric streetlight. In the 1930s, streetlights
were large incandescent bulbs protected by a cone-shaped metal
cover which directed the light downward in a larger cone shape,
making a fairly distinct circle on the street and up on part of the
sidewalk. The bulb was akin to what might have been found in a
barn or warehouse. Directly underneath it visibility was quite
good, but twenty feet away the intensity had gone, and beyond
that it was too murky to see much except in silhouette. Hide-and-
seek was the best of games in such a situation, because objects
which offered little in the daylight served well as cover only thirty
or forty feet away from the light pole. Whoever was "it" had to
peer out into the darkness made the more obscure by the bright-
ness of the light itself. The hushed urgency of finding a hiding
place once the counting began was followed by the breathless
attempt to stand motionless while calculating the odds of dashing
to the pole before being discovered and tagged. Being tagged
ended the round and made the unfortunate one "it," but being
the last one to come in was risky, too, because there was always someone who wanted to give away someone else's position because they had already made it in safely. Kick-the-can
and kick-the-stick also worked well under the light, and made
for short evenings before the summertime bedtime of 9 P.M.
The school night bedtime was eight o'clock. Mothers allowed
their children to go only so far, and these rules they enforced
very strictly, should word come back about a violation. When
George Wright skated into 21st Street from Plum, he put himself
in jeopardy twice. The immediate danger was the car driven by
Mrs. Quigley, a teacher at Weir Elementary School. Fortunately,
George survived being knocked down in the street by the teacher
who did her best to avoid him. Then Sarah and George faced a
dilemma: Should they report the good fortune that George had
escaped with only minor scrapes and bruises? Or was the offense
of venturing into 21st Street so serious that it was better to try to
hide the whole thing from their mother, who was sure to visit her

wrath on the survivor? Mrs. Quigley took Sarah off the hook by reporting the incident to their mother. George suffered severely at his mother's hands.

Religious Practice

The residents of Plum Street were a religious lot, on the whole, and mostly Protestant. The Moles family attended the Nazarene church, and it was from this church that the occasional small loan or gifts of clothing and food came. The Nazarene church was a little less than five blocks away, so they usually walked. This church became the major social outlet in their lives. They went nearly every Sunday, and it took sickness or a visit from relatives to suspend it. There was solidarity there. Most of those who attended were about as well off as the Moleses, and the strict moral teachings of the Nazarenes fit well with the tone at home. The message from the pulpit was stern, and visiting evangelists and revivals were common. These were advertised in the New Castle *Courier-Times,* in the hopes of swelling the crowds and the numbers of the saved. The sermon each Sunday tended to steer toward the depravity and inclination to sin that was part of being human. This came from Adam's fall, and it was part of every man, woman, and child from birth; there was no escaping it. The burden of this guilt lay upon everyone, whether they darkened the doors of a church building or not, and made for morose forebodings on the part of children and adolescents. God grew angry and held a terrible punishment in a lake of fire in hell for those who failed to avoid the temptations that the earthly life offered. Attempting to resist sin was hopeless, nevertheless, and the only sure hope of salvation was to make sure you had accepted the cleansing power of Jesus into your heart recently. To think that you were once saved, always saved was a mistake people made in their self-delusion and arrogance. Revivals came to the Nazarene church often because they were needed to keep those who were weak (everyone) on the straight and narrow. The Moles family went to their share of these as well.

Sarah Wright went to St. Anne's Catholic Church a block north of Broad on 19th Street, about seven blocks away, with her brothers. Eva sent them on Sunday mornings, and they went back in the afternoon for catechism. Sarah's mother did not go to church anymore, and her father was not Catholic, but Eva insisted the children go. This was the only Catholic church in town because most of the factory workers like Jess and Ethel Moles had come from Kentucky and Tennessee where Catholic churches were scarce. Because Sarah and Gemma were such close friends, this gave Gemma an opportunity that few who attended Protestant churches in New Castle had: a regular experience in a Catholic church. Sarah returned the favor and sometimes went to the Nazarene church with Gemma and her family. At St. Anne's, the Wright children were at about the bottom of the social order. Sarah was sometimes ashamed to go because the holes in her shoes showed when she had to kneel for prayer. She tried to spread her coat over them so no one would notice. She was confirmed in the Church and took Holy Communion, as did both of her brothers. During the worst times in the depression, the priest visited many Catholic homes in New Castle, but did not come to the Wright house, and there was no help from the parishioners. Sarah saw her grandmother and aunts and cousins there on Sundays, but her mother's exile from the Church was a permanent thing, neither discussed nor understood by her children.

There were other islands of alternative belief in town also. A few Jews lived in New Castle, mostly business families like the Zetterbergs, Goldbergs, Rapps, and the Dann family who owned the scrap yard on East Broad. As there was no synagogue in town, they had to go to Muncie for services and fellowship in a congregation.

3. The Slow Pull Upward, Late 1930s

AFTER THE WRIGHTS and Moleses and others on the street had descended so near to ruin in the early 1930s, what followed seemed like recovery. It was not, of course, and they all continued to struggle in the effort to pull themselves up a little further each year. There were mixed results. For many, work continued to be irregular, or at least not completely dependable. For most, wages had declined since 1929 in the face of the adjusting pressure of the depression, which few understood. At the same time, rent or house payments still had to be met, and there were people who lost their homes on Plum Street before 1935. Banks or noteholders hesitated to foreclose on a property because of the costs, and it was the rule that a debtor could go for several months or even a year in arrears if there was some hope of recovery or if token payments came in regularly. Most managed to find the rent or note payment somehow. Cars became commonplace in the 1920s, but not every family owned one, in spite of the efforts of men like Henry Ford, who made automobiles in the price range that millions could begin to think affordable. There was a thriving market in used cars in practically every town in America, on used car lots, around garages, and between individuals. Jess always had a car from the time they got on their feet in New Castle in the later 1920s. Purchasing a new car was far beyond his capability, but there were bargains to be had if one had the eye and the patience to shop carefully. He probably had a Model T Ford first, as so many did, because they were abundant, having been made from the 1910s to 1925, and about the cheapest as well. By the time Wanda was born in 1929, he had an old Chevrolet, recognizable everywhere by the noise the brakes made when slightly worn. Although he worked at Chrysler, the company did not make cars for the common man until the 1930s, when the Plymouth and DeSoto lines began to come within reach. Consequently, he drove other makes until the mid-1930s, when he bought a used 1934 Plymouth. He traded this later for a 1936 Plymouth.

Owning a car was a tradeoff Jess decided was worthwhile. The six of them lived in one of the smallest houses on Plum Street, on a tiny lot with no garage. Nearby, the Wrights lived in one of the biggest houses, paying more than three times the rent Jess and Ethel paid, but had no car. This made some people ask questions about Jess's priorities, because a car was something that could almost always be sold for a sum of cash. Even the price of an old T might pay their rent for half a year, and most used cars sold for far more than this. But the car, almost any car, was a symbol of status and mobility with which he was not willing to part. If the tires remained in good condition, a car could be operated for very little money, because gas cost under 20¢ per gallon in those years. It could always be left sitting, with no expense save a license plate, when circumstances demanded. Occasional questions arose about this later, when he drove cars that were only two or three years old, at considerably greater expense than many people thought he should be able to afford.

One of the sights that became familiar on Plum Street in those years was the bill collector. Installment buying grew in popularity in the 1920s during enthusiastic economic times and continued as many people accepted the idea that it was not dishonorable. This fueled the temptation to buy on credit when times were good but little money was available for a down payment. A sizeable sum in down payment could practically guarantee credit terms, but for many items under $30, a few dollars down and a dollar a month would put a coveted item in one's home. Payment was to be made at the cashier's window at the place the credit had been obtained, but when money was short, people stayed home to avoid admitting they could not pay. As a result, businesses began to send collectors out to extend that face-to-face pressure at the front door of the debtor family. Every collector knew it was unusual for there to be no money at all in a house. Even a partial payment helped. Twenty-five cents a week made for a dollar a month. If someone kept up with payments, no collector showed. If they fell behind, the knock started sounding at the door. Anyone who cared to look out the window could see who was having difficulty because they recognized the collectors. When Sarah Wright announced to her mother that George Stubbs, the collector for Shuffman's Furniture, was coming up the walk, Eva told her daughter to tell him she wasn't home. Sarah spoke right up when Mr. Stubbs knocked: "My mommy told me to tell you that she isn't home right now." He was there to collect for the rug Fred bought on credit in 1929. The bill collector came to the Moles house, too. Most of the time there was a little bit to give him, but sometimes there was not.

What money there was had to be used with the utmost care, and Jess and Ethel and the girls learned where their money went the furthest. When buying shoes could not be put off any longer, they usually went to Clift's on Broad Street for the Buster Brown brand. These were inexpensive, but well made, and they lasted longer. A coal man brought their coal from Daley's coal yard on 12th Street. This went onto the ground at 2028 Plum because there was no basement and no garage. In the winter, the coal froze together and had to be broken apart before it could be taken into the house. They rarely bought furniture, but when they did they usually went to Brammer's store, although an occasional item might come from the more prestigious Shuffman's. Jess did the grocery shopping by himself at the A&P on Fleming Street when he could, but Ethel and the girls went to the neighborhood grocery because they could get credit there and because it was closer. At all the grocery stores customers asked for the items they wished to buy and a clerk reached for them on the shelves. Ethel went every morning to get the food items they needed for that day, because they had no icebox. They had a window box in the cold weather, but no way to keep things cold in the summer. In 1935 Jess found a used icebox, just about the time people in town began to buy the new electric refrigerators with the big condensers on top. Ice for the icebox came from Consumer's Ice and Fuel, and the ice card in the front window was a familiar sight at their house as it was all over town. Mr. Evans, who had been their next-door neighbor on P Avenue, was the ice man. They had an oil range for a while on Plum Street, then switched to natural gas because it was cheaper. Real progress came when Jess consented to buy a Maytag wringer washer for Ethel. It was used, of course, but it allowed her to do other things while the wash agitated. The water had to be heated to make the soap work well, and afterward the dirty water had to be dumped, but it was a big advance from the washboard. The Jersey Creamery milkman came to Plum Street with his horse and milk wagon on a regular route, which the horse knew as well as the milkman. As he took shortcuts between houses, the horse pulled the wagon along the street to keep up, stopping at the right moment without being told. There was a wood Jersey Creamery box on the porch, and into this the milkman put the quart and pint glass bottles with their cardboard stoppers and paper caps. The empty bottles would be sitting beside the box. The milkman carried his bottles in a wire basket which made a characteristic tinkling sound when he walked up on the porch before dawn. In the winter, the snow creaking under the wagon wheels also told the residents the milkman was coming.

Inner Thoughts

People generally did not lock their doors, so confident were they that few if any would risk prison for burglary in such a neighborhood. But the children might not be so confident. The sensational kidnapping of the Lindbergh baby for ransom in 1931 planted a fear in Sarah that would not go away. Sarah slept in an upstairs bedroom, and it was to just such a room that the kidnapper had raised a ladder to enable him to snatch the baby. The picture of the ladder leaning against the upper window frame at the Lindbergh's home went into every newspaper in the country, and Sarah saw it in the *Courier-Times* that came to their house on Plum Street. It terrified her, and she lived in fear of the noise of the ladder against her window, lying awake for hours in order to run for her life if she heard it.

Wanda, the youngest, acquired some fears because of stories her sisters sometimes told to scare her. Wanda hid under the bed when she heard sirens, afraid that something terrible was about to happen to them. The older Moles girls terrified Wanda on occasion when they took her to the grocery with them. On the way back they would sometimes tell her that "that old man" was coming after them, and run for home, much faster than she could. She would arrive shaken and crying after they had rushed in and shut the front door. Ethel always held her and told her not to pay attention to those girls.

Jess threatened on many occasions to send his daughters to the "reform school" when they misbehaved. He was well known for going over and over an incident day after day, pounding home the same message of correction until they could not bear to hear it anymore. They did not know where the reform school was, or what happened to girls who were sent there, but they knew from the way their father spoke that it was a terrible place they were just about bad enough to be sent to if they didn't change their ways. He could drive a lesson home in a way that none of them could escape.

In Jess's mind there were dangers children could be expected to experience if not watched carefully. There were "certain things" kids might do, after all. Maxine remembered the first time this dark side of children came to her attention. She and other children had been playing kick-the-can for some time as dusk began to fall. She and a boy hid carefully in a darkened part of 20th Street. When they saw the opportunity to run home free, they jumped up and over a bank of earth into the light and ran into Maxine's father. He grabbed her by the arm and said, "I'm going to take you to the reform school tomorrow!" as she wondered what she could possibly have done to warrant it. He practically dragged her to the house and informed Ethel she was to take Maxine to the doctor first thing in the morning and have her examined. Downstairs, Jess and Ethel talked long into the night about it as the girls upstairs tried to catch a word here and there. Maxine, terrified that something terrible was wrong with her, cried a lot and was upset for days. Gemma did not know what the doctor was going to do. Maxine asked her mother what she was going to go to the doctor for, but Ethel knew Jess's ways. "He's just saying that," she told Maxine. They did not go to the doctor, and it eventually blew over, but Maxine remained puzzled about "going to the doctor" for several years until she learned more.

Jess was always going on about things like that. He would say, "I was in the Navy, I know what's going on!" But the girls never knew what he meant by these dark words. To Jess, the shameful, dirty side of a person was always lurking just below the surface, and it was always on the mind. One reason church was so impor- tant was that it was one of the few ways to fight this tendency to temptation outside the home. Morality was a virtue that had to be taught and supported at every possible opportunity. A life of misery and vice was the sure reward for those who gave in to the attractions of sin.

It was not a good idea to mention anything of a sexual nature, they soon learned. Gemma and Maxine began to put their obser- vations together to come up with a partial answer to the question of where babies came from. Mrs. Filson down the street got fat, then there was a new baby and then she wasn't fat anymore. Maxine asked her mother why Mrs. Filson got so fat. Jess, stand- ing nearby, slapped her face hard. Maxine did not bring the sub- ject up again. Marie was not present to absorb this lesson, how- ever. They had a mother cat who bore a litter of kittens on a regular basis, and on one occasion she chose a quiet area behind the dining room door. Jess called Marie over to see, and she informed him that she knew that the cat was going to have kit- tens. He asked her, "How did you know that?" Marie replied, "Because she's getting so fat!" Whack! She reeled from the slap to her face, and ran for consolation to her mother and sisters. Later, they all learned that when parents mentioned that someone like Mrs. Filson was "in a family way," that pregnant was what they meant. The word "pregnant" was forbidden. If Ethel objected to this kind of correction, she said nothing. Jess was used to having his way about disciplinary matters around the house, and to op- pose him would probably have been unsuccessful at any rate. What would she have done with four little children in the de- pression if she had taken a stand and he had walked out? It just was not done. Certain other words, they soon learned, also bet- ter went unsaid. One of the girls uttered the word "jazz." Jess stormed at them to never use language like that, and hammered at the theme for days afterward. "Jazz" was a dirty word, for some mysterious reason. When Jess was in the navy, he and his shipmates had been stuck in New York for over a year while workmen finished the USS *Tennessee*. During this time, the venereal disease rate skyrocketed among the crew, and there were strict warnings about the kind of places this kind of thing could be picked up. Jazz was new in 1920, and was probably associated in his mind with the dangers of a fate worse than death.

The worst corporal punishment for the girls was whipping. This was done in the time-honored upper South way with a switch, a supple, thin branch from a tree or shrub. Once the leaves had been removed, a good switch made a frightful sound when whipped through the air, which children heard with dread. Properly applied, a good whipping with a switch left red welts wherever it struck. For the Moles girls, this was on bare legs. The intense pain and the tears did not last too long, but the welts took two or three days to disappear. Other children on the same street got the same thing, or got whippings with a father's belt, or with a mother's hand. Swift and sure punishment for violations of rules kept these outbreaks to a minimum. Sisters and friends who saw or overheard these incidents got the message as well. Maxine and Marie thought they got most of the whippings. Gemma, older and wiser, had gotten most of hers before her sisters remembered them. Wanda, the baby, got away with more, the way the other girls saw it. There was a tension, a comparative factor that all of the Moles girls resented. Jess and Ethel used each of the girls to keep the others well behaved by citing the behavior of another as an example. This tended to sow some discord among the four of them, which would have been present naturally at any rate. Thus, each had some complaint about the others, as siblings do. But there were comments that hurt sometimes, even though their parents probably did not intend them that way. One of Gemma's most painful memories came on several occasions after Ethel gave birth to Maxine. Her father told her that she was not the baby anymore in a way that crushed her feelings and led her to believe that she was an outsider in her own family from that moment on, at least in his eyes. One's own family was the only connection to survival and the only protection against all that they feared most. It was an unhappy time to be an exile in one's own home, excluded from the attention that the younger ones got. Baby Wanda was such a pretty little girl and she seemed to get much of the attention. Maxine endeared herself to relatives and visitors with the little dance she did, but Gemma, the oldest, thought of herself as an ugly child. She was supposed to shepherd the other girls to school and back safely, but she rebelled against this duty one day and ran ahead to school without waiting for the others. She got in trouble at home when they reported this to Jess and Ethel, and she did not do it again, but some anger remained. The natural resentment of the younger children in the family was something that she tried to suppress, but which came out sometimes. They were all sensitive to words spoken without consideration of their full impact.

Life in the Hollow

By 1938, the routine in the hollow began to change gradually as they became more settled and Kenny grew old enough to do a man's work on the farm. He turned seventeen in the summer of 1938. Fred had bought fifteen acres of the higher ground behind the house from the Brennemans the previous summer for $1,300. This land was gently rolling and already cleared, so they began a crop rotation on it immediately. Fred planted more corn and oats and wheat in the late 1930s and into the 1940s. A new crop, soybeans, was introduced in the late 1930s, and Fred planted a few acres himself about 1940. Hay production and pasture were important for Ollie and her calves, and for the beef cattle that Fred enjoyed caring for and feeding. When they made more hay than they could use or store, Fred hired a custom baler to come to the farm to bale the excess. This was the first time Kenny had seen hay baled as they fed the stationary baler with forks and admired the big bales they wire-tied by hand.

Kenny had the allowable activities of boys to amuse him. In the lot near the creek he and the Burden boys or Phil Smith and other friends would ride the calf and hunt for frogs and tadpoles, or try to catch minnows. There were always farm cats, with kittens in the summer, and a dog. About 1939, Fred adopted a pup of uncertain ancestry he named Cap, who subsequently became the stuff of family legend. The school year dominated Kenny's routine. Fred and Lillian did not allow him to start school until the fall of 1929, when he was eight years old. This gave him an advantage over the other kids, because he was stronger and more mature than they, but it meant that when he graduated from high school in 1941, he was nineteen years old. After the loss of their daughter, his parents clung to him in a supportive way, and always wanted him at home or close at hand. They feared losing him at a time when the loss of children of any age was neither unusual nor particularly remarkable. It happened all the time. His time was divided between farm and house chores and school-work. He got average grades in school, usually Bs, with a scattering of As and Cs. Occasionally, a teacher would write on his report card, as happened in 1940, when the comment came home that "McKendrick could do better" in American history.

Kenny had a natural interest in history and current events nurtured at home by his father, by the newspapers, and by the radio. He enjoyed spinning the radio dial to bring in distant stations at a time when there were relatively few of them to be heard. Through the radio and the papers, at school, and at home he became aware of the events transpiring in Europe in the aftermath of the Great War that his father had been sent to help finish. From the radio came the voices of William L. Shirer and other reporters who sent their stories from the world's capitals as a new Germany began to define itself under the German chancellor, Adolph Hitler. The victorious allies of the Great War were now only Britain and France. Italy, which had been knocked out of the war in 1916, had come under the control of a new premier, Benito Mussolini, and he had set up a socialist republic with his Fascist party in the early 1920s. The Russian armies had collapsed in blood and rebellion in 1917, and Russia had given up the fight that fall, when the Bolsheviks took over. In 1936, 1937, and 1938, only France and Britain reacted to events in Germany and the countries of the old Austrian Empire. The Smiths watched these events with a greater-than-average interest, but it was all so far away. Fred had gone to France, it was true, but that was approaching twenty years ago. Russia, Austria, Turkey, even Germany were different now, territorially, politically, and in terms of their armies. How could another general war in Europe, with the trenches and the shelling and the slaughter, ever be started again? Surely the world had learned a lesson from that war that would keep it out of anything like it again. The League of Nations might not be doing much, but the great powers would avoid another trip through the charnel house. What madness could possibly make the sacrifice of another generation thinkable yet again?

Domestic news was a major interest at the Smith place, and in the 1930s there was no shortage of it. Fred emerged from the little Kentucky valley a steadfast Republican, as his father had been. Smith ancestors had lived in Kentucky when it was a slave state, but it was still a point of pride that no member of the family had ever owned a slave. They had been Union Republicans in the Civil War, and Fred's grandfather Martin Van Buren Duvall had served as an officer in the 12th Kentucky Volunteer Infantry, a Union regiment. Considering that a Confederate guerrilla had killed Captain Duvall a week after the end of the war in 1865, when Fred's mother was only five months old, there were good family reasons to dislike Democrats in general. No Smith in living memory had ever voted for one. Lillian was not old enough to vote until the 1924 election, but she followed Fred's lead and always supported the Republican ticket. The depression and the upheaval which followed in the 1930s made political news important to the Smiths. Hoover's vision of a partnership between business and benevolent government collapsed in the wreckage of the financial blunders brought on by the Great War and the attempts to smooth out the "business cycle" in the 1920s. Herbert Hoover was activist, but temperate. His successor Franklin Roosevelt, once in power, was activist and liberal, and that was very different. The New Deal set a leftward course for the country which troubled Fred. There might have been differences with Hoover's business cronies in the government, but that had been much better than the new type of people which Roosevelt brought in to run the New Deal. These were liberal academics, activists, and social workers who had first experienced the exercise of power in the War Industries Board and other government agencies during the economic emergency declared after America entered the Great War in 1917. They relished a return to the exhilaration of the days when the government had taken over the nation's economy to gear it up for war production. This offered them unprecedented power to shape American society in ways that had been impossible before the war. Industrial workers, farmers, shopkeepers all had been set to their tasks on terms dictated by the government under the banner of winning the war and defeating the Hun. These Progressives–turned–social engineers reveled in the exercise of regulation, police powers, and the power of a nearly free hand with Congress, backed by a willing president in Woodrow Wilson. These people went home after the war lighted with the glow of having served on a mission to make America over in their image. The election of Franklin Roosevelt to the presidency in November 1932 sent their hopes surging again. FDR promised bold, persistent experimentation, after admitting that he was not really sure what to do or what would work. Surely they would hit on the right solution if enough ideas were tried. To hammer out and implement these experiments, an army of New Deal administrators went to Washington in the spring of 1933. No depression in American history had ever lasted more than four years before. The "Great Depression" (as it became known) had gone on for three and a half years when the first Congress of the New Deal met early in 1933. Roosevelt's staff and a flurry of assistants hastily hammered out bill after bill as the inauguration approached, and Congress passed dozens of them in the first three months of the new administration. Still, the depression dragged on, with no end in sight. Fred did not like the arrogance of the new president, and he did not like the meddling policies which the New Deal agencies promoted and FDR championed as his own. Agriculture Secretary Henry Wallace proposed and Congress passed a bill creating the Agricultural Adjustment Administration, or AAA, which immediately began to try to boost farm prices while reducing production. The government urged farmers to plow under parts of their crops and reduce milk and cotton output, and began paying them not to grow crops. They paid farmers to kill baby pigs and slaughter breeding stock, and pictures and stories of these activities became front-page news all over the country, including New Castle. Interfering on behalf of labor unions and encouraging corporations to cooperate with each other by enacting NRA (National Recovery Administration) codes which relaxed the antitrust laws was one thing, but Fred knew in his heart that there was something fundamentally wrong when the government began paying farmers for grain that would have been harvested had it been planted. Fred would have nothing to do with them. These policies were combined with new taxes and deficit spending and inflation that government officials assured everyone would bring a speedy end to the depression. Fred became and remained fundamentally opposed to the New Deal and all that it stood for, and to its architect, Franklin Roosevelt. What they were doing was not right, and even though FDR might be elected and reelected, there remained the conviction that he was taking the country down an unprecedented and very dangerous path which had not been marked out for it by the framers of the Constitution. Roosevelt's blatant attempt in 1937 to pack the Supreme Court with justices favorable to New Deal programs did nothing to convince anyone at the Smith household that FDR was anything but bad medicine. Fred voted for Hoover in 1928 and 1932, for Landon in 1936, for Willkie in 1940, and for Dewey in 1944. New Castle voted for Roosevelt, and helped elect him to four terms as president. Being part of a minority opposition to popular Democrat presidents bothered Fred not at all. It became a family tradition.

Times were tough for many in New Castle in 1937 and 1938. There had been a slight improvement in the national economy in 1935 and 1936, but things had again turned sour after FDR's reelection in 1936. The next two years were almost as bad as 1933 had been. During the Great War and in the 1920s, all but two of Fred's siblings came to New Castle from the valley. Lillian's sister Mabel and her husband Casher moved up, too. They made their livings in various ways: Walter and his wife Rena at the boarding-house; Tom at the Hoosier, at Maxwell, and at Chrysler; Molly as a housewife married to a hard-drinking man from Clinton County. Mabel raised their seven children while Casher worked at the Chrysler. Molly, in particular, had had a hard life. Her husband Will Ed Duvall had met with a disabling accident, keeping him at home. Molly struggled to raise their children and make ends meet through the early years of the depression. Duvall had ties to many people in Kentucky, however, and he used them to supplement his family's income. He arranged for delivery from Clinton County of pint fruit jars of good moonshine whiskey. The boardinghouse in which they lived fronted directly on I Avenue near 18th Street, one of the busiest corners in New Castle. Duvall sat in a rocking chair in the room next to the street, and from there sold jars of bootleg whiskey from a bushel basket through the window to customers who walked up on the sidewalk. These sales were no secret, and were apparently tolerated by the authorities, because Will Ed was never harassed or arrested during the many years he did it. Sunday was always his best day of the week. The Smith relatives came through the hard times of the early 1930s fairly well, but with occasional difficulties paying bills. They often adapted by moving to cheaper lodgings when money got tight, and they helped each other when they could. Fred and Lillian could supply eggs and butter and meat sometimes. Walter had helped all of them with places to stay when they had first come to town, and he had connections with the Gernsteins who ran the grocery store. When Walter ran the coal yard, he could supply coal on credit, or buy it himself for a family member who might be out of a job. Tom and Molly kept gardens, offering surpluses to the others who might need vegetables to can or to supplement that day's meal.

The New Deal spent taxpayer money for jobs directly in front of the house in the hollow. In 1938, WPA (Works Progress Administration) workers came to the little bridge over the creek on Route 2 to do their part to end the depression. That summer they tore out the old culvert which carried the water under the road and hauled dirt to widen the road there, then built a new concrete-and-steel bridge two lanes wide across the creek. Much of the dirt came from the hill next to the old barn that had been there when the Smiths had bought the place. The workmen dug it out with picks and teams of horses pulling slip scoops, hauling it up to the road along the driveway. WPA did not pay for the dirt but merely gave Fred free excavating in exchange for it. Every year after it was finished, swallows built nests against the beams that supported the bridge floor and flew their graceful rounds in the hollow searching for flying insects.

The late 1930s were momentous years in America and in the world. German troops marched into and reoccupied the Rhineland in 1936. This included the area along the Rhine that Fred had helped garrison during his occupation duty in 1918 and 1919. The

French, who were vastly superior militarily to the Germans in 1936, decided not to intervene. In 1937 there was the terrible sit-down strike against General Motors, which ended with rampaging mobs and broken heads as police battled strikers in the streets of Detroit. The dirigible *Hindenburg* burned that year at Lakehurst, New Jersey, and Roosevelt had his problems with Congress and the Supreme Court. The big international news of 1937 and 1938 was the Spanish Civil War, and accounts of the fighting filled the papers in those years. Many reporters had a stake in the outcome because of sympathies for one side or the other, and the stories were written with a passion that was remarkable for the time. The descriptions and photographs which came out of this war held the world in their grip, and dominated the news of the day. By 1938, Adolph Hitler had built his National Socialist German Workers Party into a powerful political machine whose members were terrorizing Jews and those who lacked sufficient enthusiasm for the Nazi cause. The party sponsored huge rallies at Nuremberg to whip up enthusiasm and glorify Hitler. These events came to the Smith household on the console radio upstairs above the kitchen, and Kenny and his mother and father heard them through the filtering of the shortwave bands. That year, Hitler made known his belief that all Germans should be a part of a greater Germany, whether they lived outside Germany's borders or not. The first to receive this attention were the Sudeten Germans living across the mountainous border between Germany and Austria. If this area were annexed to Germany, there would be no geographical barrier to entering the rest of this remnant of the once great Austrian Empire and Vienna, Hitler's birthplace. When Neville Chamberlain, the British prime minister, went to Hitler's retreat at Berchtesgaden in September, there were promises that Germany had no such expansive intentions. Hitler assured Chamberlain that he had no further ambitions in Europe after adding the Sudetenland to Germany. Chamberlain, in what has since become the classic act of appeasement, took him at his word and agreed that Britain would not interfere. Chamberlain flew back to Britain and, clutching his umbrella at the airport, waved the signed agreement in the air and solemnly announced that, with Herr Hitler, he had achieved "Peace in our time." The Sudetenland, then all of Czechoslovakia, was soon in German hands.

In the hollow, as their customer list grew, Fred bought a hand-operated milk bottle capping machine which pressed the foil covers over the bottles to seal them after Lillian had washed them and filled them with milk. Improvements also came to the process of separating the cream from the milk for butter making. They bought a "water separator" for this purpose, which did away with the need to laboriously turn the crank on a standard cream separator. It held three or four gallons of milk, and was so constructed that when icy cold water was poured into the tank, the cream would rise to the top where Lillian could skim it off. This allowed her or Kenny to do other things while the milk was separating.

The Moles Family in the Later 1930s

After they had passed the crisis of 1933–1934, the situation on Plum Street grew no worse, but still was not what most would call good. It took nearly two years to pay down the grocery bill with Ethel's work, and Jess had fallen behind on the rent, leaving a significant debt to pay off to their landlord. Work still was not dependable, and there were times when he again got word that he was laid off. These became shorter now, and they were able to hold their own at this level for the most part. This did not allow for any savings, and extras or treats remained scarce.

On Saturday evenings, when the lights along the "White Way" on New Castle's Broad Street illuminated the hundreds of people who made the weekly pilgrimage to the stores, the Moles family went too. But in these difficult times, they did not have the money to buy much, so Jess created their own entertainment. He took them down to the business district and drove up and down Broad until he found a parking space in front of one of the big stores, or close to a busy intersection. Jess would go into one of the dime stores and buy chocolate candy, bringing it back in a paper bag for Ethel and the children in the car. Then they would sit and watch their fellow citizens go about their business, offering occasional comments on who someone was or what they did for a living. Their entertainment was a kind of human cinema, observation of the variety of other New Castle residents passing in front of them as they did what the Moles family could not do. Jess and Ethel could not afford shopping as a luxury. It was an occasional necessity, performed because it had to be done, but cut short because the bounty within the reach of others only reminded them that they could not afford much. But seeing this played out in front of them somehow eased the deprivation, vaguely assuring them that they would be able to join in one day if they could be patient and keep working hard. It is entirely possible that on one of those Saturday nights Jess and his family may have seen Fred, Lillian, and Kenny making their way into the Sears and Roebuck store.

The weather added to America's difficulties in those years. The high prices paid for grain during the Great War convinced many farmers to move out onto the marginal dry lands of the Great Plains and turn under the sod for bigger crops. Gasoline-powered tractors appeared in large numbers during and after the war, enabling farmers to plow faster and farther than horses and the old steam traction engines had allowed. By the middle of the 1920s, this boom had collapsed on the high plains from Montana and the Dakotas to Texas in a wave of bankruptcies and fore-closures, but some clung to their dreams and tried to farm their way back into solvency. By 1932 and 1933, Okie farmers and other red-necked producers faced a new menace. The weather cycles on the plains west of the hundredth meridian brought unpredictable changes. This time the rain failed over fields of cotton, wheat, and corn, and ground already plowed for planting wheat in the fall. The winds picked up the exposed soil and sent it up into the air in dirty storms that blew all the way to the East Coast. These "red rollers" hit New Castle from as far away as Missouri, Kansas, and Oklahoma, coating cars and window-sills with gritty red dust and making people sneeze. In the Dust Bowl area of the Oklahoma panhandle around Guymon, top-soil drifted around abandoned farm buildings like snow, burying crops, fences, and cemeteries, and making the landscape unre-cognizable in some areas. There were pictures in the paper of the Okies' cars heading west for California on Route 66, mattresses and clothing tied on top. These weather patterns made for severe thunderstorms in New Castle, and two summers in a row of un-bearable heat. Air conditioning had not yet come to their town, so shade, screened windows, fans, and ice water remained the primary means for keeping cool. Only eighteen inches of rain fell in all of 1934, half the usual amount. The summer of 1935 was especially hot, with many nights so stuffy that the Moles family slept on the little front porch. Sometimes a week might pass with entire nights when heat lightning flickered in the sky and there seemed to be no air moving, not even enough to move the leaves on the trees. No one feared strangers, because they would be recognized as such immediately, and strangers did not come to Plum Street much. Only on the hottest nights they would sleep on the porch, when the heat in the upstairs rooms became too much to allow sleep. On other nights thunderstorms would slash sheets of rain onto the street and sidewalks and thunder rumbled. In the hot summertime when he was laid off or on Sunday afternoons, Jess sometimes took the girls to Greensborough, southwest of New Castle, to a place where Duck Creek crossed the road on the way down to Blue River. There they could go down the bank and wade in the shallow water while Jess and Ethel watched out for them. Someone that Jess knew at work gave them a Boston Terrier puppy about 1938 that they named Toby. This marked a change in attitude for them all. Jess and Ethel no longer feared that they would not be able to pay the rent or buy groceries. Work had become steady enough that the luxury of a dog, even if it was a small one, could be considered. Toby became an instant favorite with the girls, and they considered him their dog. He began to appear regularly in the family photographs. In 1935 another person who would become a dear friend came into Gemma's life when she met Martha Fatzinger at church. Martha was born in 1923, so she was slightly younger than Gemma, but they quickly became close friends. Martha always drew attention with her bright red hair and pale complexion, and her bubbling personality and ready chatter always made friends. Martha got to know Sarah Wright through Gemma, and they occasionally chummed together.

Gemma Finds Work in the Depression

Jobs at the Chrysler or the Hoosier could be very hard to secure, but there were non-industrial tasks that might be found. For someone unskilled and still in school, part-time or occasional employment was the best that might be hoped for. Even this kind of work could be hard to discover in a small town like New Castle. Gemma, being the oldest, began the search first. She knew how to do housework, she had learned to cook with her mother, and she sewed on their treadle sewing machine. She got very good grades at school, and she was reliable, polite, and respectful to others. These constituted her skills. She began in the neighborhood. As many girls did, Gemma took babysitting jobs when she could, but the people in the neighborhood did not go out much, so one needed a large territory to make steady money in that line of work. The Cunninghams, who lived a block over on Lincoln, asked her to help Mrs. Cunningham, who was sickly. They could be seen walking around the block most evenings, Mr. Cunningham helping her along in an effort to build up her strength. She hired Gemma to do odd tasks for her just when needed, not on a regular basis. Gemma mopped the kitchen floor, helped in the kitchen, and assisted her with their two small boys. Mrs. Cunningham usually gave her a quarter when she finished, but she also sewed, and she offered to make Gemma a dress. Never before had Gemma had anything made of real linen. Gemma treasured the turquoise dress and wore it often. Gemma also helped on a more regular basis at the Poston home a few houses west on Plum. This occasional work served as experience and reference. Gemma, now a sophomore in high school, wanted regular work, so she drew up all her courage one day in the new year of 1937, and walked over to the Edwards home on the corner of South Main and Walnut, about seven blocks away. Ray Edwards was a jeweler in town, with a store on Broad Street and a reputation as a solid citizen. She knocked on the door, and when Mrs. Edwards answered, Gemma asked her if she needed any help in the house. It so happened that she did. She hired Gemma on the spot. The Edwardses lived just a block farther than the high school, so Gemma went there before school and made beds, then returned after school. In the afternoons, she watched their son, Morris, who could be a little trying sometimes. She tried to entertain him as best she could, and occasionally Mrs. Edwards would give her money to take him to the movies. She washed Mrs. Edwards's hand laundry and hung it up to dry, and performed other cleaning tasks. As compensation, Gemma received a meal prepared by the cook that the family kept, in addition to the $1.50 per week pay. This was during the school year. In the summer, she spent most of the day there, and so she received $3 a week, practically a fortune.

The Edwardses were among the wealthiest people in town, and there was never any doubt that they were far above those who lived on Plum Street. Judge Morris, Susan Edwards's brother, lived in the big prairie-style brick house with them. They always drove new Dodges and Chryslers. Judge Morris drove a Chrysler roadster, and they had a farm outside of town. Gemma was astonished to find that everyone in the house had their own bedroom. There were closets full of sheets, blankets, and bedspreads, and more closets full of linen (linen!) towels, wash cloths, and bath mats. When they had visitors, Gemma put special bedspreads on the beds and helped with the extra preparations in the kitchen. When the family vacationed, Gemma stayed overnight in the house, even though she did not like to do so.

Susan Edwards liked to go to Indianapolis to the big department stores downtown, especially Ayres and the William H. Block Company. She occasionally asked Gemma to go along, and it was the first opportunity Gemma had to go to another city for any purpose other than to visit relatives. Indianapolis, fifty miles distant, dwarfed New Castle, of course, and the excitement in the air on Washington and Meridian Streets and around the soaring Soldiers and Sailors Monument on the Circle left a deep impression. Cars and trolleys were everywhere, and even the cavernous Union Station, where they arrived on the train, was far larger than any building she had ever seen. In the stores, there seemed to be plenty of people who had money to spend in spite of the depression. Gemma had never seen anything quite like it. Ray Edwards was kindly, but he stayed at the store all day, making appearances only at lunch occasionally, or at suppertime. He was a veteran of the Great War, with all the status in the community that came with the distinction. When a teacher asked for ideas for someone to come to class to speak about the Great War, Gemma approached Ray, and he was pleased to come and make the presentation.

By contrast, Susan could put a domestic employee in her proper place very quickly. Sometimes Jess picked up Gemma when she was finished there, and Mrs. Edwards noticed that their tan 1936 Plymouth was only four years old. She asked how her father could afford a car like that, and Gemma, miserably uncomfortable, muttered something about how hard he worked. She once asked Gemma if her parents had gotten married so that he would not have to go into the army in the Great War. Even worse, she asked her if they had gotten married because her mother had become pregnant, a horrible thing to suggest in those days. Mrs. Edwards once mentioned that there was a job opening at Public Service, the gas company in town, but she quickly added that Gemma "wouldn't be able to do that." By the time she graduated from high school, Gemma was more than ready to find other employment. Little Morris Edwards had gotten in the habit of kicking her and doing other things that hurt, and getting away with it, and she had grown tired of being a servant. Gemma came to dread going to work there, but she got no allowance at home and she had no other source of income. She continued working for Mrs. Edwards until about two months after she graduated from high school. Although there was sometimes a negative side to working there, Gemma was always grateful to Susan and all of the Edwards family for allowing her to work for them. The added money she earned there was an important factor in maintaining them all.

Social Divisions in Town

For those who lived on Plum Street and in the other industrial neighborhoods in New Castle, there existed an easily understandable system of social order. The large majority of people of all ages belonged to the industrial, laboring part of their world. The men who worked at production jobs at the Chrysler, at the rolling mill, at Hoosier Cabinet, in the grocery stores and lumberyards, or on the farms all were part of the lower strata of society. These people worked hard and wished for the time when they might be better off, or for the day when instead of paying rent they would make the last mortgage payment. They hoped that their children might be happily married and get hired on at the plant, never having to worry about layoffs or strikes. Everyone who lived on Plum Street would have assumed that they were part of this group, at least on the rare times when they thought about such things. Clearly they were not what most people called the "upper crust." For the most part, it was this negative which formed the basis of the definition. To everyone in the Moles family, there was the upper crust, and there was everyone else.

The elite of New Castle set the pace for the town, and owned significant parts of it. Chrysler belonged to stockholders and to Walter Chrysler, and they did not figure on the local scene, but other major employers like the piano company and Hoosier Cabinet did have local owners. The Zetterbergs owned the rolling mill where Sarah's father worked, and there were the Jennings, Bond, Goodwin, and McQuinn families. A few managers at the large factories fit in with these families as well. There was a merchant elite, and the Edwards family was a prime example. Cliff Payne the clothier was another of these, as was George Dann, the scrap dealer. Even the paperboy was a source of embarrassment for the Moles girls. Son of one of the upper middling families, he had the paper route which included Plum Street, providing a daily reminder of their comparatively low status and practically advertising the down-at-the-corners condition of the neighborhood.

It was in the paper that everyone not in society saw what the elite enjoyed. The society page chronicled the daily activities of those who had money to spare in the worst days of the depression. The moneyed families in town went way back for the most part, and seemed to be utterly unaffected by the economic tide that had brought hardship to everyone else. It seemed that the people at the paper took the time to write about practically everything they did. They all belonged to Westwood Country Club, of course. There they had their bridge parties, college send-off dances, and ladies' golf days. There were sororities like Sigma Phi Gamma which had founders dinners and where bridge was played regularly. Even the names of the bridge partners and the prizes they won would appear in the articles. There were Christmas parties for children, and birthday gatherings for the kids who were too snobby in school to even speak or say "excuse me" if they bumped into you. Reading about the themes and party favors and expensive flowers was almost too much to stomach sometimes.

The children of these families dated each other and moved easily in the circle of each others' homes. Such a boy or girl might be given a car, an unmistakable sign of affluence, and their clothing came from the best stores that New Castle or Muncie or Indianapolis could offer. They of course formed the inevitable high school cliques, as did other students excluded from them. The elite families seemed to go to the Presbyterian church for the most part, except for the few wealthy Jews and Catholics.

The End of School

Gemma started school at midyear in 1929, putting her a half semester behind most kids her age. By the time she got to high school, she decided to take additional classes to speed up her graduation. Her work made her eligible for graduation with the Class of 1940, a year ahead of most people her age. Always a good student, she joined the National Honor Society and maintained her high average in spite of work and a heavy academic load. Honor Society met during school, so she could belong. She did not participate in other activities because they met after school when she had to go to the Edwardses' to work. Only during senior year did she join the *Rosennial* (yearbook) staff, arranging with Mrs. Edwards to come to work a little later after school.

Sarah and Martha and Gemma were close friends now, sharing the outlook and experiences of growing up together. They enjoyed going to the soda fountain at Denton's Drug Store at Main and Race for a break from schoolwork, siblings, and home routines. Miller's was a good place for ice cream or a Coke, too, and the crowds streaming out of the Castle Theater next door arrived in waves after the show. Walking and talking became a favorite pastime for them. It was during their high school years that going to the train depot to sit and watch people became another habit.

They double-dated among themselves because there were not too many boys within their social circle who had cars. Neither Gemma nor Sarah drove. Martha had learned to drive, but did not have dependable access to a car in high school. One of these dates to the famous Indiana Roof in Indianapolis ended early when one of the boys she and Martha were with put something in Gemma's Coca-Cola when she was not looking. Not only did it taste awful, but a line of propriety had been crossed which indicated a lack of respect. They went home and did not repeat the experience.

Martha's cousin Farrell Hendricks liked Gemma and they dated several times during junior year, and she went out with Ed Brenneman and Harry Beard once or twice. Farrell's mother and father thought Gemma was a good match for their son, and made their intentions clear enough, but Gemma was not sold on the idea. Soon it was David Locker who took a special interest in her and took her to the prom senior year and to the Commencement Dance.

The 1930s Become the 1940s

Kenny was eighteen years old and about to start his junior year at New Castle High School as the summer waned in August 1939. Fred had sown a rented field in hay east of the house up the road a little ways, and they had mowed it the last week of August. The weather had been good, so Fred took Friday off, and once the dew had dried, they spent the better part of the day hauling hay to the barn where they hoisted it into the mow. Loose hay accumulates quickly on a wagon when two men are forking, and they must have been on the second or third wagonful when the Robinsons across the road offered them cold water to drink. For several days, radio news commentators had been speculating about a possible German move against Poland, a move hinted by the Nazi propaganda ministry. After last summer's domination of Czechoslovakia and Austria, some thought it possible that a similar move might be in the offing for this other neighbor of Hitler's. Fred and Kenny were talking with Elmer Brenneman about this very situation while they stood on the Robinsons' porch and drank their water. As they spoke, one of the Robinsons came to the front door and brought them news that would change their lives forever. Word had just come over the radio that Germany had invaded Poland. It was Friday, September 1, 1939. No, they hadn't heard the news. Hitler had been making some noise about the Polish Corridor and the German-speaking people in East Prussia, but there was no sense that there was a crisis. This development came on the heels of the shocking news just a few days before that Nazi Germany and Soviet Russia, of all nations, had signed a non-aggression pact. Considering the way that Hitler and Stalin were supposed to mistrust each other, this had taken everyone by surprise. And now German armies were driving into Poland. Soon they would learn that the Russians had attacked Poland from the east at the same time. It made more sense then. The Germans and Russians had gotten together in an unholy alliance to divide Poland. There on the porch Kenny and his father drank their water, but they talked about the news very little on the way to the barn. Britain and France had pledged to go to war if Hitler acted aggressively against Poland, and they would probably do so. So this meant that just twenty years after signing the treaty at Versailles the Allies would go to war with Germany again, and this time Russia was on Germany's side. It was only twenty-five years since the Great War had started. What would happen now? Would America be dragged in again? When the Great War started in August 1914, Fred was twenty. Three years later, he was called to that war. Now it was September 1939, and his only son was eighteen. What would the next three years and 1942 bring for him? Thank God all that was very far away, but it must not have seemed so distant to Fred. He had already been sent on one such errand. But to Kenny, it all seemed very remote indeed. His history teacher talked about it some in class that fall when school started, but there were other lessons to be learned, and time was limited. Even though the Germans and Russians met with some resistance from the Poles, it only took four weeks for the German Blitzkrieg, or lightning war, to conquer the western two-thirds of the Polish nation. Russia took the eastern third as her share. Luckily, no one seemed too anxious to fight after Poland was finished. Instead of France and Britain attacking Germany as one would expect under a declaration of war, all sides maintained their positions and waited to see what would happen. To be sure, the British Expeditionary Force (BEF) was sent to France, and France always kept her army in the east, near Germany, along the impregnable fortifications which the French called the Maginot Line. But when they got there, no one moved to attack in either direction. Soon newspaper wags were calling it the "phony war" and the "sitzkrieg," and an uneasy calm fell over

Europe. At least this time there was no sign of another trench war. With luck, they would work this all out. Nothing much changed here at home, and as the winter passed, it seemed that perhaps the phony war would turn out to be a fizzle.

The high school years were happy ones for Kenny. His family had a late-model car which he could borrow after he obtained his driver's license. His friends Marvin Snider, Harry Ridout, and Charlie Purvis also had access to cars, making the circle of friends mobile at any time. None of them smoked or drank, and they somehow avoided the usual vices which tempted high school boys. Kenny was allowed the responsibility of driving the family car, and he was careful not to squander the privilege. It probably helped that he could expect close inspection upon his return home. He and his friends were all from upright, middle-class homes where the standard of behavior was well understood by all. Stepping outside these rules had consequences which they did not care to bring upon themselves. Kenny drove to work, to school activities, and to ball games. For fun, they sometimes drove out to the various isolated spots where boys and girls would go to park and neck, to hassle the participants and make embarrassing noises to irritate them. The hot spots in town were a soda shop called the Yukon, and later the Miller Dairy Store at Main and Central Avenue. Miller's had four rows of booths which kids jammed after games at the Church Street gym or movies at the Castle and Princess theaters across the street. The Denton Drug Store and soda fountain, another major venue, was just a block north, catercorner from the courthouse. Wednesday nights were popular for borrowing a car and riding around because the Lucky Strike Hit Parade, with Kay Kyser and his orchestra, was on the radio. Car radios were not yet standard equipment, but the cars that Kenny and his friends drove all had them. School games and activities dominated Friday nights, and Saturdays and Sundays were the best nights to go to Indianapolis to see and hear the big bands at the big theaters and hotels there. There were roller-coaster hilly roads around New Castle for cheap thrills, and there were also the hot spots at nearby towns like Muncie, Richmond, Hagerstown, and Connersville.

There was no demand that Kenny take a job as Jess demanded of his girls. But he wanted to do it anyway in order to have his own spending money. Kenny was not on familiar terms with the principal at the school, but he routinely smiled or said hello when he passed him in the hallway. Out of the blue at school one day when Kenny was a sophomore, the principal, Mr. Mitchell, walked up to him and asked him if he was looking for a job. When Kenny answered that he was, Mitchell suggested that he go see Freeman Vickery, who ran the Red Dot Cleaners on Broad Street. Kenny went that afternoon after school, and Vickery hired him to work part-time in the shop and make deliveries using the delivery hack, a 1935 Plymouth two-door with the back seat out. It became his regular employment through high school, until he hired on at the Morris 5 & 10 as an assistant manager trainee the summer after graduation. He thought it would be a good thing to work at Myers Implements assembling the new farm machinery that came in, and he considered approaching the Macer Funeral Home to be a driver for them, but the assistant manager job at the 5 & 10 came along, and it seemed like a better deal. He worked regularly, showed up on time, and got along with people.

This, then, was the world that the Smiths knew and it was the world in which Kenny grew up during the 1920s and 1930s. It was all very understandable and well-ordered. The Moles daughters and the other residents of Plum Street knew a similar world colored with more uncertainty and a more marginal existence. So bitter and deprived for many at the time, it would be remembered by most as a happy era in their later years, long after the hard edges had been worn smooth by the passage of time. It was this world which the coming tempest destroyed forever, so it became accessible only through relics and the memories of those who knew it themselves.

4. Into the Storm, 1939–1941

GEMMA CONTINUED TO work hard to keep her grades high during senior year. With the yearbook, work for Mrs. Edwards, and chores at home, she had time for little else. On Saturday nights she went out with Martha or Sarah or double-dated. Martha always had a boyfriend, and she often found dates for Gemma. This was the time when David Locker was Gemma's primary suitor. Gemma had dated Ed Brenneman and Harry Beard, and when she lost interest in David, she dated Martha's cousin Farrell Hendricks. His parents thought that Farrell and Gemma were a good match, and urged Gemma to marry him. Gemma decided she wasn't ready for that step yet.

Sarah had taken an interest in Clay Grubbs early in 1939, her freshman year at New Castle High School. Clay was almost four years older than Sarah, and had his own troubles at home. After Clay's father died in 1930 when Clay was twelve and his brother Orrin was only eight, their mother Erma married a man named Vitatoe in 1933 who kept company with the bottle. The boys' stepfather made life miserable around the house when he went on drinking binges, and Erma tried vainly to keep their home life on an even keel. Even before their father had died, the boys had gone to stay at the Indiana Soldiers and Sailors Home down at Knightstown because their mother had more than she could handle with a sick husband, a small baby born after Orrin, and another child on the way. Their father, Clay Sr., had been a veteran of the Great War, so the boys could be taken care of at the home when things got bad enough. As they got older, Clay and Orrin were at home on B Avenue most of the time. Clay found a job working part-time for Western Union. When a wire came into the office next to the interurban station, Clay delivered it on his bicycle. In 1936, when he was a sophomore, Western Union offered him a full-time delivery job. In the middle of the Depression, and with the financial burden that his stepfather presented to the family, Clay jumped at the chance to make a steady wage. He quit school to take the job in the fall of 1936.

For almost two years, Clay worked steadily for the telegraph company, but on his evenings and Saturdays he ran around with friends who spent their days in school. In the fall of 1939, he decided to go back to school and quit his job, taking an early morning paper route to make a little spending money. This put him in the same class as Orrin, who took over his job at Western Union part-time, delivering telegrams on his bicycle. Clay joined the circle of friends that included Sarah Wright, and she took an immediate liking to him. Girls did not ask boys to go out, of course, so Sarah made it clear enough to Orrin, whom she knew already, that she wouldn't mind being asked out. Orrin thought this was a good thing, too, and they began to date, but Sarah's object was to get closer to Clay.

When school started that fall, Sarah was in marching band as usual, and Clay joined as a drummer. Orrin, now working at the telegraph office, had less time to dote on Sarah, and this was the opening that Sarah had hoped for. Clay began to walk Sarah home after band practice and games. Orrin soon discovered that she seemed interested in Clay, and this did not set well. Orrin began shadowing Clay to determine whether he was taking Sarah out. When Clay put on his band uniform and left the house, Orrin would speed to Sarah's house on Plum Street by a different route and watch to see if Clay went there. Sarah was aware of this, of course. In February, while she was getting ready to don her own uniform and go to a basketball game, she heard the bell ring and asked her mother to see if it was Orrin, and if it was, to tell him that she had already gone. Her mother said, "Oh, Grubby, she's gone," but Orrin noticed that Sarah's uniform was hanging on a door where he could see it. "Mrs. Wright, you wouldn't lie, would

you? What's her uniform doing up there?" Caught, her mother
said, "Yes, I was lying. She told me to tell you that. Come on in."
While Orrin waited, Clay arrived and they traded glares. They
both walked her to the game at the YMCA gym.

Orrin refused to give up. A few weeks later, Clay said he
would come over, and Sarah agreed. Orrin was in the habit of
asking Clay where he was going when he left the house, and he
did this time, but Clay had gotten used to giving vague answers.
They both showed up at Sarah's house. By this time, Fred and Eva
thought the whole process thoroughly comical. They got out the
Chinese checkers and Sarah and the two suitors began to play.
When Clay and Orrin both tried to hold hands with Sarah under
the table, they found to their surprise that Sarah put both her
hands on the table and they were holding hands with each other!
Eva shook with laughter when Orrin said, "Keep your damn
hands to yourself!"

Months later, Orrin showed up on the porch long after the
Wrights were accustomed to be in bed. Eva told him to go home,
but he refused, asserting that Sarah must be out with Clay. Eva
woke Sarah and asked her to put her robe on and go down and
send him home, which she did, but Orrin sat there long enough
for everyone to give up and go back to bed. Sometime during the
night, he left. At home, Clay and Orrin were having trouble. They
shared a room and sometimes got into fights or sought other
ways to antagonize each other.

Company I, 38th Division, and
the Clouds Begin to Thicken

In April 1940, word appeared in the *Courier-Times* that there
would be changes made in the makeup of New Castle's National
Guard unit; a new detachment, Company I, could be added if
local recruitment efforts secured at least sixty men who would
sign up. The school superintendent voiced approval in the paper,
as did Cliff Payne, head of the American Legion and veteran of
the Great War. It would be a good thing to have some prior training if war came. Parents should welcome this training for their
sons. Clay went down to the armory and signed up.

Those who watched the news from overseas during the winter of 1939–1940 had reason to be concerned. After the declaration of war in September, German submarines regularly sank British shipping in the Atlantic and North Sea. Surface ships of the German navy, like the *Graf Spee,* also roamed the seas. Hitler incorporated the western two-thirds of Poland into Germany, giving the country a rough oval shape which included Austria and Czechoslovakia. Mapmakers began to acknowledge these changes in the maps published in newspapers and sold in stores.

In Britain, as the war began to come home, meat rationing began for the general population in December, followed by restrictions on bacon, butter, and sugar in January. British troops in France held trench positions much as they had in the Great War, but this time with no shelling. War had been declared between Germany and the British and French allies, but there was no fighting along the border. For a while, practically everyone referred to it as the Phony War.

In April, as spring began to show in New Castle, the Germans invaded Norway, and British naval forces did their best to try to disrupt the landings. As the German operation continued, the British troops sent to help resist the attack did not do so well, falling back from their positions and finally withdrawing back to England. By early May, Allied efforts in Norway had obviously failed, bringing on a political crisis for Britain's Prime Minister Neville Chamberlain. The government fell, and on May 10, 1940, Winston Churchill became Great Britain's new prime minister. That same day, German forces crossed the frontier into Belgium and Holland. For the third time in seventy years, French and German armies met in battle in the east and north of France. The French and the small BEF moved forward into Belgium and Holland to take up positions in anticipation of the onslaught, just as they had in 1914. German air forces devastated Rotterdam on May 14, and the paper carried word received via shortwave that the Dutch had surrendered on May 15. The same paper brought word that the Germans had crossed the French border and driven into Sedan, site of the French Army's humiliation in 1870. By the 18th, German armored units had pushed halfway to the channel coast and taken St. Quentin and Cambrai, and threatened to isolate French forces in the south. Newspaper analysts thought that the German drive would falter as it had in 1914, but the wave moved on, trapping hundreds of thousands of French and British soldiers on the Channel coast.

With these ominous events in the back of everyone's mind, on Friday evening, May 17, the high school gymnasium took on a southern plantation theme for the Junior Prom. Chet Curry, president of the junior class, crowned Gloria Ann Davis as prom queen. Gemma attended with David Locker. Her friend Martha Fatzinger was there, as were Clay and Orrin Grubbs. Also in the crowd were Kenny Smith and his date Jean Spears. For Gemma and the Class of 1940, graduation was just ten days away.

In Europe, the battles continued. Commentators still expected the German drive to slow from sheer fatigue, but the attacks which had already cut off the BEF in the north, along with a French army, continued. On May 28, King Leopold surrendered the Belgian army, surprising his own government and the rest of Europe. The British and French forces in the north of France and in Flanders scrambled to fill the gaps in the Allied line while British ships of every kind began to evacuate troops from the beaches at Dunkerque. The German radio began to boast that nearly a million men were cut off, virtual prisoners which had only to be put in the bag.

While the Germans pounded the Flanders pocket, the high school gym filled with parents, family, and graduates of the Class of 1940. Martha took Gemma's picture that afternoon in her black cap and gown in front of the house on Plum Street, and the underclassmen in the band played *Pomp and Circumstance* as the graduates marched in. Jess and Ethel watched their eldest daughter graduate from high school, something neither of them had done. The Parent-Teacher Association (PTA) held a dance for the seniors after the commencement exercises. Gemma went with David Locker, and Martha had a new beau, Phil Perry. It was an unsettling time to graduate from high school, but everyone still hoped that things would calm down in Europe. The problem was that America's allies from the Great War were in trouble. The last time this had happened, the United States had held back, then joined in, as every family in New Castle knew.

The evacuation continued from Dunkerque until June 3, when the city and the remaining French troops fell to the Ger-

mans. At the same time, preparations began for the final with-
drawal of Allied forces from the hopeless effort in Norway. It, too,
would soon be completely in German hands. Although the press
began to refer to the "miracle of Dunkerque," evacuating a third
of a million men could not win the war, as everyone knew. Of the
French isolated with the British in the north, a little over one
hundred thousand escaped, along with over two hundred thousand British troops. Once Dunkerque fell, the German Panzer
divisions turned toward the west again and prepared to do what
they had failed to do in the summer and fall of 1914. The Germans now attacked from the stalemate line of the Great War,
broke the French defensive line almost immediately, and made
rapid gains toward Paris. On June 10, the Associated Press reported that 100 German divisions, counting 1.8 million men,
were battering the French positions and were within 35 miles of
Paris. Just four days later, on June 14, the headlines told that the
Germans had occupied Paris just nine days after launching the
new attack. German armor and troops poured into France in an
unstoppable wave.

On June 21 everyone in New Castle learned that Hitler himself had gone to the Forest of Compiegne, to the same railway
car where the Germans had signed the Armistice in 1918, to
humiliate the French with his unconditional surrender demands.
The next day, the French surrendered and agreed to turn over
their industries and resources to the Germans. When the terms of
the surrender came out on June 25, the residents of New Castle
learned that the Germans would occupy all of the coastal areas
opposite Britain on the Channel and the North Sea. Speculation
about air attacks on Britain began almost at once.

But what had happened was beyond believing. In just five
weeks Germany had won the war. With all the slaughter of millions in the Great War of 1914–1918, the Germans had ulti-
mately lost and been sent home but not this time. They had
conquered France, Holland, Belgium, Denmark, and Norway and
driven the defeated British Army across the channel, just as the
Kaiser had tried to do. For the Fourth of July, the editorial cartoon in the paper showed Uncle Sam safely viewing a storm destroying the European democracies from across a stretch of water. Thank God it was all over there. The British called up men up

to thirty-two years old, the papers announced in July. Seven thousand men per day were going into the British Army.

Roosevelt accepted the Democrat nomination for an unprecedented third term as President on July 17. In spite of failing to end the depression with his New Deal, Roosevelt became the convention's choice to run again because of his solid popularity with the coalition that had put him in office. He had sent a message to the convention that no one believed, saying that he had no "desire or purpose" to run again. They ignored it, and roared approval when he won the nomination on the first ballot. Jess could not have been happier.

New Quarters

Late in the spring of 1940 Gemma noticed that someone had put a For Sale sign up in front of a house on Plum Street nearer 18th Street, at 1828, and she told her father and mother about it. They had been overcrowded practically from their first day in the house at 2028 and they had felt squeezed more and more as eleven years went by. Jess had by now worked out of his financial difficulties and had a little cash saved up for emergencies or car expenses. Ethel had gone to work at the Clinic, next to the police department, which was the primary medical facility in town, working in the kitchen. She soon became a nurse's aide, helping with routine chores around the patients. They put the better part of their small savings into a down payment and the owners took his note and a contract, and they could finally move to a bigger place late in the hot summer. It was only two short blocks away, so they carried many of their belongings, and carted the rest.

The lot seemed twice as big, and there was a real upstairs of two bedrooms, not just a glorified attic. For Jess, there was a garage with a little driveway. In here he could finally keep the car out of the weather, and the coal could be kept dry. The backyard would allow for a much expanded garden, and there was a willow tree there for shade. But there were no trees to shade the front of the house, so he soon found two Norway maples about an inch in diameter, and set them out, one on each side of the front walk. There was a little bank up to yard level, with concrete steps and a low wall made of brick around the porch. Round wood columns held up the porch roof. There were houses on either side, but not so close as they had been down the street.

The rest of the house amounted to two rooms on the second floor over a small living room, small bedroom, small dining room, and a hall below, with the front door in the center. Jess and Ethel had one of the upstairs bedrooms, while Maxine and Marie shared the other. Attached to the back were the cramped kitchen and bathroom. The coal stove, which served as the primary source of heat, was in the dining room. In the kitchen, a four-burner kitchen range with oven below helped heat the house in the winter, and made the kitchen uncomfortable in the summer.

Facing the house from the street, the living room was on the left with the hall next to it, and across the hall was the bedroom which Gemma shared with Wanda, the youngest. When anyone talked in the living room, it was hard to go to sleep. Opening or closing the front door made noise that could not be hidden very easily. Wanda offered the aggravations that could be expected from a younger sister, but she and Gemma were close nevertheless. Gemma had hoped that she, being the oldest, would be able to have the room to herself, but she had no say in the matter. This she resented, but there was nothing that she could do about it.

Gemma also had no alternative when Jess informed her that because money was tight, she would have to buy bedroom furniture for the room she shared against her will. She tried rebelling on this point, but lost. All the money was going to groceries, utilities, house payments, and the other expenses, he said. It was her obligation. Besides, she had noticed the house in the first place and had encouraged them to buy it. She would have to help out, because she was out of school and working. Gemma shopped around, and selected an oak veneer bedroom suite with curved headboard and matching dresser at Frank's Furniture. She paid the entire cost, $73, with dollar-a-week payments from her own money. The alternatives were impossible. She could not afford to find her own place, and anyway, girls did not do that kind of thing in 1940.

In the fall, the presidential campaign pitted FDR against Wendell Willkie of Indiana. There were quite a few "No Third Term" buttons to be seen, but those who loved Roosevelt were happy to see him run again. After all, the two-term limit was just a tradition, not a law or a part of the Constitution, so what difference did it really make? Democrat politicians from all over the country loved FDR for his ability to sweep local Democrats into office on his coattails. He destroyed Willkie at the polls, then asked him to be a roving ambassador for the White House. Willkie accepted, and went abroad.

The National Guard Goes to Camp Shelby

President Roosevelt had many things on his mind by the beginning of 1941. He and his military advisors probably knew that the odds of staying out of a European war like the one that had developed were going to be slim, but at the same time, there was no way to tell when the point might be reached that would allow the United States to justify getting involved on an all-out basis. Wilson had faced the same dilemma just twenty-five years before, and had taken three years before he had asked for a declaration of war. Three years into this war would be September 1942.

There were many who opposed having anything to do with the war, and they said so when the Lend-Lease Bill was introduced into Congress early in January. Important senators like Wheeler and Nye were violently opposed, and Charles Lindbergh, still a hero to millions for his transatlantic flight just thirteen years before, came out strongly against it. The America First organization was holding rallies and trying to show that most Americans were against having anything to do with the war over there, and was having some success.

There were plenty of people who still hated Roosevelt, and they were not surprised when in January after the 1940 election that won him a third term, he ordered the National Guard to undertake a year of training just in case war came. There had been numerous military appropriations bills that had passed Congress in 1940, and they kept coming in 1941. There would be no shortage of money for building tanks, guns, and ships, and for training soldiers. FDR's campaign promise not to send the boys to fight in any foreign wars notwithstanding, he wanted stepped-up

On January 27, 1941, in front of New Castle's Armory, Sarah Wright saw Clay Grubbs off to Camp Shelby, Mississippi, for a year of duty with the 38th Infantry Division.

training to begin. Clay Grubbs was affected by the call-up, and so Sarah was too. Clay could have been exempted because he was in his senior year and was due to graduate with the Class of 1941 but, because his home situation was as bad as ever, he went with Company I, Indiana National Guard, when they were ordered to Camp Shelby, Mississippi, in January. He would worry about finishing school later. Sarah had mixed feelings. She knew that Clay's mother needed the money and that it would be coming in regularly now that he would be serving full-time, but of course she hated to see him go. Going to Mississippi was about the same as going to the North Pole. She would only be able to see him if he got leave to come home. So off he went. Orrin assured his brother that he would look out for Sarah while he was gone.

Looking for the Future

Gemma had worked for Mrs. Edwards for more than three years, and she was anxious to move on to something different. She had begun to dread having to deal with the routine that seemed to never change. Morris Edwards did not need a babysitter so much now, anyway. Ethel had heard that Mrs. Newby, who lived in the affluent part of town on 12th Street, needed domestic help. Having worked for the Edwardses for three years was reference enough for anyone, and Gemma took the position. She told Mrs. Edwards that she would not be coming back. Mrs. Newby seemed rather arrogant to Gemma. She sang the praises of her affluent daughters, but she paid $3 a week for Gemma's being at the house from 8 A.M. to 1:30 or 2:00 in the afternoon, six days a week. Gemma's job was to cook breakfast and lunch for her, clean around the house, and do such chores as she was assigned. It was one of the rules that the toilets had to be cleaned by hand with soap and water and a rag instead of with a bowl cleaning brush. This part of her chores galled Gemma, but she buckled down and did it anyway.

The status that came with having a servant girl pleased Mrs. Newby, and she enforced the distinction by insisting that Gemma enter the house by the servant's door. The work continued throughout the summer, but early in the fall, Gemma learned that she would have to wear a maid's uniform starting the next week. This was too much. Too proud to be seen in town that way, she quit abruptly, and was pleased with herself that she had done so. It was early in the fall of 1941, and it took her only a few days to find a position at one of New Castle's five-and-dime stores, the Morris 5 & 10 on Broad Street just east of 14th.

It was important to Gemma to have work. She was expected to contribute at home, and she had bought or made her own clothes for some time. To be without work for any length of time would be unthinkable. At the Morris 5 & 10, Gemma worked where she was needed, primarily in hardware. She was an eligible young woman now, finished with her education, employed, and fetching in appearance with her shoulder-length dark hair and quiet manner. She met Bob Robbins there and dated him a couple of times. When Bob went into the service he wrote to her. Soon after she arrived, the Morris 5 & 10 hired a new assistant manager, McKendrick Smith, recently graduated from high school with the Class of 1941. He first saw Gemma in the basement, where he was unpacking newly arrived merchandise. Kenny took a liking to her, and a few weeks later they began to date. At the store, they helped each other clean the fish tanks and move stock up to the sales floor from the basement.

The Germans attacked Britain by air after France fell, although the intensity had let up a little since the fall of 1940. In the meantime, the German submarines continued their attacks in the Atlantic, sinking thirty-nine ships in February 1941 alone. There was word of this in the paper in New Castle, but it had become almost routine by this time.

The United States moved a step closer to possible war in March when President Roosevelt signed the Lend-Lease Bill. Most people thought that it was a good idea that the program would expire in the middle of 1943. It made them nervous to be helping one side so openly, even if it was already clear that Hitler had gone way beyond his limits. Under the agreement, the United States agreed to lend and lease equipment needed by the British in their war against Germany. It freed the British from having to pay for everything immediately, and it contained authorization for the president to offer other war materials on his own judgment, without getting authorization from Congress. It looked as though they might need it. The air raids against British cities and industrial centers picked up. By April, the Germans were pushing the British back across Libya, and they also had invaded Yugoslavia and Greece. The Greeks resisted with British help, but had to give ground rather rapidly. By the end of April 1941, the evacuation of British forces from Greece was well under way as the Germans first hesitated, then rushed southward. Athens fell on April 27. In North Africa, Rommel pushed the British and Australians back toward Cairo. As Kenny and the Class of 1941 went through graduation ceremonies in May, the Germans continued their airborne attack on Crete, and secured it by June 1.

The headlines in the paper on June 22, 1941, stunned everyone. Massive German armies had attacked the Soviet Union!

Since the conquest of Poland, Germany and the Russians had been allies for two years. The Germans advanced very rapidly, and there were reports in the paper that some Russian cities, especially in the Ukraine, welcomed the Germans because they hated Stalin so much. Because the Soviets were now at war against the Germans, did that mean that we would help them as we were helping the British?

During the fall, when Gemma went to work at the Morris 5 & 10 and met Kenny, the Germans continued to push into Russia, and everyone tried not to think about it too much. But it was there in the paper every evening. By the end of September, the Germans had already driven five hundred miles into the Soviet Union, and they weren't slowing down. They were only a little over two hundred miles from Moscow, Leningrad was almost surrounded, and the line of the front stretched south all the way to the Black Sea. Who could ever have any hope of stopping these people anywhere?

The War Comes Closer

There had been talk in the papers if one wanted to read it, and there were ominous speeches from time to time about the United States entering the war. In July 1941, Roosevelt ordered that the limited embargo against Japan be given teeth, and cut off shipments of scrap metal and oil to them. This resulted in a severe blow to the ability of the Japanese to obtain materials they needed to make ships and guns, and to produce fuel. After the Atlantic Conference in Newfoundland in August 1941, Churchill and Roosevelt issued warnings to the Japanese to keep hands off British possessions and the oil of the Dutch East Indies. In September, fifteen countries, including Russia, signed the Atlantic Charter, making for partnerships between the United States and Britain and most of the governments-in-exile of the occupied countries of Europe. From New Castle, it had the appearance of an alliance of the lost.

With German columns deep inside Russia, the administration laid plans to send the Soviet government aid in the form of Lend-Lease supplies. But still, in the fall of 1941, most people here did not think that war was imminent. The focus of life was not convoys in the Atlantic, runs to Malta, or Panzer divisions. Life consisted of having a steady job, a respectable home, and planning for the near future. Gemma felt the unspoken (and sometimes spoken) pressure to find a husband and settle into a domestic routine, just as her mother and father had done. Above all, Jess made it clear to her and her sisters many times that they were never to do anything that would embarrass him or threaten the economic position of the family. She understood that it was her duty to find a proper way to begin a life of her own and cease being a financial burden to her parents as soon as possible. Thus, she kept on the alert for a better job. No man who might be interested would be upset that she was working, although the expectation was that once she had married, she would quit her job to stay at home. Once married, an outside job would be a last resort, and a clear indication that a husband was unsuccessful in his role of providing for her and any family there might be. It had been a mark of shame when Ethel had to take in laundry in the 1930s. Although she had offers, Gemma was determined to make a careful decision, one that she would not regret later. She had seen such matches on Plum Street and had heard about others from her friends at school. It was clear enough from the sermons she heard in church that marriage was a permanent thing, not to be undertaken lightly, and never to be escaped. She would bide her time.

Thousands of miles away, and months before, a plan had been set in motion that would change the lives of everyone in New Castle forever. The result of this plan struck the town like an earthquake, and sent people scrambling for news reports and atlases to try to find the place where it had happened. Everyone heard about it on the day it happened. Sunday, December 7, 1941, was a chilly day in New Castle, a little misty with a gray overcast, and Gemma had walked to a friend's house after church to spend the afternoon. Walking back home about 5:30 in the afternoon, someone she did not know asked her on the sidewalk if she had heard that Pearl Harbor had been attacked by the Japanese. No, she hadn't heard, but she picked up her pace and soon arrived at the house on Plum Street. Jess and Ethel were not home. They had gone to visit brother Walter and his wife Marie for the afternoon, and heard it on the radio over there. Gemma was in a daze, just like millions of other Americans. They knew that the chances of getting into a European war might be pretty good, considering that the same thing had happened in 1917. But no one she knew had dreamed of going to war with Japan. Why would they do such a thing, and where was this Oahu island where it had happened? Even the radio announcers had trouble pronouncing it in the news flashes. She had to wait with her sisters to see what Jess and Ethel would have to say about it when they got home.

Sarah had gone to Clay's mother's house to babysit because Erma and her husband wanted to go to Muncie. She did not have the radio on, so she did not hear of the attack until they told her when they returned early in the evening. Sarah went home immediately, because she knew her father would know as much about it as anyone in town. After the fall of France, Fred Wright had warned that if the United States did not "go over there and whip them, they'll be over here." They talked about it, and he asked Sarah if she wanted to call Clay at Camp Shelby. She did, of course, although this was a thing that was done only on very rare occasions. It was costly and extravagant, and Fred made it a condition that it would be part of her Christmas gift. When she called, Clay had to tell her that they didn't know anything more down there. They had been put on alert, and were to "be prepared," but even that alarmed Sarah. She began to think that they were really going to be in a war. Her father confirmed that we would have to do something, because we had "them" on both sides of us now.

The next day, she listened to Roosevelt's speech before Congress, and heard him ask for a formal declaration of war. She remembered Roosevelt promising during the campaign the year before that he was not going to send our boys overseas to fight in anybody's war. That was before the Guard had been sent to Mississippi. And now this. She and Gemma and most people in New Castle began to pay closer attention to the news. All during the day of December 8, the town's residents could hear the drone of aircraft flying west. No one knew how far the Japanese would go in their push eastward, but there were cities, oil refineries, factories, and shipyards on the West Coast that they had to be interested in taking. The Pacific was such a big ocean, after all, and they had sneaked up on Pearl Harbor easily enough. Gemma saw twin-engined P-38s flying west from somewhere, maybe Wright Field in Dayton, Ohio. Everything in the air that day seemed to be heading for California and the Pacific Coast.

For most people, the days that followed Pearl Harbor were filled with confusion. Casualties had been heavy; that much was clear. All of the great battleships of the Pacific fleet that were there had been sunk or heavily damaged, but the worst appeared to be the *Arizona*, which had taken a bomb in her magazine almost at the first moment of the attack. The picture in the next day's paper showed her death agony as she exploded and burned. Jess's ship *Tennessee* was there, next to *Arizona*, but protected by *West Virginia*, which caught fire from torpedoes and bombs and sank next to *Tennessee*. Oil poured into the water and caught fire, threatening other vessels and making it difficult to see. The heat made some parts of the ship too hot to stay in. Doomed *Arizona* sank as she burned out, with horrible loss of her crew. To the outside of her neighbor *Maryland, Oklahoma* took a battering from torpedoes and capsized. These ships pinned *Tennessee* in place, although the crew managed to get up steam and keep her screws turning to move the burning oil away. It was a small consolation for Jess. Most of the Pacific fleet lay in ruins, and as he well knew from his own navy service, it took a long time to repair a battleship and get her ready to resume active service. In the meantime, what was left of the fleet would have to suffice to protect other islands like the Philippines, as well as the West Coast. Britain joined us in a declaration of war against Japan.

The Japanese attacked in the Philippines the next day. The United States had owned these islands since 1898, and there was an American army division there under General MacArthur's command, but it was very small. Soon a large Japanese ground force supported by its navy began a major push after destroying most of the American aircraft on the ground. By Christmas, MacArthur had withdrawn into the Bataan peninsula across the bay from Manila. Corregidor, the heavily fortified battery island in the outer bay, would be the last fallback position. We had lost the war there almost as soon as it began.

All over the western and central Pacific, Japanese forces advanced, seeming to take a new island or launch a new invasion practically every day. Chaos and paralysis reigned at home, as the government frantically tried to organize war production, find land for plants, get ready to train all the soldiers that would be needed, and coordinate it all with the Allies. As Christmas came and went that year, the picture in Europe and in the Pacific got worse with every passing day.

The generation which had been told that there was nothing they could do about the depression except hunker down and hope that the government would straighten things out now had to face a new and much more sinister crisis. The president told them they had a "rendezvous with destiny," and the same generation which had been powerless to escape the economic grip of the depression just a few months before would now have to defeat fascist socialism and its empires. It would surely be a far longer and costlier undertaking than the one that had cost so many millions of lives in the carnage of the Great War, which had ended only twenty-three years earlier.

5. Duty Calls Every Citizen, 1942

Don't You Know There's a War On?

THE YEAR 1942 dawned with very little hope for most people in middle America. There was no certainty that the United States would win the war, and very little in the papers to suggest that we could expect much good news anytime soon. The Japanese were a mostly unknown quantity. They had struck with great power at Pearl Harbor, and even if no one knew where Oahu was, a great fear settled upon the West Coast that they would soon swoop in from the fog to strike at places that we had heard of before. The draft was already firmly in place, and had been since 1940. Every young man knew that there would come a time, and probably very soon at that, when he would either be expected to join up or be drafted. Many chose to enlist. But many others waited quietly, looking for jobs in vital war plants with the dim hope that their work would be so important that Uncle Sam would choose someone else. Others simply continued the daily routine, working at the shop, or the diner, or the 5 & 10. When the call came, they would go, but the call would come soon enough without jumping the gun. In the meantime, there was home, or school to finish, or hay to make, or chores, or that girl up the street. The irony, of course, was that most of the defense plants, once they had expanded and began to add a full third shift and to extend the work week, refused to hire the young men that they all knew would soon be called to wear the uniform. It became a kind of awkward stage for boys over eighteen. They were already old enough to join up, but still young enough and afraid enough to want to stay around home for a few more weeks.

That spring and summer, the lists of the draftees in the paper grew longer and longer. Many were city boys, but a growing percentage came from out in the county, where the abandoned farmhouses of a later time each still held a family with children. Many of these rural folk led a hardscrabble life, clinging to the dream of farm-based prosperity that their fathers had known before World War I. Even of these, more and more left quietly for work in town, before light most of the year, returning in the late afternoon to milk and feed the chickens and tend to the garden or carry firewood before the evening light faded into night-long shadows.

There developed a routine of induction for draftees and enlistees alike. There was not just one departure with leave-taking and grim good-byes. Would that there had been, because loved ones and boys embarrassed to be choked up would have had to endure it only once that way. The draft notice went out to a group of anywhere from ten to seventy-five across the county, announcing with the familiar "Greetings!" that they had been selected and were to report at a given date and time to the bus terminal for transportation to a given military facility for physicals. So there was a first departure.

Part of this trip was seeing that there were others one knew from school, or from up the road. When there was a stop for a meal, Uncle Sam paid, which wasn't so bad. At the place where the physicals took place, there was a packinghouse mentality. Those who had gotten the free bus ride and lunch had to strip naked and stand in lines while they were looked over, tapped, and made to cough for the army doctor. Stethoscopes allowed the inspectors to listen for signs of a weak heart or bad lungs. They judged eyes, ears, and feet, and looked for signs of venereal disease. The doctors did not say much, but noted on paper forms the important data that would determine whether each man would be accepted or rejected.

Usually they returned home late that night or the next day. At this point they were wanted, but not yet accepted. The impression at the time was that few failed the exams, but those who did often tried to enlist to avoid the stigma of staying behind. Some hid defects they feared might disqualify them, and this was sometimes successful, at least for a few. Back home for a few days, sometimes a week or two, most used the time to take their leave of friends and family. Sunday dinner took on a new significance as everyone savored the sight of a family circle that would soon be missing someone.

To those in this in-between life, it seemed strange that kids still arrived at the two-story brick high school every morning, just as they had done before the war. The old frames of reference were beginning to fade already, as the war took over more and more of people's thoughts. Those inside the high school felt the pressure and weight of events accelerating behind them, huffing to overtake them before they could even graduate. Many of these enlisted or were drafted with the provision that they could finish out the school year and graduate before they were to report for duty.

The second leave-taking was the one that counted. For nearly all of them, the departure was by bus or train, at a time appointed by the War Department. It was a schedule that would not be changed. There were very serious consequences if one failed to report on time with the group to which he had been assigned. It was at this second leave-taking that there occurred the tearful scenes of saying good-bye to dad and mom, sister or girlfriend. For many of New Castle's young men who left to report to training camps, this took place at the old interurban station on the southwest corner of 15th and Race Streets. Now the bus terminal, it offered transportation links to Indianapolis, Cincinnati, Fort Wayne, and all points beyond. When they left, they did not know when, or whether, they would return. For most of the draftees of 1942, it would be a long war. Their enlistments were for the duration, not for just two or three years, and they knew it. They would be in uniform until it was over. And victory or armistice was nowhere in sight that summer and fall.

Hoosiers turned their calendars to a new year just three weeks after Pearl Harbor. It was 17 degrees when most people got up Thursday morning, January 1, 1942, with the temperature headed down to 5 degrees that night. The afternoon's *Courier-*

Times was loaded with more news than an average Thursday might have brought. Children in Millville, a little burg in the county, were down with diphtheria, and at least two families there were having farewell dinners for sons who were leaving for army camps soon. On the back page of the paper were the day's pictures. One of these was a map of the situation in the Philippines. The Japanese were only a few miles from Manila. American and Filipino forces were being pressed between two battle lines to the north and south, fighting against what the report called "overwhelming odds."

The next day's paper had worse news. Japanese troops had taken Manila and the Cavite naval base. General MacArthur was on the fortress island of Corregidor, outside Manila. And right there on the front page was a bad sign. Daniel Griffin, a boy who had been born in Henry County down in Spiceland, had been killed during the first few minutes of the attack on Pearl Harbor. He was the son of preacher Pearl Griffin, and people in Spiceland still remembered him in spite of the fact they had moved away twenty-six years earlier, when Daniel was five. He had a wife and two children.

On January 2, the Office of Production Management in Washington suspended ordinary purchases of new cars and trucks. Word of this prompted the car dealers in the city like Herman Redd to quickly offer their used cars for sale. Myers Implement Company on 18th Street had used Farmall F-12s, F-20s, and F-30s for sale, some with steel wheels and some on rubber. Other officials debated the wisdom of moving important manufacturing plants away from coastal areas where they were vulnerable to enemy shelling. The navy announced plans to begin recruiting at once throughout Indiana, particularly in the smaller towns. Already production was reaching the peak levels of the world war just twenty-five years before, or at least that's what they were saying in the paper.

The paper on Monday the 5th brought more grim news. President Roosevelt announced that February 16 would be the deadline for registration of all men aged twenty through forty-four who had not registered previously. Those aged forty-five through sixty-four were to register later. The government expected nine million names. This included everyone born after February 17,

1897, and before December 31, 1921. Aliens also would have to register. An editorial reprinted from the Indianapolis *Star* urged the government to quickly demand that all aliens turn in items bearing on the war such as cameras and shortwave radios. No one wanted to take a chance on the Japanese here acting as spies. It was grim news from Europe as well. The Russians, six months into their war with Germany, were fighting the Germans outside Moscow, Leningrad, and Rostock. The Germans still held Kharkov, Kursk, and Orel, and showed no inclination to give them up.

The next day the president called for a one-year budget totaling an unbelievable $56 billion to help produce 60,000 planes and 8 million tons of shipping in 1942 alone. The goal for 1943 was to be 125,000 planes and 10 million tons. At the same time, county civilian defense officials announced plans to collect all of the 1941 license plates to conserve metal. Tires were expected to become so scarce that the police chief asked everyone in the city to register their tires at headquarters, including size, make, and serial numbers for positive identification. Police would keep the files. In other news, labor leaders of the American Federation of Labor (AF of L) and the Congress of Industrial Organizations (CIO) agreed in Washington to cooperate for the war effort, and a close-up map of Manila Bay showed Corregidor Island and the Bataan peninsula. The Japanese were massing for attacks on the island. More up-to-date word could be had on Tuesday, Thursday, and Saturday nights at 6:45 when H. V. Kaltenborn read the news on the radio. One mother in town had some good news. Mr. and Mrs. Anson Saunders got word that their son Herschell was safe at Schofield Barracks, one of the army airfields near Pearl Harbor, after the attack. It was the first word they had from their son for four weeks.

Not two weeks into the new year the heroes of sport began to appear in the *Courier-Times* as they joined up or reported for physicals. Bob Feller, the fireballing Cleveland pitcher was first, along with Mountain Man Dean, the Georgian wrestler. Ted Williams, the American League batting champion with the Boston Red Sox, signed up as well, and an army physician in his hometown of Minneapolis pronounced him fit for service. On the 12th, Joe Louis appeared shaking the hand of an army officer as he enlisted in New York.

Eleanor Roosevelt, who according to an article was a housewife above all else, asked the housewives of the country to keep on keeping house, as the serenity of the American home was the third line of defense after the Armed forces and the civilian defense agencies. Give up the jitters, she urged, and fix a good dinner for your husband. Other articles urged everyone to take care of aluminum cookware, because no more would be made for the duration of the emergency. Conservation was the watchword.

On January 14, President Roosevelt appointed Donald M. Nelson to be the production czar for the entire country. One man would dictate levels of production for the entire economy from an office in Washington, D.C. Not since America's entry into the Great War of 1914–1918 had this kind of control been exercised over the businesses of the country. The clamps had really been put on certain kinds of civilian consumption. The few new cars that were available were to be allocated to buyers by the tire rationing boards. The Office of Price Administration (OPA), headed by Leon Henderson in Washington, announced that the following people would have priority in buying the cars: physicians, surgeons, nurses, veterinarians, fire and police departments, other law enforcement and public safety and health agencies, mail carriers, and those who had arranged purchases before January 2. But even these people would have to obtain purchase certificates from the OPA through the local office. There were about 650,000 such new cars to be allocated. The approximately 130,000 cars to be produced the final eighteen days of January would be "held" by the OPA for "future needs."

The editor noted in an article on army inductees that the Selective Service System had relaxed its rules, allowing the papers to print the names of those drafted into the services from Henry County. This was a relaxation of the rule adopted after Pearl Harbor, which kept the names and numbers secret, lest the Japanese or Germans gain information on potential troop strength. Thirty-seven boys from New Castle and the county appeared on this list of draftees. There was no word of where they were going or the branch that had taken them.

After the previous day's news of the draftees, it came as no surprise on the 15th that the army would expand its numbers to 3.6 million men, double the January 1942 strength. Three new divisions were to be organized by March 15. For the year, there were to be thirty-two motorized divisions added to the twenty-seven infantry divisions presently in existence, and a doubling of armored divisions. This meant an increase in anti-aircraft, engineer, and other special units. Fifty Military Police (MP) battalions would be added to guard important installations all over the country. A bulletin on the front page of the paper announced that the war was getting closer. German submarines sank a freighter off the Long Island shore, the second attack in two days. The previous attack was off Hampton Bays, seventy-five miles from New York City.

The big city newspapers realized that many of their Sunday paper sales were outside of the metropolitan areas they normally served. On this Saturday, the Chicago *Tribune* hoped to lure paper buyers with a special spread on Captain Colin P. Kelly, the B-17 bomber pilot who sacrificed his own life in the Pacific by crashing his crippled plane into a Japanese ship. The *Tribune* included a full-page color portrait of Kelly, suitable for framing, in Sunday's edition.

By January 21, there were only nine days left to get the federal automobile use stamps from the post office that everyone was required to display in their cars. Most people used the plastic-covered wraparound holders that fit over the steering column. There were reports of thefts of these stamps now and then. No one is sure why, but the number of marriage licenses was up sharply in 1941, while divorces dropped slightly. Some thought it was the war, but others believed it was the change in the blood test law that brought the increase. There were 142 more marriages than the 345 in 1940. The New Castle police department had gotten its second new DeSoto police car but, under the wartime metals restriction, it had painted black hubcaps and a painted grill instead of the traditional chrome.

The wire services reported on January 23 that the Japanese had landed on New Guinea, in the Solomon Islands, and captured Rabaul, the capital of New Britain. This brought the Japanese perilously close to Australia and threatened to force Allied shipping to pass to the south around Australia in order to supply Dutch, British, and French friendly forces in the East Indies. With this news, it came as no surprise that the two county draft boards had received their quotas for 1942, and they were grim. The county was at war, a fact mentioned in the article. The New Castle board's quota was 979 for the year, but credit was given for the 295 who had already enlisted. The rural board had a quota of 328 for the year, but 111 had gone in so far from outside New Castle. If Henry was an average county, this could mean that more than 120,000 Hoosier men would be required just in the year of 1942. As if to make it all easier to take, comedies were the rage at the theaters in town. Abbot and Costello were at the Castle in *Keep 'Em Flying* with Martha Raye. The newsreel was titled *War Clouds in the Pacific.*

By January 27 there was news that the first convoy of American troops made it safely to Northern Ireland without a loss. This was in spite of the fact that there was a great deal of U-boat activity in the Atlantic at the time. Somehow they got past the submarines which had sunk the ships off Long Island the previous week. The government formed boards with the British to coordinate the production and movement of munitions, shipping, and war materials. The experience of the world war of twenty-five years ago was being put to good use once again. The high school honor roll list was in the paper. Gemma's dear friend Sarah Wright was on the honorable mention list, as was her sister Marie.

There was more bad news when people turned their calendars to February. The British had been driven back upon the island of Singapore, the Associated Press reported. They retreated 350 miles in just two months but an allied convoy got through, which helped. General Percival indicated that they would resist in the fortress until help arrived. If this weren't bad enough, there was news that here at home, three hundred thousand auto workers had been ordered to halt the production lines in order to begin retooling for war production. The layoffs might last until midsummer. No more cars of any kind could be made, but production continued in medium and light truck plants and their suppliers for the next two months, and a six-month supply of replacement parts began to go into stockpiles. The trucks manufactured, however, would only have temporary tires to allow them to be delivered to the dealers. No one knew whether the government would release tires for them later. Coming in the Sunday Chicago *Tribune* was something many wanted to read: advice from expert sociologists about war marriages and whether to have children.

In the picture section on the back page were the twenty-four army nurses who accompanied the convoy which recently made it to Ireland. None were from New Castle, but one was from the neighboring town of Richmond in Wayne County.

The war was not going well in the late winter of 1941–1942. By the end of February, Washington had judged the situation in the Philippines hopeless, and ordered General MacArthur to Australia, where he was to establish a new headquarters. From formerly French Indochina, the Japanese overran most of the East Indies, forcing the Dutch to surrender on March 12. With this conquest, the Japanese had taken over the world's entire rubber production. The Germans held on against the Russians in the snow.

Throughout early 1942, stories in the paper gradually made clear what everyone already suspected. It was just a matter of time until every young man in the chosen age categories would either be inducted into the army or would be rejected as physically unfit for duty. The lists of names of those ordered to report for their physicals began to appear in the paper in the spring. Kenny Smith joined the rest of the millions in his age bracket who decided to wait for the call. Others went sooner. Harold Lovelace, longtime manager of The Corner Drugstore in New Castle, reported for active duty in March 1942. He was a lieutenant in the artillery, having served in the early 1930s, and Uncle Sam needed him now.

Chrysler announced that it would increase capacity by expanding its production facilities with $66 million in new plant space. Chrysler was already making tanks, tank engines, antiaircraft gun parts, and subassemblies. Aluminum forgings and bomber parts also were in the works, along with a considerable list of items that were secret. No details were given about which plants would make which items, of course, because that would allow the enemy to begin sabotage efforts in key production areas. It was clear, though, that New Castle's humming Chrysler facility would be in the thick of wartime production efforts. The men there might not know what they were making, but they would be making plenty of it.

There were hints that production would have to get rolling soon. Pictures began to appear in the photo section on the back page of the *Courier-Times* showing the impact of the war. German U-boats sank a Gulf Oil tanker within sight of the New Jersey shoreline, and its prow remained above water to remind everyone that the Germans were at times very close indeed. The strong arm of the government began to appear on the local level, too. In Valparaiso, up near the Michigan line in northern Indiana, a junk dealer refused to sell scrap metal to steel mills at the price set by the OPA because he thought it was too low. A picture showed the dealer surrounded by a U.S. Marshal, uniformed MPs, and other official types as he was read the order requisitioning one hundred tons of scrap. The message was clear. Play by the government's rules and do it with a smile, or face the consequences. The government was not about to let the increased demand for certain items enable anyone who held them to make "excessive" profits.

Everyone would have to cut back on important materials. Cliff Payne, new president of the Chamber of Commerce and prominent clothier in town, announced the restrictions being placed on the men's garment industry. Baggy pants and amply cut coats had been the fashion for most of the decade of the 1930s. This was about to end. Suits could no longer be sold with two pairs of pants, and double-breasted suits could not be sold with vests. Trousers would lose their cuffs, could not be pleated, and would have to conform to official lengths specified by government agencies. Patch pockets, vents on coats, and belts for topcoats would be forbidden. Wool was the item in demand for uniforms, and everyone else would have to do with less. In the middle of March, Payne still had plenty of the old style full-cut clothes, but there would be no more when they were gone. The government had given him until March 30 to sell what he had, and then the new regulations would go into effect.

There was plenty to occupy the thoughts of people on Plum Street as the spring of 1942 turned into summer. Ads began to appear in the paper offering jobs and job training for work in factories making war supplies. The Swallow Airplane Company agent came to a hotel in New Castle to recruit students for its aircraft mechanic school. It did not take too much hard thinking to figure out that if one had a vital skill, wartime duty might consist of clocking in at a war plant for the duration. Many young men sought out this training, and Kenny Smith was one of them.

In March 1942, Kenny quit at the Morris 5 & 10, paid his tuition, and went to Wichita, Kansas, for aircraft production training. It was a six-week course, and the primary assignment was to build a wing strut out of sheet metal according to the specifications on the blueprints. Wichita was already a center for plane manufacturers, and many young men went there to see if they could gain a needed skill before the War Department got all the training camps built. Kenny finished his strut in three weeks and came home early with a certificate that he had successfully completed the course. When he got home, Fred and Lillian had been saving articles and ads out of the papers, and he soon went to Akron for more training and another certificate. After returning from this trip, he went to Buffalo, New York, to look for work, but finding none, went to Detroit where he could stay with his cousin while he continued the job search. Kenny turned twenty-one on July 3, 1942. Even with his production training and a rapidly growing need for factory workers, no plant would take him on, not even in New Castle. Every shop boss and hiring agent in the country knew that every young man twenty-one years old and in apparent good health would soon be in the service. There was no sense hiring and training them just to have them drafted a few weeks later.

Only farm boys might have an advantage. Kenny's friend Harold Rothrock fell into this category. Born and raised on a farm about two miles south of where the Smiths lived on Route 2, they had attended the Riley school together, then the junior high, and were both in New Castle High's Class of 1941. Harold's brother Howard was already in the army, so Harold did not get a notice from the draft board because he was considered irreplaceable on the family farm. He tried to enlist but was prevented from doing so by the ruling of the draft board. He stayed at home during the war, helping the vital agricultural sector produce the food and fiber needed to feed and clothe our fighting men and allies. Farm women helped even more than they usually did. Mrs. Rothrock received severe injuries when she got caught in a corn picker on the farm later that year.

Farmers got into the war effort. The July 1942 issue of *Farm Journal* arrived at the Smiths' house with a cover showing the flag waving from the porch of a farmhouse while the farmer patiently cultivated his corn across the road. "United We Stand" was the cover theme, and it contained a declaration of war by the Unarmed Forces of the United States on partisanship, political intrigue, special privilege, blindness, and bickering. It would be a war of production, and labor was needed on the farm. The articles included suggestions for cutting back on tire wear, a piece on the supply snafu here at home resulting from too many pork purchases for Lend-Lease, a call for nurses, and the usual stories and recipes in "The Farmer's Wife" section. Already, *Farm Journal* reported, 4,290 of the 6,460 farms in California taken over from the evacuated Japanese had been turned over to new operators. The local paper had previously printed pictures of the camp being built for them in the California desert at Manzanar.

Because war production had already shifted resources away from consumer goods output, OPA announced new maximum prices for goods such as refrigerators, typewriters, vacuum cleaners, washing machines, irons, radios, and stoves. The list continued to grow during the year. The government could only move so fast, however. Other items continued to be abundant. At the end of March, the Hoosier Pete service station at Grand and A Avenue put regular gas on sale for 14.9¢ per gallon. At Denton's Drug Store, anyone could buy Mum deodorant for 42¢, a pint of Peptona tonic for the stomach for $1.25, a pound of Borden's Hemo malted milk mix for 59¢, and Sal Hepatica for 49¢. Deodorants like Mum and Odorono were relatively new and intended for women, of course, but it did not take long for men to start dipping their fingers into the small glass jars and using it themselves. It even helped the problem a little bit.

After years of reading the society page to see what the elite in New Castle were doing, Gemma found herself listed prominently in the March 26, 1942, issue of the paper. "Miss Gemma Moles, assisted by her mother, Mrs. Jess Moles, entertained Wednesday evening at their home on Plum Street with a surprise linen shower for Miss Martha Fatzinger. Miss Fatzinger's marriage to Philip D. Perry will take place on Easter Sunday, April 5, at the Brick Church of the Brethren west of Hagerstown." Phil's mother and sisters, Mrs. Lineback who had rented part of the Plum Street house from the Wrights, Gemma's cousin Pauline Koger, Sarah Wright, other friends, and Wanda, Marie, and Maxine all made the list of those who attended. The wedding was just ten days away.

Martha and Phil overcame considerable difficulties to arrive at the point where they would take the leap into marriage. They began dating seriously early in 1941, when Martha began to want to go alone with Phil instead of double-dating so much with Gemma. Although Martha graduated with the Class of 1941 in May, she was still just seventeen during the summer of 1941, and although serious thoughts went through both their heads that year, both their families urged caution. Martha had a job at J. C. Penney on Broad Street. Phil was from Hagerstown, Indiana, eleven miles east of New Castle, and had graduated with Hagerstown High's Class of 1939. Tall, lanky, and handsome, Phil worked at Perfect Circle's piston ring plant, Hagerstown's most important employer.

The strongest opposition came from Martha's father and mother. In November, Phil bought an engagement ring and took it to the house when he went to see Martha. He thought it proper to ask her parents if they would consent to Martha marrying him, and as he asked them, he told them he had the engagement ring. Would they mind if he gave it to her? The answer was an emphatic yes, they would mind. Phil retreated awkwardly, and they waited.

Pearl Harbor changed everything. Now the expectation that young men would be needed by the millions altered everyone's perspective. Phil's brother had joined the army in 1938, and knew what the life of an enlisted man was like. Enlisted pay was meager, and it was difficult to support a wife, so he was waiting to marry his girlfriend until later. With the war on, everyone knew that being sent overseas was practically a given. His brother urged Phil to wait at least until he found out where he would be assigned. There would be time after it was over to get married.

Martha's father put it on the line to her when she and Phil pressed again to become engaged. "You get married, and then you'll be pregnant, and he'll go away, and you don't know if he's coming back." Everyone was struck into silence for a terrible moment while the words sank in. He had said the thing that everyone tried to avoid saying or even thinking. They all knew that anyone who went into the service might not come back. It was the one unspeakable possibility that hung over them all. For the sake of morale and individual sanity, most took care to keep the thought out of their heads. Yet here Martha's father had said it out loud, hoping to discourage them from a course of action that might result in Martha's being a young widow with a child. The implication was that her parents would have to support her if this happened, and she would have difficulty finding a good husband in those circumstances. Of course, they hoped to spare her the possible pain of losing a husband. In the face of these protests, they agreed to wait a while. But having decided that they ought to get married, it was very difficult to just wait for those opposed to come around to their point of view. In January 1942, with alarm about the Japanese at its height, they decided that they would go ahead with their plans. Martha was eighteen now and of legal age to get married even without her parents' consent. They made plans for an Easter Sunday wedding, and Phil gave her the ring. Her father cried and carried on and thought her mother should put her foot down and insist that Martha wait. But it was too late. The couple asked the preacher at the Brick Church to marry them on Easter Sunday afternoon, and he agreed.

Their courtship, brief engagement, and marriage were instructive for Gemma. Although the same age as Gemma, Martha played the role of an older sister in going through the steps leading to marriage. They shared confidences, and Gemma knew all about the problems with Martha's parents. Gemma gave the shower for her, and when the wedding came, Gemma was Martha's bridesmaid. By April 5, Martha and Phil's families had gotten over their concerns and everyone who could do so attended the wedding, coming from as far away as Missouri. Farrell Hendricks was there, as were all the Moles family. Gemma's cousin Pauline Koger, Mrs. Linebeck and her daughter, from Plum Street, and McKendrick Smith also attended.

Martha's wedding dress was beige silk crepe, with Gemma dressed in light blue wool crepe with beige accessories to match Martha's dress. Phil was somber in his dark suit. It was a simple single-ring ceremony. Two standards of flowers decorated the altar, and there were piano selections and a solo of "I Love You Truly" as the guests arrived. After the ceremony and the throwing of rice, Martha and Phil left for a "short wedding trip." They went to the Leland Hotel in Richmond, twenty miles to the east, where they spent the night. On Monday, they returned to New Castle to a house they had rented at 424 South 15th Street. The next day, Martha's picture appeared in the paper as an Easter bride, Mrs. Philip Perry.

In the *Courier-Times,* the editor wondered why there had to be such a long delay between events and the receipt of news about them. Wake Island had fallen to the Japanese two days before Christmas 1941. Newspaper files showed that the Japanese radio had announced an American attack on Wake Island in the Pacific on February 24. The American force had been successful in damaging the Japanese shore batteries, had sunk two patrol boats, and had destroyed some aircraft. The Navy Department had denied knowledge of any action at that time. The day before this editorial appeared, the navy had announced that there had indeed been an attack on February 24 after all. There was no explanation why it had taken a month to make the announcement. It had taken almost four weeks for word of the death at Pearl Harbor of the Griffin boy from Spiceland to reach the papers, too.

Mostly the news of the war was bad, anyway. A week after Martha and Phil were married, MacArthur left the Philippines but vowed, "I shall return." The only significant American areas left were the Bataan peninsula and the fortified island of Corregidor. On April 9, the American and Filipino forces trapped on Bataan surrendered, giving the Japanese seventy-five thousand prisoners, twelve thousand of them Americans. It would be a long time before word got out, but the Japanese marched these prisoners, many of them sick and wounded, one hundred miles to a prison camp. Thousands died along the way in what became known later as the Bataan Death March.

At home, Petroleum Coordinator Harold Ickes, former Secretary of the Interior, took over the nation's tank cars due to an oil shortage on the East Coast. His agency began ordering the railroads to deliver so many cars of fuel here and so many there. Word was that it was oil tanker sinkings in the Atlantic and Gulf of Mexico that had caused the shortages. The Department of Agriculture announced April 5–11 as 4-H mobilization week to encourage members to increase the nation's food production and assist with its preservation by canning at home. The Army Air Corps ended the tourist trade in Miami Beach by taking over the flashy art deco hotels as barracks for air trainees. The good news for the owners was that thirty thousand men would be stationed there for the duration, courtesy of Uncle Sam.

In New Castle, "job insurance" payments dropped dramatically as spring turned into summer. Local factories were already receiving war orders and unemployment dropped like a rock. For the first time in several years, Henry County Sheriff Cash Robinson reported that there was no one in the jail. A new "Men in Service" column appeared in the interior of the paper for the first time. By the middle of April, it would be on the front page every day. Robert Winter, manager of the Rose City Airport, urged young men to learn to fly in the Rose City Aero Club. On April 9, the two county draft boards announced that forty-three young men left that morning for Fort Harrison, east of Indianapolis, for induction into the army. Twenty-six were from New Castle and seventeen were from out in the county. Pictures of three county men appeared early in the month. One, Roy Ruddell, had won his wings as a naval aviator at Pensacola and had been assigned to active combat duty on an aircraft carrier. The other two were going to report to the marine base at San Diego for training. Chief Water Tender Oscar Popejoy wrote home to his parents in New Castle that his ship, the carrier *Lexington,* had survived an attack from nineteen Japanese planes by destroying sixteen of them. A fourteen-year navy veteran, he expressed hope that at that rate, the war would soon be over.

Wartime restrictions eased their way into the daily routines of New Castle's citizens. The Chamber of Commerce began working to have the community declared a "defense area" because of the hardships that would result from failing to receive that designation. The War Production Board (WPB) sent word to the water plant early in April that it would be allowed to install only six new water meters for the entire year of 1942 unless New Castle became a "defense area." With the designation, homes could be built for defense workers, the only exception to national restrictions on residential building. The Board also announced that if styles dictated shorter and tighter skirts, that was okay but they could be no longer than the official maximum of twenty-five inches. The Board established measurement standards for all sizes. Homemade dresses and skirts did not have to conform to the rules unless they were to be sold. The WPB's reach was far and wide. Arvid P. Zetterberg, manager of the Ingersoll Steel and Disc Company's New Castle plant, received appointment to a WPB advisory committee on the hand shovel industry, and had an official notice from Washington, D.C., to prove it.

On April 22, the OPA announced that rationing would begin on May 5. Sugar was the first item to come under OPA's restrictions, and the allotments for hotels and restaurants were cut to half of the previous year's consumption. Bakers, ice cream makers, and soft drink bottlers were restricted to 70 percent of past use. The first civilian ration stamp allowed citizens to pay for the purchase of one pound of sugar during the period May 5–16. Three other stamps allowed one-pound purchases every two weeks until the end of June. Household consumers had to register at their local schools from May 4–7, and wholesalers and retailers had to sign up with the government on April 28 and 29. The government gave schoolteachers the task of signing up the millions of family representatives who would show up to obtain ration books. One adult member of the family could go to the registration site to register for the entire family. Each family member received a ration book, so that if there were five members of a family, they could obtain five pounds of sugar upon payment of the cost and presentation of the ration stamps from war ration book #1 for that period for each member of the family. No one who already owned more than six pounds of sugar could get their ration book yet. They had to wait until ration stamps equal to the weight of the sugar on hand had been authorized for other people. Children born after the start of rationing were entitled to normal rations upon application of their parents or guardians to the local ration board. Over 7,800 people in the county registered for their war ration books the first day and 7,300 actually received books because they did not have six or more pounds of sugar at home. Within the month, the state ration board notified the local ration board that there was more sugar being sold in New Castle since rationing began than there had been before. People were using their ration stamps before they expired whether they needed sugar or not. Although it was against the law, there arose almost immediately a quiet trading of rationed items. Better to stock up while it was possible and legal than to have none later.

Already the fear of shortages loomed. Used car dealers advertised their inventories with a notation about the condition of the tires. Crow Implement Sales announced that they had only two Ford tractors on rubber tires rather than steel wheels, and that there were to be no more when these were gone. OPA administrator Leon Henderson warned the nation that unless a large part of the supply of spendable income could be immobilized immediately, severe inflation could result from too much money chasing too few goods. The *Courier-Times* editorial staff summed up the attitude that the government hoped everyone would take: "There may be some disposition to argue as to whether there is a sugar shortage and the necessity for the complicated program of receiving rationing cards. But after all we are in a war and if the proper authorities deem rationing wise, there is nothing else to do but fall in line and be sweet about it." The rationing boards had another duty, as well. They would be responsible for enforcing the price ceilings established by OPA.

Men between the ages of forty-five and sixty-five had to register at the armory in New Castle on Monday, April 27. Even Fred Smith would have to sign up this time. There was no telling what use the government might have for the country's able-bodied men, but all the nations at war had already instituted such measures. Roosevelt announced that women, however, would not have to participate in voluntary registration for wartime activities.

The war continued to go badly. The navy announced the overall casualty figures for the war to date on May 2, 1942. There had been 2,991 killed, 2,495 missing, and 907 wounded for a total of 6,393. Already, in just five months of the war, the navy had lost half again as many men as it lost in the Great War of 1914–1918. The uncertain fate of crews of the cruiser *Houston* and three destroyers, lost in the battle for Java, had swelled the total of missing. Already the cost of the previous war had been exceeded. The government had spent $26 billion on war preparations since 1940.

Profiles of Japanese planes began to appear in the paper, beginning with the Kawasaki Type 97 light bomber, and perhaps it was just in time. Word appeared on May 6 that Corregidor, the last American stronghold in the Philippines, had fallen to the Japanese. Only the miraculous Doolittle raid on the Japanese home islands offered any lift to the progress of the war. Our B-25s, launched from the pitching deck of the carrier *Hornet*, ranging far into waters controlled by the Japanese Navy, managed to bomb targets in three Japanese cities, including Tokyo, and fly on to a friendly reception in the part of China controlled by Chiang Kai-shek's pro-American forces. The Japanese, caught completely by surprise, suffered a largely psychological blow which Americans cheered. The raid had little or no impact on Japanese war production, but it served as a small repayment for the attack on Pearl Harbor. There would be more payback later.

There was a war on, but the 1942 Junior Prom at the high school drew the usual very large crowd of over four hundred. As in past years, this included the administration, practically all the faculty, and school board members and their guests. There were some from Plum Street. Maxine and Marie Moles attended, as did James Capshaw, whose family had moved to Plum Street in 1939. Marie had begun dating Orville Hammond, a handsome, lanky, sandy-headed lad from Hagerstown, and they went together that night and to the commencement dance, too. Sarah Wright went alone. Clay was in camp in Mississippi, and she was trying to keep Orrin at an arm's distance. In spite of Orrin's pledge to take care of Sarah while Clay was away, she had managed to shake him for this occasion. Kenny's good friends Harry Ridout, always sober-looking with his wiry hair and wire-rimmed glasses, and dark-haired, rakish Charlie Purvis went, too.

It was senior year for Maxine Moles. She had dated Norman Rust during much of that school year, but he had a jealousy problem that caused considerable difficulty. He was simply insanely jealous of anyone who even talked to Maxine. He was not so bad when he went on dates with her, because he had her full attention then, but other times he could make life a little difficult. He constantly scoured the school and her circle of friends for information about her. She went to Junior Prom with him, and to the commencement dance, but a few days later she began the process of breaking up with Norman, and soon terminated the relationship completely. Marie had promised that Orville had friends that Maxine ought to meet from Hagerstown. So there were prospects. Even though she was about to graduate from high school, there were jobs to be had, as Gemma had shown. She would wait for the right boy to come along.

Two weeks later, 197 seniors made up the New Castle High School Class of '42, Sarah Wright, Clay Grubbs, Orrin Grubbs, and Maxine Moles among them, along with the Moles girls' cousin Glenn Cowan. None of them probably noticed it, but Edsel Ford, president of the Ford Motor Company, announced that day that the first of the four-engined bombers that Ford would manufacture for the Army Air Corps came off the assembly line at Ford's new Willow Run assembly plant at Ypsilanti, Michigan. These were the first of the odd-looking B-24s that would become a mainstay of strategic bombing forces in both Europe and the Pacific. They would touch the lives of both Glenn Cowan and Maxine Moles.

Clay took advantage of the opportunity provided by the state of Indiana to take his diploma in spite of the fact that he was a couple of credits short of the required total. Men in service could graduate from high school if they were three or fewer credits short due to the wartime emergency. Clay got a ten-day leave, his first in many months, to come back to New Castle for this occasion. Dressed in his green infantry corporal's uniform, he and several others got their diplomas before heading back to Camp Shelby. This leave gave him the opportunity to take Sarah to the commencement dance after the diploma ceremonies. Orrin took a date, too, but it wasn't Sarah. Gemma went, although Kenny could not go. His friends Harry Ridout, Marvin Snider, Charlie Purvis, and Harry's good friend Robert Pitts all attended.

An editorial cartoon offered service and patriotism as "Another Chance for the Role of Honor" to the Class of 1942. Many of them met this obligation, and more. The class officers turned the $75 profit on the Junior Prom over to the United Service Organization (USO). Those who attended also bought $50 worth of War Savings Stamps at the door.

For Sarah, Clay's visit flew by at a furious pace and he was soon gone again on the train from the 18th Street station. They wrote and kept each other close as best they could from that distance. Upon his return to camp, Clay learned that he had been promoted from corporal to sergeant. Clay's mother Erma immediately sent word of his promotion to the paper so everyone would know.

6. Bearer of Bad News, 1942

ORRIN STILL WORKED for Western Union and still pined for Sarah, but she tried to give him no encouragement. Orrin brought good news and bad to Western Union's customers. There were the usual birth announcement telegrams and news that relatives would be coming to visit, but there was bad news, too. That was only a trickle for now, with few casualties from New Castle this early in the war. But it would not be long before the sight of the uniformed Western Union boy pedaling down the street would send a chill down the backs of those who saw him, and instantly halt conversations. Neighbors knew which neighbors had boys in the service from the stars in the windows, and everyone peered out of their doors or turned to see where the telegram might be headed. If the messenger rode down the street out of sight, there was a sigh of relief and a return to normal. But if he parked his bicycle in front of a house with a banner in the window with one or more blue stars indicating family members in the service, then a hushed tension gripped all who watched. Those who had seen called others to the window to see the drama played out. The Western Union boy handed the envelope to an adult who answered the door, and left immediately. Usually the door closed, making it impossible for neighbors to gather any information about its contents until later. A telegram directly from the family member might mean that he had been given leave, had arrived somewhere, or was safe and sound and out of danger. The most dreaded message was from the War Department, because that meant that something had happened to a loved one in the service. The word could be that their GI was missing, or wounded and recovering nicely, or seriously wounded, or dead. There were always trembling hands when such a message, sealed in its envelope, traded hands at the door. In the next few months, Orrin would deliver all kinds of wires, including the worst kind, in New Castle.

Three days before the Class of '42 graduated, word came from the Navy Department that Lawrence Corum, whose family lived in the 2300 block of Plum Street, was either dead or a prisoner of the Japanese. Corum, thirty-three years old, had been a chief petty officer on the minesweeper USS *Quail* in the Philippines. Her crew scuttled the vessel before Corregidor fell to keep it from falling into enemy hands. Corum's wife received the message in Hawaii, where she lived. Corum attended New Castle schools, leaving to join the navy in 1926 in his junior year in high school. His brother, on a hospital ship in Manila Bay at the time of the war's outbreak, had escaped, because the family had received word from him in March. Corum's sister thought it might be better if he were dead rather than in a Japanese prison. Only Corum himself knew that he was in fact a prisoner, and there was no way for him to notify his family that he was, in fact, alive. It would take years to learn that he died a prisoner without ever knowing whether they would find out.

With the war less than six months old, New Castle had already given lives at Pearl Harbor and in the conquest of the Philippines. On June 12, 1942, the navy announced that the carrier USS *Lexington* had been lost in the Coral Sea, off the east coast of Australia, on May 8. One New Castle man on the crew was known to have survived, and the navy reported that 92 percent of the crew of 3,300 had been saved, but there was no word yet on Oscar Popejoy or Rex Lovett. The United States lost the *Lexington*, a tanker, and a destroyer. The Japanese lost fifteen to seventeen ships sunk and twenty damaged, including a carrier, three heavy cruisers, and others. Troubling as always was the fact that it had taken almost five weeks to find out.

In April 1942, Gemma left the Morris 5 & 10 for a job at the hosiery counter at Penney's. Gemma's friend Sarah Niles had worked at Woolworth's, then got on at Public Service, the local power company. She encouraged Gemma to apply there, and she did. Gemma started her new job at Public Service in July, putting bills into envelopes. She was soon assigned to help Martha Schultz, who was always behind, to figure partial bills for customers who moved in or out. Martha then became a cashier, and it was expected that someone would have to be hired to help Gemma with the partial bills, but she never got behind. It became her regular place. Ten or twelve girls worked in the office with Gemma, and they were mostly of the society class in town. It had been a breathtaking rise for Gemma by local standards. Even though she graduated high in her class and had been a member of National Honor Society, she did not think she was qualified for an office job. Many people went to business college to prepare for this kind of work.

Summer of '42

By the summer of 1942, Gemma and Kenny were seeing each other regularly. She told her friends that she was not in love with him, but Martha noticed how excited she became any time she thought she saw Kenny driving up Plum Street. It was plain to all by now that theirs was more than a passing interest. In July, Jess took their picture in front of the house at 1828 Plum Street, standing in the clover near one of the Norway maples that Jess had planted. Gemma was nineteen, and Kenny had just turned twenty-one. They were about to go out on a date, Gemma in open-toed shoes and anklets, light-colored skirt and jacket, Kenny in a cotton knit shirt and pleated pants. Gemma appeared pleased, but a little uncomfortable as Jess centered them in the viewfinder and snapped the picture. Kenny smiled good-naturedly with his hands on his hips. Jess had never taken her picture with a suitor before.

That summer was the waiting time. Kenny knew as the lists of names continued to appear in the paper that his name would have to be drawn before too much time went by. When the list of all registrants appeared in the paper, he discovered to his surprise that his name was not included, in spite of the fact that he had

In the summer of 1942, just before they went out on a date, Jess took this picture of Gemma with Kenny in front of the house at 1828 Plum Street, the first ever of Gemma with a suitor. Gemma is nineteen years old, Kenny has just turned twenty-one.

signed up at the proper time just like all the other young men. Another opportunity for staying out of it presented itself. But he knew that it wasn't right, so he went to the draft board and pointed out the fact that he had been omitted from the list. They corrected the mistake. He helped his father on the farm, and lent a hand when his mother needed assistance breaking beans or doing other kitchen chores. They did not know what was coming or just when, but they all cherished the days of that waning summer.

It was a time when "victory gardens" were the rage, offering common citizens and even children a chance to contribute to the war effort. Scrap drives were ongoing, but gardens helped reduce the number of men needed on farms. The Moles and the Smiths always planted gardens, but they expanded them during the war. There was no way to know what might be rationed later on, and seeds were cheap. Rationing and price controls did not apply to produce out of the garden. What had been an economic necessity in the depression became military assistance in the war. A weekly column began to appear in the paper to advise novice gardeners when and what to plant.

Just when it began to get really hot in the summer, the government ordered the ice industry to cut back on trucks, tires, and gas. Consumers Ice and Fuel, which supplied the Moles, and Burke Ice and Coal stopped delivering ice on Sundays, ended special deliveries, and refused to honor call-backs or more than one delivery on a given day. The city's dairies cut deliveries from six days a week to four days in accordance with rules published by the Office of Defense Transportation. Official word had it that coffee, tea, cocoa, and clothing might be on the rationed list soon.

One shortage kept women cooler, however. Silk and nylon were already becoming scarce, so leg makeup ads began to appear in the paper. This product included foundation applied all over the leg to give the appearance of a stocking that was a different color than the skin and to hide freckles or other blemishes, and a pencil which women used to draw a line straight up the center of the leg on the back to simulate the seam in the hose. The line was hard to put on straight and was usually put on by someone else. The Armand company claimed that it stayed on all day. It cost 49¢.

The housing shortage in New Castle helped earn it a designation as a critical defense area. Combined with the rubber and automotive manufactures in town which were already hiring rapidly, the population was growing beyond what had been adequate in the depression years of the thirties. Chrysler was already a major defense contractor and would remain so throughout the war. The Chamber of Commerce and other organizations helped provide the local data to the WPB, which merited the designation. The main advantage was that local building suppliers could now bid for construction materials on the national market in order to provide contractors what they needed to build in New Castle. The only sizeable area available within the city limits which had already been supplied with the sewer, water, and power needed to accommodate major building was the Sunnyside addition on South 14th Street. Earlier construction plans had halted when the war brought tight controls on metals for wiring and plumbing, and lumber.

At the end of June, Maurice Goodwin, New Castle's postmaster, announced the government's new guidelines for mail going to servicemen overseas, known as V-mail. It consisted of a one-piece letter and envelope of a lightweight paper, with special markings on the outside to identify it as V-mail. People wishing to write got these forms at their local post offices. The main advantage was in the weight saved, allowing many more letters to be sent on ships or aircraft in the same amount of space. Writing was to go on both sides of the page, then it was folded over and sealed. Postage was 3¢ by surface transportation, and 6¢ to get the letter to the port of embarkation by airmail. There machines opened it, the censors read it, and other machines microfilmed it, so that the recipient got a 4×5 photo card of the actual letter, or at least that was the government's plan. V-mail soon became a familiar part of keeping in touch with the millions of men and women who went overseas.

Another familiar sight in 1942 was the community scrap drive. The government needed massive quantities of rubber, aluminum, scrap steel and iron, and other metals. The Boy Scouts, 4-H clubs, community groups, and service stations all participated in this effort as housewives gave up their aluminum pots and pans, kids searched garages and trash areas for old tires and inner tubes, and everything from bedsprings to sewing machines to engine blocks accumulated at designated collection points. One enterprising group of kids got free movie tickets for the 930 pounds of rubber they brought in. Rubber was particularly critical. With the Japanese in control of practically all the natural rubber plantations in Indochina and the East Indies, rubber scrap became critical to the war effort. While scientists worked frantically to develop an alternative, manufacturers tried to match booming truck production with very scarce tires. In New Castle, Homer Smith's Standard service station, a landmark at 520 South Main, led the city in rubber collections with more than four tons. Junk and scrap dealers like the Danns on East Broad Street played a pivotal role in collecting and shipping critical materials to the plants where they could be made into planes, tanks, and jeeps. County residents found and turned in more than 160 tons of rubber by the time the drive ended. Even Fala, President Roosevelt's Scottish terrier, had to give up his rubber dog toys for the war effort.

The war effort was so important that on July 1, 1942, the government abolished three New Deal agencies: the Civilian Conservation Corps (CCC), the WPA, and the National Youth Administration (NYA), which was a youth training program. Nearly 500,000 people lost their jobs, but there was so much hiring in the wartime agencies in Washington and at defense plants around the country that few of these were out of work for long if they desired to work. The government was having trouble building office buildings and ordering desks fast enough to keep up with the demand for space and new employees.

Orrin Grubbs surprised his mother and everyone else by enlisting in the Marine Corps at the end of June, apparently through the Indianapolis recruiting office. He had until August 5 to put his affairs in order. That would be the day he would leave for San Diego for basic training.

William Bartling, the naval aviator from Henry County who had served with the American Volunteer Group, or Flying Tigers, in China, ended his career there as the group disbanded. Now that America was in the war, there would be plenty of enemy planes to fight as a navy, Marine Corps, or army pilot officially in the employ of Uncle Sam. General Chennault had gathered the volunteers to serve the cause of free China, including several who became famous as Flying Tigers before Pearl Harbor, and secured P-40s and supplies with contributions and with the help of the U.S. government in order to battle the Japanese in their drive against China, long a friend of the United States. After Pearl Harbor, the pilots reentered their original branches of service, or chose others, but nearly all continued to fly.

Local pride rose to a new pitch when, over the July 4 weekend, the Chrysler put on a display of the war products the firm made in New Castle. A medium bomber and its bombs were a highlight, as was the tank, with treads made locally. It was good that these products could be seen, because there were no more Chryslers, Plymouths, or Dodges coming off the line in Detroit with parts made in New Castle. Herman Redd, a major new car dealer in town, announced that he would suspend business for the duration. The defense plants had hired his mechanics, there were no tires or gasoline, and repair work alone would not keep the business afloat. Redd himself was a captain in the Army Air Corps, having left operation of the business to his wife and brother. When there were Chryslers to sell again, he would be back at the old place.

Enlistments and inductions continued as more and more entries in the "Men in Service" column appeared every day. The two county draft boards assigned priority numbers to county boys aged eighteen through twenty, determining the order in which they would be called. In July 1942, only men over age twenty were eligible to be drafted. For the time being, these could wait or enlist, but would not be called. Every day brought them closer to the time when they would turn twenty-one, of course. Some, like Charles Loer of A Avenue, joined up with the idea of training for a job that might keep them safe on the ground at an air base while others flew off and got shot at by German or Japanese fighters. Loer and 105 others from Indiana signed up the third week of July for aviation mechanic school at Kessler Field, Mississippi. There was a lot of calculating. Everyone knew, of course, that certain units, infantry, bombers, and marines were likely to see action on the fighting fronts. These troops had to be supplied with everything they needed, from rations and blankets to razor blades and bullets. To do this would take thousands of truck drivers and supply clerks. Mechanics would repair trucks, engineers would build runways and repair bridges, transport pilots would fly supplies over tedious routes and land far away from the fighting. Company officers almost always placed those who had taken typing classes in high school or business college in the operations shack or supply depot, where they typed orders, checked inventories of supplies, and maintained communications with other units. These soldiers, sailors, marines, and airmen spent the war in boring but vital routines of record keeping and paperwork so familiar to every GI. Every unit needed them. Frederick Walker of New Castle, assigned to the operations section of the 59th Troop Carrier Squadron along with four other enlisted men from Ohio, Florida, Maryland, and Georgia, not only learned about the homes, hopes, and dreams of his buddies but participated in important paratroop operations in the war. As a company clerk commanding his section as a Tech Sergeant, he had a typewriter, unlimited supplies of paper, and time to record his duties and thoughts every day after he left for duty overseas. His and other accounts created a record intended only for their own use, and as Walker wrote: ". . . to keep me posted on what day and month it is for it isn't long in the service until one day seems to be the same as the last."

Some in the forward areas got many chances to look death in the face. Destroyer crews ran endless convoys across the Atlantic and Pacific protecting freighters, tankers, and troopships. Bomber and fighter pilots and crews flew mission after mission over enemy-held territory. The infantry often suffered the worst from shelling, tanks, and machine-gun fire. Tanks or aircraft might help take a position, but only the infantry could hold it. Crew members of capital ships like battleships and aircraft carriers engaged in campaign after campaign, especially sought out as targets by enemy submarine commanders, bomber and fighter pilots, and surface vessels. Oscar Popejoy, rescued from the water after abandoning USS *Lexington* in the Coral Sea, came home to New Castle for a month's furlough in August. Experienced carrier crewmen were too scarce to stay home for long, however. The paper carried a picture of the hull and deck of the new carrier USS *Essex* at Newport News, Virginia. Popejoy already knew he would be Chief Water Tender on her when she was finished and went to sea, and he would have more opportunities to confront the Japanese. The government might not say much when it lost a carrier, but it wanted the country, and the enemy, to know it was building plenty more.

While Popejoy was at home on leave, Admiral King announced that American forces had attacked in the steamy Solomon Islands, north of the Coral Sea and east of New Guinea. Marines and army troops were battling the Japanese on Tulagi and Guadalcanal, and it was tough going.

OPA regulations began to take hold with an iron grip. Two longtime New Castle meat markets went out of business because of meat shortages. One could get only lard from a long list of needed items sent to a supplier. Shortages and supply chaos had begun showing up all across the country as Leon Henderson, the commissar of prices, enforced his agency's maximum price guidelines and other food directives. Bananas disappeared from store shelves in town because banana boats had been pressed into more important uses as U-boats prowled the Caribbean. The local editor urged consumers to direct their ire toward Hitler and Hirohito, not at grocers. Sugar rationing continued to create chaos. Officials set up rationing to encourage efficient use of food, but it took large quantities of sugar to preserve the nation's home-grown fruits, which the government also encouraged. A few pounds a month for a family of four did not cover the quantities needed by the same family when canning season came around in early summer. Consequently, crops of berries, peaches, and plums which ripened on trees across Indiana and the Midwest often went to waste that year because there was a limit on sugar purchases. It took seven cups of sugar, half or more of a five-pound bag, to make four pints of raspberry jam. If there was plenty of sugar in the house, people were accused of hoarding and dealing on the black market. If there was none, the crops that could not be eaten fresh simply rotted. Toward the end of July 1942, a special form, OPA R-315, appeared in the paper. Presentation of this form to the local ration board, if they accepted it, allowed families to receive extra sugar for canning, but it was not quite that simple. Applicants had to list everyone's name in the family unit, their ration book numbers, the number of quarts of fruit canned in 1941, sugar obtained already in 1942, quarts of fruit already canned with 1942 sugar, number of quarts of fruit currently on hand, amount of fruit to be canned by the end of the year, and the amount of sugar being requested. Canning fruit in light syrup required one cup of sugar for each three cups of water, and it might take two or three cups of syrup to fill a jar already filled with peaches or pears. The heavier the syrup, the better the fruit flavor usually was when the jar was opened. The Ball Corporation "Blue Book" for 1943 suggested that a family of five alone would use about 225 quarts of fruit in a year. They estimated nearly nine hundred quarts of vegetables and fruits of all kinds to feed the family. A baby would use 80 half pints of strained food the first year, and 150 the second. In spite of this, OPA limited sugar applications to one pound of sugar for each four quarts of fruit to be canned, and only one pound per year for each family member to make jams, jellies, preserves, and fruit butters. Jams and jellies instantly became a luxury item for the duration of the war. Mothers allotted supplies already on hand very carefully. OPA did not recommend falsifying the information on the application, either. "NOTE: Presentation of incorrect facts on this application represents a violation of Rationing Order No. 3 which is a crime punishable by a fine of not more than $10,000.00, or imprisonment of not more than one year, or both." The neighbors were not very fond of hoarders or ration cheats, either. Anyone intent on bending the rules had better make sure that no one found out.

Greetings!

Kenny Smith's waiting ended the second week of August 1942. The now familiar envelope from the War Department arrived in the mailbox at the house in the hollow, informing him that he was to report for his physical the following Thursday, August 20, at the National Guard Armory in Indianapolis. In the paper he was no longer McKendrick; it was Edward M. Smith. The friends he would make for the rest of his life would know him as Ed. Only the people he had known in New Castle would call him Kenny. He boarded the bus at the interurban station at 14th and Race early that morning and headed, with the other ninety young men from the county and city, for Indianapolis. Gemma's cousin Glenn Cowan and Elmer Pfenninger, one of the older Pfenninger boys from the corner of 18th and Plum, also went that day. As so many would do, they stood in line naked and underwent the humiliation of being treated like so many sides of beef. They passed. After shots, an officer swore them into the army for the duration of the war, the same terms that those who enlisted accepted. Now they could go home. The next day, the *Courier-Times* informed everyone who cared to look that the three of them and most of the others had been accepted for service and had been placed in the reserves. They were to report for active duty training in fourteen days. Fourteen others had enlisted, including Herbert Heller, a social studies teacher in whose class

Kenny had been in high school, and Cortis Selke, vice president of the Class of 1939, both of whom had gone into the navy. Guy Amburgey, familiar all over town as the Railway Express Agency deliveryman, joined the navy. The Class of 1941 decided to hold a reunion on August 30 while there was still time. Its members were already being scattered across the country by the war. Who knew who might return and who might not?

Kenny did not have much to wrap up as far as his business matters before leaving for camp. He had been expecting the call anyway, so he had time to get ready for it in his mind. Fred, who had entered an army training camp just twenty-four years before, offered him not a single word of advice for getting along in the army. The subject did not come up in their conversations. The army would teach him what it wanted him to know, and there was nothing he could add to that. There was already the realization that this war would not be doughboys in steel hats charging barbed wire and pillboxes. The aircraft and the tanks, both of which were introduced in the war that Fred had known, had come far by then, and any battlefield would be more complex that the ones he had known. It was better to let the army do what it would. They would have to trust in the Lord to bring their boy back. Kenny told his friends who were still around good-bye, and went out with Gemma for the final time the evening before he would be leaving. Gemma had to work just a couple of blocks away at the Public Service office the morning he left, so Fred took time off and drove him to the bus station. His father told him to be careful, and to take care of himself, and to write when he could. With the crowd around, they shook hands gruffly, then he climbed aboard. Fred held his son's steady gaze as the door closed and the bus began to move. They went a block, turned the corner, and disappeared. Their only child was gone, like Fred had gone, to the army in time of war.

It was a hot ride in early September westward toward Indianapolis. The government had them, and the government paid all the way. The draftees went to Fort Benjamin Harrison in Indianapolis, where they were turned out of the buses and drew their first army clothes. Two days of tests followed to determine intelligence, aptitudes, and weaknesses. Officers assigned the group of draftees from New Castle to various training camps all over the country. Those in Ed's small group boarded trains in Indianapolis for the slow trip to Fort Bliss, Texas. Their route took them to St. Louis, then through Texarkana, Ft. Worth, Big Spring, and El Paso. They tried to grab what sleep they could in the hot cars, but it was a sweaty, gritty trip into the Texas heat, made bearable only by the wind that blew in the open windows when the train moved. The army assigned Elmer Pfenninger to Fort McClellan, Alabama, and he eventually went into the infantry. Glenn Cowan went to the Army Air Corps. Two weeks later, Ed's friend Harry Ridout passed his physical and got ready to leave home. At the same time, Robert Pitts, who would become Harry's close friend, reported for duty. Ridout and Pitts ended up at the same training camp for medics in North Carolina. About a dozen, including Herb Cook of New Castle, went with Ed all the way to Fort Bliss, which was an anti-aircraft artillery center. When they got there, their new lives began. After almost four days on the train, army trucks met them at the railway station to take them to their new barracks.

The sparse population, dry, clear air, and long desert vistas at Fort Bliss made it an ideal place to teach soldiers to operate a variety of weapons designed to destroy enemy aircraft. But first they would have to learn what every schoolkid who would become a soldier would have to learn. They drew their supplies of ill-fitting fatigues, shoes, helmet, and a pile of other items that would be their sole possessions for the next several months. Once they mostly looked all alike, they got down to the business of soldiering. They marched, made and remade beds, mopped the floors, and polished buttons and shoes until they got it right. They lived in barracks that were little more than board-and-batten boxes with asphalt shingle roofs, with the rafters visible inside. The corners of the buildings sat on concrete blocks, making neat rows on the flat, dusty ground. In the spaces between the buildings that served as roads and parade grounds, sergeants taught them to march, halt, and about-face, going over and over it until they could, and did, do it in their sleep. They learned quickly, and soon found out that they should not expand the scope of their responsibilities. When one man in the battery decided to polish the square-headed brass plug in the drainpipe in the latrine, the sergeant made no notice of it. A week later, when it had tarnished, it cost them all extra duty because it had not been kept polished. They learned not to borrow trouble.

The army broke them into hiking gradually. In the intense heat, starting raw recruits on a ten-mile hike would only add to the sick list the next day. They started marching two hours at a time, and became toughened, but not everyone could take it. As they grew accustomed to the routine, the sergeants increased their endurance and the weight in the packs that they had to carry. They all got sunburned and learned to deal with the desert creatures they could encounter. Night marches began, and they camped in the Texas and New Mexico desert. Coming from the humid Midwest, Ed found the desert beautiful and full of interesting sights. At night, if there was any moon, everyone cast a shadow and the countryside would be illuminated almost as though it was daylight. He could even read in the soft light. Although the sun blazed in the daytime and made heat waves that looked like water in the distance, at night the desert was cold, and the blankets they carried felt good. He remained at Fort Bliss through most of the winter, and it even snowed while they camped in the open. There was sand in the food and in the bottom of the coffee cup sometimes, but their muscles grew hard and their waistlines shrank as they tanned and grew up into citizen-soldiers. The sergeants stayed with the units they trained after basic training ended, so there was a sense that they were all going to be together for a while. The men did as they were told and most caught on quickly, with only an occasional "ironhead" lagging behind the others and drawing kitchen patrol duty. Most of them got along well, and there were always interesting characters. One, Sergeant Swenson, a tall, blond Swede from Chicago, entertained them all by quoting at length from Kipling's poems. It was not a bad life.

To learn to fire on aircraft, they first learned to fire other weapons. Some recruits had never held a firearm before, so they all started with .22 caliber rifles. These offered the basic bolt-action mechanism and dangers of more advanced infantry weapons, and they were lightweight. This took an afternoon, then they started on the standard weapon of the Great War, the Springfield Model 1903. This was a real infantry rifle that was extremely accurate, but unforgiving if one was sloppy in using it. In the kneeling, standing, and prone positions they learned the great recoil it offered that took more than one trainee by surprise. Firing prone, they all learned to use the covers from their canteens as a pad to prevent the kick from skinning their elbows on the rocky ground. Ed gained respect for his father's training with the weapon years before. He scored 92 out of 100 on the range. They all took turns serving in the target pit as other units practiced their target firing. It was a good way to learn to keep one's head down as the bullets tore the earth just a few feet above them.

From rifle practice they went to a real anti-aircraft weapon, the Browning liquid-cooled .50 caliber machine gun. These spit a bullet as wide as a thumb with great force that would penetrate brick buildings and most anything else that was not armored. Belt-fed, they were simple to operate, but the ammunition belts had to be hand-loaded before they could be fed into the guns. Brass from spent cartridges had to be taken out of the belts and carefully saved for reloading.

At Fort Bliss, Ed was thrown together with other recruits from all over the country. Italians, Hispanics, Jews, hillbillies, and others found themselves in the same barracks scrubbing the same floors. He wrote home to Gemma, to his mother and father, and occasionally to friends. He took the time to write letters home for his friend Rodriguez from California, because he could not write. They all learned to get along, to keep their ties straight, their uniforms pressed, and their shoes shined. They even learned to carry empty cans in their packs so there would be less weight to bear on marches.

Ed's unit was Battery B, 448th AAA Automatic Weapons Battalion, also known as AA or "ack-ack." The 448th was a new unit created the previous July 1. At Fort Bliss, he rose quickly, moving up the ranks from private to private first class, to corporal, to sergeant. He had been there only two weeks and he was still a private when word went around that there would be a math class offered for anyone who had ambitions to attend Officer Candidate School (OCS). Ed thought he might just try that. He took the class in the evenings, and passed it. After a call to headquarters and a brief interview, he heard nothing for a few days. Then his commanding officer, a West Pointer who had washed out of the Air Corps, told him to come see him when he could fill out the

Ft. Bliss, Texas, the fall of 1942. Ed's AA battery in the desert, L to R, Kramer, Louis Link, Paul Borgman, Frank Natale, Ed Smith, Rod Rodriguez, Simpson. This was their main weapon, the 40 mm anti-aircraft gun, pictured here with dust cover over the barrel and range finding equipment.

paperwork for OCS. This he did, but he heard nothing more for months. After a month at camp, he made corporal, and six weeks later, sergeant. He kept his nose clean, did his job, and avoided kissing anyone's butt. The officers watched those who had shown the ambition to try for OCS, and waited. Sometimes he thought luck might be with him, but it was hard to tell what might have advanced his cause. When still a corporal, an officer asked him what he would do if someone expectorated on the barracks floor. Ed had no idea what the word meant, but he reasoned that if something was on the floor that they had all helped wax by hand, the only thing to do was to "Clean it up, sir!" The officer nodded approval. At the first opportunity, he looked the word up in a dictionary and discovered he had guessed correctly. Was this a test? He would never know.

He kept up a regular correspondence with Gemma, and their ardor increased as the months apart went by. They now faced the dilemma that Martha and Phil and so many other young couples faced during the war. Should they think about getting married, or wait until things settled down after the war? What would the world be like then, anyway? There was no way to know. Gemma and most of her friends believed that only one real chance at true love came along in a lifetime. It could take a while before the right man came along, but when you felt sure, then you knew. Gemma was getting close to the point where she was sure.

As Ed headed for camp, Secretary of Agriculture Claude Wickard announced that meat would be rationed within four months to assure "equitable distribution" of what even he admitted was the "largest livestock production in history." As in the Great War, there was the likelihood of meatless days ordered by government officials. With employment roaring at full capacity, the government feared that Americans would use their record paychecks to buy up meat to replace other foods in short supply. It would also help remind people that there was a war on, and that sacrifices would have to be made. The Smiths had eaten meat on a regular basis because they raised it on the farm, but the Moles did not eat much of it, especially during the difficult times in the 1930s. When the government placed meat on the ration list, they began to buy it every week with Jess's substantial paychecks. Under rationing, the Moles family ate meat on a regular basis, far more than they had done before it was restricted.

Every defense plant needed war workers and wages began to rise accordingly. The Kaiser shipyard in Oregon hired three New Castle men in September 1942 after they took welding classes as part of the National Defense Training program. A bus line began making three round trips daily from New Castle to the giant Allison aircraft plant in Indianapolis. If one could show evidence of health and was not likely to enter the service soon, there was a job available. During 1942, as the need for workers skyrocketed, men and women from the South began to arrive in northern cities to find work. Ethel's younger sister Hazel, who had remained in Wilder, Tennessee, after Ethel went north with Jess, answered the call and went to Detroit to work in a defense aircraft plant. Millions of other women did the same thing, sharing apartments, sleeping in shifts, and sharing rides to work because of the shortage of housing. In Henry County, school officials excused students working in the bumper tomato harvest and in the canneries until the crop was in. Cannery officials feared that as much as 25 percent of their labor force would be lost if the truant officers began enforcing the attendance laws. If food was to help win the war, school would have to wait if there was to be plenty of catsup, tomato juice, and sauce.

There was a regular flow of men out of New Castle as they reported for duty at the various camps around the country, and a slower return flow as those who had been in for a while came home on leave. Sarah Wright was delighted to learn that Clay had gotten a five-day furlough in September. He arrived on the train on September 2. They had begun thinking about a future to-gether, too, and they used this precious time to talk about their plans. In the same day's paper, everyone found out why Clay had been given leave. The 38th Division, of which his 152nd Infan-try was now a part, was going to Louisiana on maneuvers. Mail would have to go to the field address at APO 38, Leesville, Loui-siana, after mid-September. The division would be field-tested in preparation for assignment overseas.

On the political scene, President Roosevelt ordered Congress to get to work passing the legislation he wanted on taxation and the establishment of parity prices on farm products, long a goal of the New Deal that was never achieved in the depression. Impa-tient with the pace of politics on Capitol Hill, Roosevelt declared that if Congress did not act soon enough, he would assume emer-gency war powers and take control of the government himself. Herbert Hoover, discredited on every issue by the Democrats and the press unless he spoke out to support the administration, had announced earlier in the year that the president would have to be given dictatorial economic powers in order to win the war. Hoover, entrusted with similar powers over the food supply in the Great War, believed that an unpleasant truth had to be faced. "We must start our thinking with a disagreeable, cold, hard fact. That is, the economic measures necessary to win total war are just plain Fascist economics." He hoped that they would not be frozen into the American way of life after the war, but he insisted they were necessary to win it. Roosevelt blasted the legislative branch for political fighting instead of acting on the nation's urgent busi-ness. No one spoke up to protest that seizing dictatorial powers would make Roosevelt rather similar to Hitler and Mussolini. The bills he wanted soon passed and the matter dropped.

It seemed as though every month there was something new

on the ration list, and new orders from Washington to enforce the rules. Gasoline came next. OPA established a scheme for priority allocation. Stickers in a car's window would tell everyone the amount of gas that could be purchased, and ration stamps would be required to buy it. The A sticker was the lowest priority, limited to 240 miles per month, and was by far the most numerous. B stickers were for those who had no other means of transportation and agreed to share rides with three or more passengers. These drivers got an additional 320 miles per month for driving to and from their occupations. C stickers were for people in very important positions whose work was considered vital to the war effort. These jobs included official government business, mail delivery, school officials, wholesale newspaper delivery, carrying photo equipment for public information reasons, medical personnel, clergy, farm product transportation, farm, marine, and transportation workers, construction and maintenance, farm and industrial machinery salesmen, medical supply salesmen, and message delivery services. There were a very few X stickers, which carried unlimited mileage privileges. People with questions about the details of rationing looked to the papers for guidance, asked the grocer, or went to the local ration office and stood in line. Gasoline rationing especially changed the way Americans lived during the war. Carpooling and sharing rides to work began immediately. Those within walking distance of their jobs often walked, while those in rural areas, like Fred Smith, rode with a fellow Chrysler employee who lived even farther out of town. Everyone cut back on driving, and many cars simply went into the garage and stayed there. Trips, even short ones into downtown New Castle, had to be carefully coordinated to avoid having to come back after a forgotten item. Men often stopped for a needed item after work rather than drive the car back after going home. There was still joyriding and pleasure driving, but there was only so much gas that could be bought, and when the month's allotment was used up, the car sat. The following month, a national 35 m.p.h. speed limit went into effect for privately owned cars. Fuel oil restrictions followed soon thereafter. Homes could only be heated to 65 degrees, and the OPA divided the country into fuel oil ration zones according to the severity of the climate. Coffee shortages began in most midwestern cities.

Rationing was not the only sacrifice. Editor Chambers of the local paper pointed out that before the war, the government collected about $7 billion in taxes each year. In 1943 it expected to collect $25 billion. There had been no tax on a respectable income of $2,000 per year up to 1942, but next year that same person would pay close to $300 in taxes. There was nothing to do but get used to it. "After all," he wrote, "doing without things and paying high taxes are nothing compared to the family that sends its boys to war." He did not mention, of course, that the families that sent their boys to the war paid the taxes, too. In the fall, Congress lowered the draft age to eighteen.

The war drew closer in other ways, too. The Japanese landed on two Alaskan islands, Attu and Kiska, in June while the battle at Midway Island was being fought. The navy and army were too busy elsewhere, and for the time being, the Japanese held on to both of them. Americans suffered severe casualties as they began fighting on Guadalcanal in August. Both sides reinforced their positions, and large naval forces fought surface battles for months around the Solomons. A New Castle woman, Mrs. Fred Howren, spotted her son Tom in newsreel footage at the Castle Theater. He had written that he was "somewhere in the Pacific," but the narrator identified the place as New Caledonia. Phil Perry, in the Army Air Corps reserve, made his solo flight at the Indianapolis Municipal Airport in October. He intentionally neglected to tell the enlisting officer or anyone else during his physical that he had a perforated eardrum, and had gotten in. He was determined to become a pilot, and was interested in gliders. He commuted back and forth to New Castle during this phase of his training. Phil Smith, Kenny's boyhood friend, enlisted in the air corps, too. Lots of boys wanted to fly.

In early October, President Roosevelt signed into law the legislation he had demanded from Congress under threat that he would seize emergency powers. The laws gave him unprecedented authority to control salaries, prices, and wages. Citing a danger of inflation, the president signed the bills just hours after they passed. The powers given him by Congress were the same ones he had said he would seize if they were not handed over. The next day, OPA officials cut the nation's beef ration by 20 percent, and pork by 25 percent. The extra had to go to the armed forces and Lend-Lease clients. Two days later, on October 5, James Byrnes, economic stabilization director, ordered all rents rolled back and frozen at May 1942 levels. Landlords would be prevented from evicting tenants by selling their properties. Byrnes decreed that ninety percent of all food product prices be frozen to help prevent inflation. OPA announced that the thirty million pairs of nylon hose to be released for Christmas sales would be the last of them for the duration of the war. Their price had been frozen also, and some stores reportedly had posted prices above the legal limit.

The local Chrysler plant received the Army-Navy "E" Award the first week of October for outstanding production of defense materials. Everyone in the plant assembled outside on I Avenue for the award presentation, complete with army brass. National efforts to rally the people toward greater productive effort continued in the papers, at the movies, and in magazines. It was difficult to escape it.

Everyone got another reminder of the importance of production and the scrap drives on October 27, when the navy announced that a Japanese submarine had sunk the carrier USS *Wasp* in the Solomons. Even the Secretary of the Navy called the efforts there battles of attrition. A *Wasp* survivor from Middletown was already home on leave.

On November 9, headlines announced that American landings had begun in French North Africa, and for once it was fresh news, since the landings had begun the day before. Now Americans had started fighting near Europe, not just in the Pacific. The Vichy French, cooperating with the Germans in metropolitan France, mostly offered no resistance to the attacking Allied forces, according to the reports. But the Germans under Rommel still battled the British who were pushing them westward. Now they could be pressed from two directions at once. Even as the press reported gains in Morocco, Mrs. Melvina Wolfe got word that her son Roy Lee Barnes had earned the honor of being the first serviceman directly from New Castle to die in battle in the war. He enlisted January 1, 1942, and died on Guadalcanal August 21. He would not be coming home. There had been a service for him on the battlefield.

News about rationing appeared in the paper nearly every day.

Almost four thousand New Castle motorists registered for gasoline rationing and received their ration coupon books and A stickers from ration office workers. Within a week the ration office would be trying to dig out from beneath three thousand more applications for B and C stickers from local citizens who already had A stickers, but believed they needed more.

But there was a growing problem at the Railway Express Agency (REA) office because of tire restrictions. The government ordered motorists to have no more than five tires in their possession for each car they owned, and to turn the extras in to the government. Even the best tires were notorious for blowouts, so most garages had an extra or two. Officials ordered that the extra tires be taken to the nearest Railway Express Office, where agents would issue government receipts. They would be sent to warehouses where they would be inspected, and a fair price paid for them to their former owners in cash or war bonds. It all seemed straightforward enough in Washington, but local citizens flooded Fred Pope, manager of the REA office, with more than two thousand tires. Not only did he have nowhere to put them, but he ran out of government receipts and had to issue REA receipts instead. Ten days after the mandatory turn-in had started, he still had 950 tires at the office. It was evidence that the government feared a rubber shortage even more than they wanted everyone to know.

Coffee rationing started November 29, 1942. The ration boards prohibited sales for the week before, and, of course, they froze prices. The idea was that when the use of coffee ration stamps started, everyone would be out of coffee. Consumers could use stamp number 27 in war ration book #1, originally the sugar rationing book, until January 3, 1943. This allowed the purchase of a pound of coffee every five weeks, if grocers had it. The coupons from the books issued for children under fifteen could not be used to purchase coffee. Retailers had to fill out various forms and warrants, based on business in September 1942 to get supplies of coffee from wholesalers if it was available. In New Castle, people no longer poured out a half cup of coffee if it got cold. They poured it back into the pot and reheated it. Swamped with work, the ration board asked for volunteers at the end of November to help prepare coupons for fuel oil rationing.

The state selective service board ordered that the names of

men rejected for physical or moral reasons for induction into the armed forces not be published in the papers. There had been considerable embarrassment and inquiries by friends and neighbors when anyone did not qualify, but local draft board officials insisted this was why the names ought to be published. It allowed the man rejected to show that he had reported, but had not been accepted. The local boards stopped listing those who were to go for physicals, and only listed the names accepted for service.

The year was winding down. The railroads asked people to use the trains as little as possible between December 12 and January 12 in order to facilitate getting servicemen home for the holidays. Families planned for a Christmas that might be the last one with ample meat.

Many men in uniform spent Christmas Day in camp. Ed Smith and his battery had Christmas turkey and dressing out of a field kitchen in the New Mexico desert. For the Ruddell family of Park Avenue in New Castle, it was a somber holiday. In a telegram received on the morning of the 15th, their son, Lt. Roy Ruddell, a marine aviator, had been reported missing. Two days before Christmas the paper carried a picture of Ruddell with his squadron mates, including ace Joe Foss, who had already shot down twenty-two Japanese planes. Their squadron claimed 110 kills in the two months they had fought in the skies over Guadalcanal. An army transport plane crashed south of New Castle, killing all eight on board. The U.S. Employment Service office in New Castle asked that women register for work in defense plants because of the shortage of male workers. Scores of men went into the service from Henry County alone every couple of weeks, and there simply were not enough able-bodied men available to fill the needed positions.

It had been a tempestuous, disruptive, frightening year. Thousands had already gone ashore in North Africa or had been on ships that had gone to the bottom. The unlucky ones already in the service in 1941 and shipped first to the South Pacific were buying yards of rotten jungle real estate with their blood and the blood of their friends. People at home buckled down to the grim job of trying to win the war at a lathe, on a tractor, or in an office.

Throughout the year, there was little to encourage anyone to believe that we might win the war, let alone believe it might be soon. There was no end in sight, and in fact the Germans and the Japanese achieved numerous victories during the year. Since Pearl Harbor, there had been 56,075 casualties, including 7,918 killed. The navy had lost 5,900 of those killed. The year 1943 looked to be worse.

7. Urgent Preparation, 1943

Opportunities and Decisions

AFTER FOUR MONTHS of training at Fort Bliss, the 448th AA left for advanced gunnery training in the Mojave Desert in California, but four sergeants from the battalion stayed behind on temporary duty. Ed was one of them. When this happened, the four of them knew they had been chosen to go to OCS. In February, Ed went home on ten days furlough. Gemma could hardly wait to see him, but she had to share him with his mother and father, who were just as pleased that he was home. In their correspondence, Ed and Gemma had decided that their love was sure and strong enough to become engaged. Ed had saved his army pay and bought a ring in El Paso that he brought home to her. She was more than happy to wear it, and fairly beamed in the pictures that Jess took of the two of them in front of the house on Plum Street. The ring showed on her left hand as they stood on the sidewalk in the faint February sunshine. It was not so cold, so Gemma had her knee-length gray wool coat unbuttoned, and in spite of the shortage of hose, she had saved some back for occasions like this. Ed wore his three sergeant's stripes on the belted dark green gabardine tunic with the matching pants, tan shirt and tie, leather-brimmed barracks cap, shined shoes, and dark gloves. Never heavy, he looked every inch the military man in the close-fitting uniform of the United States Army.

February 1943. Ed is home after basic training with the 448th AA, bringing an engagement ring for Gemma. They're on the sidewalk in front of 1828 Plum Street. The trees Jess planted in the yard are still there today.

It was no secret that Jess and Ethel were pleased that Gemma had found a nice young man for her betrothed. After all, it was their view that respectable marriage was the proper role for all women, and certainly for their four daughters. Gemma, the eldest, had set a good example for her sisters. Here was a soldier who had made sergeant in ten weeks at camp. In one of the pictures, Ethel grinned her approval of the happy couple from the porch. If things went according to plan, she would be married later in the year and be on her own. Naturally, Gemma's sisters joined in the fun with teasing and questions.

Ed spent the nights at home in his old room at the house in the hollow. In the mornings, his mother fixed coffee for him, now that he was accustomed to army coffee, and they sat and drank it together after Fred caught his ride to work. There were only a few days he could actually spend in New Castle because his ten-day furlough included travel time. There were few friends to visit because most of them had left for camp. Harry, Marvin, and the few others in his circle of friends had already gone. He spent as much time as he could with Gemma, and used his father's 1937 Chrysler Royal sedan sparingly. He had only been gone a little over five months, but they had changed him. Neither he nor Gemma knew what was ahead. He was going to North Carolina for OCS from New Castle, but even that was an unknown. If he succeeded there, he would be a lieutenant, but then what? Would he go to North Africa? The Pacific? Would he train new re-cruits? How long would the war last? Would it ever end? Would he come back? There was no way to know.

They made what plans they could while they were together and alone. OCS would take three months, with no leaves. If he made it through OCS, he would be an officer, and they could get married and be together. Wherever the army assigned him in the States, she could probably go, so they spun their dreams on that belief. After he left, Gemma had her job at Public Service to keep her occupied, but she worried about getting married, what it would be like, and tried to get herself ready. The first order of busi-ness when she got home in the afternoons was to see if any letters had arrived by either one of the two mail deliveries each day. When there was mail, Wanda or Marie often teased her about it, or held it behind their backs and demanded something to hand it over. When this ended, Gemma retired to the quietest place she could find, or went walking to be alone while she read what Ed had written. In the evenings she wrote letters and worked on putting her clothing and linen together for the day when they would be married. She dreamed about what life would bring them, and began to watch the papers carefully in order to under-stand the progress of the war. Maybe it would all be over before Ed would have to be involved too much.

OPA changed the meat-rationing plan in January. Instead of limiting consumers to so many pounds per month (the as-sumption was that everyone would choose the best steak and spurn other cuts), they were limited to a specified number of A points each month. The better cuts required more points than the cheaper cuts. If people wanted hamburger, they could get more of it than steak with the same number of points. This all assumed that the meat markets would have any, of course. Every OPA announcement always took care to note that the system would work a certain way only if retailers had meat to sell. When the new system was set to go into effect, there were no ration books available. The books had arrived in New Castle and the board had control of them, and housed them in the county jail for safe-keeping, but local officials decided to have another general regis-tration. One board member opined that the system would not start until March, in spite of the fact that the OPA said it would begin in February. There had previously been much confusion over the issuing of ration coupons for kerosene. Those who ap-plied for kerosene allotments had gone to the ration board in person at the last minute instead of mailing in the forms, and chaos ensued. The local ration bureaucrats tried to sort it all out as soon as they could. The Indiana Bankers Association announced that they had agreed to handle ration coupons for the federal government. Banks began providing auditing and accounting services for the ration coupon system so that the government could tell how many stamps of what kinds consumers actually used. The banks began to open special windows for ration point accounts. This helped the planners decide where to allocate re-sources. With price controls in place, it was the only way to judge demand.

In the first week of the new year, New Castle's war price and rationing board also urged motorists to get their tires inspected according to the gas ration rules before the deadline of January 31. Approved inspectors had to look at every car's tires to make sure that they were wearing evenly and not wasting gasoline. It also gave them an opportunity to look in the trunk at the fifth tire. Someone at practically every service station and garage in the county applied, but they could not be sworn by the board until later in the month because OPA had not sent the forms with the oaths yet. Inspectors could charge 25¢ for visual inspection, and 50¢ per tire if they had to be removed from the car for any reason. The next big drive in the county was the upcoming tin can collection. With no tin mines in the country, salvaging the tin that was already here became important. To be accepted, the cans had to be cleaned, flattened, and have their labels removed.

There were fighting men from New Castle on Guadalcanal and in North Africa. Emmit Neal wrote from a log-and-sandbag-topped foxhole on Guadalcanal that he was okay, but the flies, mosquitoes, and Japs were pretty bad. He said that writing paper was scarce so he wrote the letter to the paper to let everyone who had written to him know how he was getting along. The letter, dated November 3, 1942, took almost two months to get to New Castle. Corporal Elmer Popejoy, Oscar Popejoy's brother, told of going ashore with the American Army in North Africa and coming under machine-gun fire. Anti-aircraft fire, he said, looked just like the fireworks display at Memorial Park, except that there was more of it and it made more noise.

Word finally got to New Castle that the first county boy to die in the air war in Europe, Sgt. Arnold Pearson, engineer on a B-17 Flying Fortress, lost his life December 20, 1942. The army refused to say where it happened. He left a wife, parents, and six brothers and sisters. The next day, January 13, word arrived that Pvt. Charles Byrket, well-known Spiceland athlete in his high school years, had been killed November 8 in North Africa. That was the day the invasion of North Africa began.

The names of other local boys that the Moles girls knew appeared in the news. There was a mixup with Orrin Grubbs's enlistment. On January 8, his name appeared on the draftee list in the paper, headed for the army on January 21. Erma Vitatoe, his mother, held a farewell party for him at the house on B Avenue on the evening of January 12, and nearly twenty people showed up, including Betty Jacoby, who had been prom queen the previous May. All the family members, some of Orrin's friends, and Sarah Wright attended. Orrin spent as much time as he could with Sarah. Clay came home on a ten-day furlough just before Orrin had to leave for Fort Benjamin Harrison, then Camp San Luis Obispo, California. Elmer Pfenninger, from the corner of Plum and 18th Streets, entered OCS in January at Fort Benning, Georgia. Glenn Cowan, Gemma's cousin, came home on leave for five days after graduating from the Army Air Corps technical school in Colorado.

Everyone prayed for the five Sullivan brothers from Waterloo, Iowa, all of whom the navy reported missing after the sinking of their ship, the USS *Juneau,* in the Solomons in November of '42. All five enlisted together to avenge a friend killed at Pearl Harbor. That a family had five sons in the service was not unheard-of. There were several Henry County families who had four sons serving with Uncle Sam. But to lose all five at once was another matter. People swallowed hard, went on with their business, and tried not to think about it too much.

Churchill and Roosevelt met in Casablanca, Morocco, in January to discuss war plans and strategies. Dispatches from the meeting indicated that the decisions made would affect whether more men would be drafted, how much food everyone would have, how warm houses could be next winter, and how much higher taxes would go. The army had about 5.5 million men in uniform as of the beginning of the year, with a goal of about 7.5 million by the end of 1943. More went almost every week from New Castle and Henry County.

Taxes happened to be on the minds of many people early in 1943 because the government had a new plan for paying for the war. American citizens had long been accustomed to figuring their taxes after the end of the year in order to send in what they owed by April 15. People saved part of what they earned in order to have the tax payment ready when it came due. The new plan called for withholding the amount that would be paid as people earned the money. Employers were to pay their employees the part of their earnings that they would keep after paying taxes. This money had to be paid by employers to the government several times a year. This way, the Treasury got tax money all through the year, instead of in a lump sum in April. The administration assured the public that it would make the war effort much easier to manage with a more dependable revenue. The government called it "pay as you go." Citizens saw a drop in their pay envelopes, but they did not have to come up with a lump sum in March or April. Instead, taxpayers paid just a little by April 15, or got some money back from the government if too much had been withheld. The plan went into effect later in the year.

While Roosevelt was in Morocco, he visited American troops there and ate with them. There was no direct reporting on many of the topics that he and Churchill discussed, but stories began to appear about the "coming sacrifice." This apparently referred to the losses that would have to be sustained if the Germans and Japanese were to be defeated decisively. There was much speculation about a settlement that might end the war, with Germany and Japan keeping some of their gains, but many people objected to this. But how to end the war? The Russians seemed to lose hundreds or thousands almost every day, and the Germans still pushed deep inside the Soviet Union almost two years after they had invaded. Maybe the leaders talked about how much their respective populations would be willing to take, or how much politicians could expect them to suffer while holding on to their jobs. One writer believed that a direct land invasion of Europe, with terrible losses, would be necessary in 1943 to confront Hitler. If successful, victory could come later in the year, at least in Europe. Of course, there was no indication that Russia, Britain, or the United States could mount such an invasion during the year. There was still heavy fighting in Tunisia by the combined British and Americans, with no end in sight. And then there was the situation in the Pacific. Furious fighting continued on Guadalcanal five months after Americans landed there. There seemed to be no end to the number of Japanese ships, soldiers, troop transports, and aircraft that had to be faced. With *Yorktown* and *Lexington* lost, half of the American carriers in the Pacific had been lost, and ships damaged in the attack on Pearl Harbor still had not returned to sea.

Perhaps there was something to all the talk of "sacrifice." Just a couple of weeks after saying that the goal was to have 7.5 million men in uniform by the end of 1943, and with a serious manpower shortage in the factories and on the farms already, the War Department announced that it would put 10.4 million in the armed forces by 1944. To do this, it began to work out rules for drafting men with children. There were not enough childless married and single men over twenty-one to last very long if the armed forces topped ten million. Officials would not say when married men with children might be called, but General Hershey, director of Selective Service, speculated earlier in the year that it could begin in October 1943. By the middle of March, there was talk in congressional committees of needing as many as fifteen million men by the end of the year.

As OPA added new items to the ration list, it began to adopt new tactics. It gave three months notice that canned milk would be rationed, giving everyone plenty of time to stock up. But on Monday, February 8, 1943, OPA froze shoe sales and announced that they would be rationed as of the next day. No one got a jump on that ration category. Finally, about the middle of February, the ration board announced registration for ration book #2. This had been planned as the meat ration book, and still was, but the new twist was that its coupons would be needed to purchase most canned goods after March 1, 1943. Like meat, canned goods would be rationed according to points. Citizens who already had ration book #1 were eligible for book #2. They had to declare, on forms, the number of cans of fruit, vegetables, juices, and soup, and the amount of coffee on hand the day they registered. Officials removed an eight-point stamp from the new book for each can over the limit, up to half of the points for any ration period. Coupons in excess of this amount would be removed from future books. The board forbade purchases of rationed goods without the required coupons. During the week of February 21, OPA suspended retail food sales to allow for a smooth transition to the beginning of rationing.

There were other rules, too. A ration book belonging to anyone who died had to be turned in within ten days, and anyone who would be out of the country for more than thirty days had to leave their ration books with the local ration board. The board reminded housewives to take the ration books with them and tear out the required coupons in front of the grocer or deliveryman. Taking loose coupons into the grocery when shopping was prohibited to prevent coupon trading. In addition, when using gas ration coupons, customers had to print their car license plate numbers and state on the back of each little coupon before using it. The service station attendant could not pump gas without first looking at the ration book to make sure there were enough of the proper coupons, to see that the license plate number on the coupon was the same as was on the car, and to see that the proper sticker had been displayed on the window. Wholesalers had to open point accounts with their local banks to keep track of transactions.

The official table of point values for processed foods appeared in the paper on February 27, 1943, with increased points required for larger cans. Some goods would be plentiful, the bureaucrats assumed. Sauerkraut in 4 oz. cans took one ration point, as did most small cans, but 3 lb. cans required thirteen points for purchase. Three-pound cans of beets took twenty-five ration points, but the same size peas or pears required forty-one points. The ration office published the list in the paper, and copies could be found in all the grocery stores, too. Fresh fruits and vegetables did not fall under ration rules. The requirements were the same for the A&P store as for the little neighborhood grocery. OPA admitted that it intended to reduce home consumption of canned goods to 57 percent over nineteen months, reserving the other 43 percent for military use and for the Allies. Nearly 95 percent of the food on a typical American table had controlled prices when people got their papers on February 23. OPA slapped many price controls on suddenly to prevent speculative price increases. Officials froze wholesale egg prices at 40¢ per dozen. With manpower shortages affecting all sectors of the economy, the army authorized the use of troops to help harvest the long-staple cotton crop in Arizona. After criticism of farm programs that paid farmers not to grow crops like wheat, the government finally suspended the programs in order to boost the wheat supply. The *Courier-Times* editor reprinted an editorial from the *Christian Science Monitor:*

THE WAR COMES HOME

This food rationing, which seems so strange to the land of abundance, may help Americans return to the more rugged virtues. It should mark the end of an era of waste; it may usher in a new period of wiser, more considered, living. If Americans feed the world, they must think of the world.

The effect on food certainly was coming home to people in New Castle. The ration board issued 17,818 ration books at the schools, while classes were dismissed for the purpose, during the registration period the last week of February. Calculating ration points and planning ahead for meals became a way of life for practically everyone.

Finally, the Japanese gave up on Guadalcanal and evacuated their forces. Of course, there were hundreds of other islands that they held scattered across the Pacific. But for now, Americans had, at great cost, driven the enemy out of at least one of them. Would there be more New Castle men reported lost there when the news finally got back? Three casualties from the county appeared on the same day on March 11, all from North Africa, all three missing in action on February 17. That was about the time of reported American losses from an attack by Rommel's forces in Tunisia. The time lag was terrible. Even after an action had been completed, there was such a long time to wait to be sure that loved ones were still okay.

Rationing of meat and butter, cheese, fats and oils, and canned fish started March 29. It seemed that OPA added a few things every time it updated the ration list. Washington officials estimated that the average American could eat about two pounds of meat per week under the new system. These items required the red coupons in ration book #2. This left milk, cereals, fresh produce, bakery goods, and specialty items still unrationed. People began to supplement with and stock up on these items where practicable. OPA called the system simple, and allowed shopkeepers to make "change" of one-point ration stamps. With the cold weather moderating in March, Secretary of Agriculture Wickard urged everyone to grow a victory garden in 1943. The city of New Castle and several area factories set aside plots of unused land for community gardens. Once again, the paper carried suggestions from the county agricultural agent for planning and planting a garden, in more detail than the previous year.

Small retailers from all over the country began letting their congressmen know about the disaster that rationing had become for them. They complained that large retailers had an advantage over them because wholesalers, to save tires and fuel, delivered orders to large chain stores first, and often left smaller retailers without stocks. Rationing, intended to cut down on consumption, was actually cutting profits at the same time. Paperwork problems added to the mess. Delivery was a service many neighborhood groceries could offer that the big stores could not. Instead of leaving a grocery order at the door if no one was home as they had done before, delivery boys now had to stop, or return, to collect the ration stamps as well as the payment. There was talk of impending shortages of refrigerator cars to transport the fresh produce that was not rationed. There were plenty of canning jars for putting up garden produce in 1943, but the rules stated that farmers who sold produce direct to consumers had to collect ration coupons, obey price laws, and make retailers' reports, just like the grocery stores. This was in the paper as official information just a few days after everyone had been assured that fresh produce was not rationed. People became confused, frustrated, and angry at the chaos, but tried not to let it undermine their support for the war effort.

William Bartling, the Flying Tiger who shot down nine Japanese planes in China with the American Volunteer Group (AVG), came home to Sulphur Springs, in the northern part of the county, the third week of March 1943. In the picture in the paper he looked perfectly at ease between his mother and father on the couch, like a farm boy instead of an ace fighter pilot home from halfway around the world. The article told some of his exploits in China and Burma, and explained his broken leg, earned in the crash of a transport plane he was testing for the Chinese government. His parents enjoyed having him around again, since he had been gone since the fall of 1941, more than a year and a half. The secretary of the number two draft board in the county lived near the Bartlings, and took his registration forms over to him so that he would not have to make the trip with his bad leg. Bartling resigned his commission in the navy in 1941 to join the AVG, so he had not been in the service of the United States since the war began. He registered for the draft and waited for his leg to heal up. Shooting down nine Japanese planes as a volunteer was not good enough to keep the draft board away.

Worry at 1828 Plum Street

The war had already begun to take a toll at the house on Plum Street. It was difficult enough to raise children and keep them on the straight and narrow in ordinary times. But the war changed the nature of everyone's calculations. Parents with children in the service wished for any expedient to win a victory before fate took them away forever. Those who entered the service played it a day at a time and never thought that they would be the one to get hit or killed. The younger brothers and sisters of servicemen looked ahead and saw the same fate waiting for them, given enough time. As the casualties began to appear in the local paper, and with practically everyone in the vulnerable age bracket in one of the branches of the armed forces, it was easy to see that they could become casualties themselves. They faced death in a way that only wartime generations could know. Even if they were girls or young women, their brothers, uncles, cousins, and the boys and men they liked and loved could all go away and not come back. How should a girl act around a serviceman who is about to leave to go to camp, or overseas? Should he remember a good time? Should he remember a modest, virtuous girl, anxious to see him return? If he wanted more than a kiss at the door, should something more be considered? What if he went to some shattered Pacific island and was buried there? Shouldn't there be something of paradise for him to take with him? How to steel him against the temptations of women in faraway places? Make promises? Write steamy letters every day? Marry him? How could one know if he were stepping out? The Moles girls faced these questions during the war. Gemma set the standard by looking for a man she loved and trusted and making preparations to marry him. Maxine followed in much the same way.

An Officer and a Gentleman

Traditionally, the United States had had a small standing army. When war came in 1941 there were not enough officers trained at the military academies or non-commissioned officers (high-level enlisted personnel with experience, usually referred to as non-coms) to fill the need. Officer Candidate School offered a way for the army to quickly train the many thousands of officers it would need to command the millions of enlisted men who would fill the ranks. OCS introduced Ed to a circle of people and a world that he had never expected to know. He went directly from New Castle to Camp Davis, North Carolina, and plunged in. Major wars tend to be leveling experiences for those involved because aristocratic members of society have to associate with soldiers from the other levels. The Revolutionary War, the Civil War, the Spanish-American War, and the Great War all had resulted in an increased awareness of different strata of American society of each other. Ed had met and knew college-educated people before, of course. His schoolteachers had bachelor's degrees and some had master's degrees. Ministers ordinarily had divinity degrees from colleges or seminaries. Some, like Dr. Turbeville of the Methodist church in New Castle, had doctorates in theology or divinity. The county agricultural agent usually had an agriculture degree from Purdue, and there was a small percentage of students from New Castle who went to college after high school. For the most part the degrees held by New Castle citizens came from the state schools—Indiana University, Purdue University, Ball State Teachers College—and a few had private school degrees, but it was relatively rare for local residents to have traveled out of state for college, although there were some who did. Most New Castle High School graduates did not go to college, and those who did not go felt that it was mostly the upper crust in town who did. At OCS, there were men from all over the United States, many of whom had attended college. A scattering of these held degrees from the Ivy League schools such as Harvard, Yale, and Princeton. The army considered a college degree a prime indicator of potential officer material. There also was a scattering of college Reserve Officer Training Corps (ROTC) graduates the army put through OCS as a way to finish them. Ed, with a high school diploma from a town no one at OCS had ever heard of, would be up against some of the nation's best.

Part of his upbringing was to believe that in America, anything could be accomplished with grit and hard work. The army intentionally made the OCS recruit classses large because the odds were that many would not complete the course. Ed learned from Gemma soon after he started that Clay Grubbs had been sent back to the 38th Division a few weeks after he began OCS at Fort Benning. Clay, like Ed, liked the idea of being an officer, and volunteered to go to OCS. The officers and non-coms there decided he was not what they were looking for, so he returned to his old unit at his old rank. Like Ed, he had an easy-going personality and a ready smile. He took it in stride.

The army spent the first few days telling the men what would be expected of them, how to do things, and how to find their way around. After that, they got down to business. The OCS routine differed from AA training at Ft. Bliss. Ed came to camp a staff sergeant, and thus had already mastered the basics of drill, proper dress, and use of basic small arms. Sergeant's stripes meant that one knew not only how to do something but what needed to be done. The army's expectation was that this would be a group of AA officers, so practically everything they did reflected the activities of AA units. At Camp Davis they had to learn to think and act like officers in a relatively short period of time. They spent much of their day in classes studying math, tactics, and military doctrine. There were courses in radio, telephone, and wire communications, and even one on proper table manners. They studied transportation procedures, small unit tactics, AA weapons, and maps. They learned how to lay fire properly, and how to figure projectile trajectories. Once they had learned all the AA weapons from 4.07-inch flak guns down to air-cooled .30 caliber machine guns, they practiced endlessly, taking them apart and reassembling them. Then they did it blindfolded and in the dark until they knew the guns backward and forward.

First and second lieutenants filled the training roles that sergeants had played at Fort Bliss. These officers, also OCS products, evaluated the candidates for personality traits, perseverance, and leadership potential. There was a great deal of pressure, because pressure was what OCS was all about. The army needed to know if the men could hold up under difficult conditions while retaining what they had been taught. Future officers had to do their work, whatever it might be, quickly and cheerfully. If anything went wrong, it was important to smile, and get on to dealing with it. Those in charge did not appreciate panic or irrational behavior. Every problem had to be taken in stride. Never an alarmist, this fitted Ed's nature perfectly.

Each day started with breakfast and classroom work. Instructors threw large quantities of information at them in the classes they sat in, and tested them on it at the end of each week. They marched for hours on a huge, sweltering parking lot. They stood for inspection to see if their shoes had the right spit-shine and if the buckles and buttons had been polished enough with the blitz cloth. Clothes had to be pressed according to regulations, nails had to be clean, and faces clean shaven. Ties had better be straight and caps at the right angle. In the barracks, everything had to be in its place and available for inspection at any time. Footlockers always stood open, with every shirt, sock, and pair of underwear perfectly arranged and properly folded. Each man's tent section, tent pegs, gas mask, and mess kit, all kept spotless, sat on shelves in a uniform line down the barracks wall. No trace of dirt could be found anywhere. The floors often shone nearly white from endless scrubbing with sand and careful washing. Sixty men with toothbrushes could make fairly rapid progress cleaning a barracks room floor when they put some elbow grease into it on Friday night. Bedmaking skills became very important. The platoon leader had to be able to get a quarter to bounce off the tightly stretched wool blanket that covered each bed. If it did not bounce high enough, the officer candidate worked on it until he got it right. Consequently, no one sat on a bed for any reason. If there was a break, the floor was the only safe place to lie down. A man could close the lid on his locker and sit on that, but it had better be open when he left the building. They had thirty minutes for lunch and any other chores that needed to be done, then it was back to the grind. All quickly learned to avoid coffee for breakfast and lunch because no one could be excused to relieve himself. The evening meal was more leisurely, allowing for slower eating and conversation.

Afternoons were spent running, performing calisthenics, and marching. It was a grueling routine with little free time. When lights went out at 11:00 p.m., no one could study or review what they had been taught that day. By that time, many of the men were already asleep. As at Fort Bliss, there was no screaming or abusive behavior by those in charge at Camp Davis. Only once in a while, when one lieutenant of particularly short physical stature noticed something out of place or done incorrectly, would he ask the guilty man if he intended to do something about it. That took care of it.

When Ed began classes, most of the other men in the neat rows beside him furiously took notes, so he began to do the same. He had taken notes in high school, of course, but there had never been this much information to digest. His memory staggered under the quantities of data that the instructors piled on, and he dutifully tried to study his notes in the time allotted for it in the evenings. At the end of the first week's classes, he discovered that he had done poorly in his classroom work. He resolved to try even harder. Many of the men smoked cigarettes or pipes on their brief breaks during the day, and the ones he talked to said that it helped steady them and get them ready for the next task. He took up smoking, and thought that it helped. Besides, the routine was comforting when he was under pressure. At the end of his second week, his classroom grades had not improved. His section leader called him in and told him he would wash out in the next two weeks unless his scores improved. At his wits' end, he despaired of making it, but resolved to try a new tactic. When he took notes, he could not concentrate on what the instructor said. Consequently, he missed half or more of what had been said because he was writing the other half down. He threw away his notebooks and never used them again. Focusing all his concentration on what the instructors said, he never wrote down a thing. At the end of the third week, he took the tests and passed them all. This became his routine as he continued to improve. The rest of the work gave him no trouble either. OCS became a manageable task that he performed ably. The section leader never again suggested that he would fail.

His friendly nature helped him get along at Camp Davis just as he had done at Fort Bliss. He made friends easily and avoided people who might give him trouble. One associate was an advanced amateur photographer from Chicago's large Polish community. Color photography was still relatively rare in the middle 1940s, but Ed's friend brought a roll of film from home and took color slides of his fellow officer candidates. They were the first ever taken of Ed in color. One showed him leaning against wooden steps shining his shoes. The other showed him sitting on the ground between the barracks buildings reading a letter Gemma had written to him from New Castle. In both, he wore the regulation khaki pants and blouse, with no insignia except for the round black pocket patch with the green OCS letters on it.

Everyone stood for inspection at noon on Saturday. The army apparently liked this schedule, because it was the same everywhere Ed was posted in the States. This invariably took place on the large, hot parking lot, where the entire class could be assembled at one time. North Carolina was sweltering that time of the year, and it was common for candidates to pass out from the heat as they stood at attention. They took turns at various duties during the week, and it was most important that every command be heard by the entire class. Men whose voices did not carry had a particularly hard time in these temporary command positions because they would have to shout themselves hoarse in order to be heard. By Saturday noon, some of them could barely whisper.

Seventy men started the officer candidate course in Ed's class, but attrition soon set in. There were relatively few men in their early twenties like Ed, and there were others as old as thirty-five. Particularly among the older candidates the physical training aspects of the camp soon began to take a toll. Several of those with the big-name college degrees fell into this category and began to be dismissed back to their old units. By the time their ninety days had passed, the seventy who had begun had been reduced to twenty-five. This was about average. Only about one-third of those who started officer training finished it. The food was good, regular, and there was plenty of it, but the activity level was so high that Ed went from 179 pounds when he got there down to 156 pounds when he left.

Ed found Camp Davis a pleasant enough place, considering that it was in a low-lying area just north of Wilmington, North Carolina. The Atlantic coast was only about ten miles from the center of Wilmington, and his platoon went down to the beach on two or three occasions to fire weapons. It was the first time he had ever seen salt water. There was a little crossroads settlement just outside the Camp Davis gate called Holly Ridge, and when time permitted, Ed and a few friends would cross the road to the store there to get something to drink. Ed loved the Mott's apple juice that was so very cold out of the cooler.

The officer candidates had a considerable amount of free time available to them after inspection ended Saturday at noon. The army provided transportation into Wilmington via buses and trucks, where the men could relax, get transportation to surrounding towns, or go to a movie. The USO in town provided a reference service to local residents who were willing to rent rooms over the weekend. This allowed the men to stay with civilians like the people back home, have a home-cooked meal, write letters or perhaps try to call home, and rest up for the return to camp on Sunday. There was a mandatory class in camp on Sunday night, so everyone had to be back in time to begin at 7:00 P.M.

There was not much rowdiness. The men all wore their khakis with the OCS pocket patch in town, and they all understood any news of problems or disruptive behavior that found its way back to camp would cause them trouble they did not want to face. Unlike at Fort Bliss and other places where he would be stationed later, there were no card games or drinking that he was aware of.

At camp, the warm rain fell often, standing on the flat, low-lying ground and flooding easily, but soaking in quickly. It seemed to rain often that summer, especially when they marched or ran. When they ran, or could move freely, the mosquitoes were not too bad. When they marched, there could be no unauthorized movements. If a mosquito landed on an arm or face while the candidates stood at attention or marched, it just had to stay there until it drew its fill of blood and decided to fly away. When it left, scratching was not permitted, either. Although there were no clouds of them, the mosquitoes that were around could be rather large. Kept out of the barracks buildings by heavy screening, no one thought much about them until one weekend three men in his class came down with meningitis. Once contracted, meningitis was very contagious, so everyone who might have been exposed had to be quarantined immediately. Ed's platoon went far back into the woods to another barracks where they could be isolated from all contact with others, and there they stayed. The outbreak happened just as Ed was about to finish the ninety-day officer training course, so he had to put his plans to marry Gemma at the end of May on hold until the army would let him go home. In the meantime, his unit went over and over the materials they had learned. They ran every day, marched, and even began surveying the area with transits borrowed from the engineers. For sport they hunted snakes. It seemed to go on forever. Meningitis was often fatal, so the army had to be very sure that no one else had it, and no one seemed to. After an additional two and a half months in remote sections of camp, they came back to their regular barracks, and got ready to graduate. It was an impressive but austere ceremony in which the men received their second lieutenant's bars and marched off to clear out their barracks area. All the men got leave to go home before reporting for their next assignment. The bars on Ed's epaulettes and overseas cap distinguished him as an officer now, and he proudly wore them home on the train. A notice in the "Men in Service" column announced to all of New Castle that he had been commissioned an officer in the United States Army. In his footlocker were orders to report to Camp Haan. They were going to California!

Difficult Times

While Ed was at OCS and Gemma worked at Public Service, the uphill struggles of the war continued. Of course the epic struggle between the Russians and the Germans continued on the Eastern Front. The Germans had not been prepared for the fearsome Russian winter and had suffered greatly from the cold and snow. As the weather warmed up and some roads began to dry out, they prepared for their third summer of campaigning in the Soviet Union. The Russians pushed them back early in the year, then lost ground to German counterattacks. The Russians gained the most, with German resistance causing terrible losses. Among the civilian population, losses had also been very high. As the Russians retreated in 1941 and 1942, they had scorched the earth. Then came the shelling and tank fighting, then house-to-house combat through practically every village in the vast disputed areas. The Germans practiced the same policies as they retreated westward, only there was little left to scorch. This process continued in sections all along the huge front throughout the year.

In May 1943, American forces landed on Attu, one of the Alaskan islands that the Japanese had held for a year. Word had it that there were three thousand Japanese troops on the island. By June 2, the *Courier-Times* reported that fifteen hundred of the enemy had been killed, but only four captured during the first three weeks of fighting on the island. It would take until nearly the end of August before American troops would regain both islands.

Labor problems plagued the nation in the spring and summer of 1943. On the first of May when their contract expired, a quarter million miners went on strike. Roosevelt ordered the fuels coordinator, Secretary of the Interior Harold Ickes, to take over every mine in which a work stoppage had occurred or was threatened. Ickes had full authority to "do all things necessary" to operate the mines and sell and distribute coal. There were rumors that the army would be used to mine and move coal if needed. After the government took action, John L. Lewis, the powerful president of the United Mine Workers (UMW) union, asked the miners to return to work on a two-week, temporary basis while negotiations went forward.

A local family celebrated their son's receipt of the Silver Star for his service aboard a submarine. Chief Torpedoman Mate Kenneth Gwinn's father operated a lunchroom across the street from the high school, and Gwinn had already served in the navy sixteen years. His wife would be arriving from Maine to be with him when he came home to Grand Avenue on the leave they hoped he would soon receive. Exactly how he won the medal was not clear, but it had something to do with sending Japanese ships to the bottom. Another family, the Pfenningers from 18th and Plum Streets, enjoyed having their son Elmer home over a weekend as he transferred from camp in Georgia to Kentucky. His wife had not seen him for some time, and she would be going to Kentucky with him.

The fighting continued in North Africa as British, French, and American forces battled into Tunis and Bizerte, trumpeted in unusually large headlines in the paper. The Allies controlled the air, and supported the advance with strikes against retreating Axis columns as the home front effort continued. The Chrysler plant won its second "E" pennant for outstanding production efforts.

The ration board hoped to avoid the canning sugar mess that rationing had caused the previous summer. Ration book holders could fill out the application for extra sugar published in the paper and send it in along with their ration book #1 to the ration board where the application would be considered. Long lines had been a problem the previous summer. This year, the limit was twenty-five pounds extra per person for canning for the calendar year ending in March 1944. As before, applicants had to list sugar on hand, amounts to be canned, and amounts of jams and jellies to be canned, along with the number of people included in the application. Everyone figured out right away that if you applied for sugar for jam and jelly, the board would refuse. The extra sugar had to go toward preserving fruit. The next day, the ration board changed the maximum to fifteen pounds after being told by OPA to do so. There would be a coupon available later for ten more pounds, but no one knew whether it would be validated before the canning season ended. People sent in the applications and their books, then in the third week of May the ration board got word that OPA would validate stamps #15 and #16 immediately for five pounds of sugar each, no questions asked, so long as it was for canning. The housewives who had sent their books in with the canning sugar applications, about two thousand of them in New Castle, then began demanding their books back so that they could use the new coupons. The ration board asked for patience and volunteer help for the two clerks working on the two thousand applications.

The board also announced that when servicemen came home on leave, they could come to the ration board to receive special authorization for as much as five gallons of gasoline. There were some strings. Application had to be made on OPA form number R-552 and the applicant had to present leave or furlough papers. Validation stamps had to be affixed to the back of the gas coupons. A sixteen-year-old stole coupons for 1,980 gallons of gas from a station at Central Avenue and South 15th Street. He waited in jail while OPA officials decided whether to charge him with a federal offense.

Nylon and silk hose had become very scarce, but there was still rayon hose. Numerous stories and ads in the paper touted the new rayon cord tires that would help win the war, but with parachute silk and nylon items taken over for the War Department, the cheaper rayon had to do for hose. The main difference was that rayon hose stretched out much faster than nylons and tended to bag around the knees and ankles. There wasn't much to be done about it. Leg makeup could be messy and it took time to put it on evenly. The OPA put ceiling prices into effect, and stores like Morton's downtown rolled prices back to comply. Morton's reduced what had been $1.35 hose to $1.05. One-dollar hose went down to 89¢. But they had plenty of all colors and sizes, and even if they were expensive, at least they worked.

On Monday morning, May 17, 1943, the war came home to Gemma in a new and shocking way when the Western Union boy

Wanda and Maxine Moles in the middle of wartime. Wanda was in high school and working part-time, and Maxine had her job back at Ingersoll Steel, each doing her part to support the war effort at home.

made a trip to the Hornaday home on South 12th Street. Gemma went downtown to the Public Service office that morning as she always did and began the day's work. Some of the girls in the office smoked, so they all took a break at 10:00 for ten minutes before going back to their desks and resuming the clatter of typewriters and calls. Sometime before eleven o'clock the phone rang at Margaret Thompson's cashier window. No one paid much attention when she picked it up and listened as the caller began talking. Then she cried "Oh, no!" and ran sobbing from the room. The other women exchanged looks of fear and foreboding, and a friend ran to comfort her and find out what had happened. It was in the paper that evening on the front page. Ten days before, Captain Warren Hornaday, Army Air Corps fighter pilot, had been killed in the southwest Pacific, perhaps in New Guinea where he had been recently. His parents had gotten the wire that morning and had called Margaret, his fiancée. He was twenty-five years old, and they planned to marry when he came home. She took off work for a few days, then came back to work at her window. There was a service for him in town the following Sunday. His death raised Gemma's fears and increased her resolve to marry Ed as soon as possible. Who lived and who died seemed so completely random and irrational.

Yet another death appeared on the same front page. Lt. James Armstrong of Knightstown died in the crash of an army transport which was en route to Indianapolis from North Carolina. The eighteen men aboard were all headed home on leave. Armstrong was in one of the glider squadrons of the Air Corps. Just a week later, two more Henry County servicemen's obituaries appeared on the front page of the *Courier-Times*. Both had been killed in North Africa, where the fighting had been over for almost two weeks. The same day, the number one draft board sent twenty-one more New Castle men to the army.

On June 1, half a million coal miners went on strike at the direction of John L. Lewis. Coal powered most of the nation's factories and power plants, including the Chrysler plant at New Castle. Labor had long had a sympathetic ear in Washington since the New Deal had come to town in 1933, and had gained much under Roosevelt. The labor boards, which set wages during the war, had already granted concessions to the unions, but Lewis and others saw the critical need for coal for war plants as so much leverage to wring more gains for their members and themselves. A large percentage of people in the country thought it was outrageous that a union president could deny required fuel to industries everywhere while American boys were fighting and dying overseas. Roosevelt ordered the miners back to work, but the strike went ahead. The Associated Press (AP) put this notice from the Army Mothers Club of Huntington, West Virginia, on the news wire: "We feel if the executive department has the power to take our sons and send them to the far corners of the earth without the consent of the parents or the sons, it has the power to force John L. Lewis and the United Mine Workers to return to work at once." A draft board in Tennessee refused to induct any more local boys until the government took action to settle the strike. Cartoons showed Hitler and a Japanese general looking at factories labeled "Essential U.S. war production" while Hitler said "Why worry about bombing it, when John L. Lewis can close it up for me?" Another showed a fresh grave decorated with a flag and a headstone that read "Died for John L. Lewis" with the caption "Next Memorial Day?" Administration and labor officials wrangled over the issue for several days before most of the miners went back to work, but a week's coal production had been lost. Many Americans began to dislike Lewis even more than they already had. After talks, the miners went out again on June 21. Roosevelt suggested that any miners who went out after this date should be drafted into the army. In the meantime, the Secretary of the Interior operated the mines under an executive order, promising to return them to the owners as soon as possible. The government went into other businesses, too. The War Food Administration ordered U.S. attorneys to requisition corn from major elevators in the country for use in vital war plants.

There was a New Castle contribution to the labor problems, too. Nearly 250 workers walked out of the Schact Rubber plant in New Castle on June 17. CIO Rubber Workers Union officials gave a list of grievances to the paper which focused on a lack of ventilation for women workers, overtime, and wages.

There were other domestic problems, as well. Naval officials put parts of Los Angeles off-limits to all military personnel after clashes between them and "zoot-suiters." Gangs of these youths had gone on rampages and two or three of them had been killed. Labor representatives and American Civil Liberties Union delegates told the U.S. attorney that law enforcement officials had overreacted and made matters worse. In the third week of June, race riots broke out in Detroit. On June 21, the wire services reported that six had been killed and two hundred injured in widespread rioting. The governor sent in the National Guard to help the city's thirty-five hundred policemen. A policeman died in a gun battle, and crowds threw rocks and bottles, overturned and burned cars, stopped streetcars, and stoned passengers. Looting began on Hastings Street and spread to other areas. By the next day, there were twenty-three dead, seven hundred injured, and thirteen hundred arrested as over a thousand troops tried to restore order. It took days for police and troops to quell the disturbances.

A new feature, POW addresses of Henry County boys, began to appear more and more in the paper. Pfc. Thomas Lee and Private Donald Klipsch of East Broad Street became prisoners in the North Africa campaign. Lee went to Stammlager VII and Klipsch went to Stalag 3-B in Germany. Merle Rawlings of rural New Castle became a prisoner of the Japanese in the Philippines, and went to Camp Kawasaki, then Camp Tokyo, in Japan. Getting this word usually came as a relief, because captured men almost invariably had been reported as missing. If they had a POW address and some word had come from them, they had at least been alive when they wrote it. Mrs. Roy Ruddell fervently wished for such a message. She and her son Roy came to New Castle from Florida to stay with Roy Sr.'s parents that summer. Roy had been missing over Guadalcanal since December. But being safe in a prisoner camp did not guarantee life, either. On August 23, the family of Chief Petty Officer Lawrence Corum, captured in the Philippines, announced he had died in a Japanese prison camp.

The Germans and Italians had finally given up in Tunisia in May, losing a quarter of a million prisoners. After that, preparations went ahead for possible Allied actions in the Mediterranean or in southern Europe. The Italian garrison of the island of Pantelleria, halfway between Tunisia and Sicily, surrendered without a fight, and the British had maintained their forces on Malta and at Gibraltar throughout the war against attempts to destroy them. Where the Allies might strike next was anyone's guess, but there were plenty of potential targets, since the entire European Mediterranean coast from Spain to Turkey was in Axis hands. Widespread speculation suggested that Allied forces would attack Sicily and then Italy.

There was good news in the photo section on June 11. A B-17 bomber had finished twenty-five missions over German-held territory with its crew intact, and would be allowed to return home. The plane, called *Memphis Belle,* would be used back in the States to sell war bonds on a flying tour of the country. A picture showed the captain and crew receiving congratulations from Army Air Corps brass in England. More and more bombers and their crews arrived in England every week to increase the bombing pressure on German factories and rail yards. A few days later the photo section showed row upon row of white wooden crosses on the graves of dead marines on Guadalcanal.

In New Castle, Civilian Defense officials laid plans for the first blackout in the city. It had taken a year to get the required number of people through the Civilian Defense classes as air raid wardens, auxiliary firefighters, control center workers, and auxiliary police. These workers had to perform twenty hours of first aid work in addition to their other training to qualify. All citizens had to observe the blackout from 8:30 to 9:30 P.M. on Monday, June 21. A front-page article described the meaning of the air raid siren signals and what to do when they sounded. It could happen. British bombers were even then delivering a series of attacks on the Ruhr industrial area in Germany, and the paper reported that civilians had been evacuated to escape the bombs. Chrysler blacked out in twenty seconds, but shut down for only three minutes in the test so as not to stop production of vital war products. Other test blackouts took place at Perfect Circle, the Ingersoll steel rolling mill, and the ice plant. Officials called the test 98 percent successful the next day. Few people ventured onto the streets during the blackout period, and neighbors helped remind neighbors that it was time to turn 'em out. When the employees at Long Cleaners on East Broad failed to turn out their lights, vandals threw rocks through the display windows in the front of the store and escaped before police could discover who they were. Few reports of violations came in from any of the residential areas.

OPA announced that shoe ration stamp #18, in the sugar-coffee book, would be valid on June 1, and would have to last until October 31, eleven days longer than the previous stamp. This stamp could be transferred to another family member, however, which was unusual. If a parent did not need shoes, the stamp could be used for children's shoes. As the expiration date for coupon #17 approached, crowds of buyers fell upon New Castle shoe stores to buy shoes before it was too late. Customers waited an hour or more to be helped. Even when the stores closed an hour early at 4 P.M., there were still customers waiting in line at six o'clock.

Two New Castle boys met in England in June. Sgt. Alvis Pfenninger, from the corner of Plum Street, and Corporal Kenneth

Moystner ran into each other in camp after Pfenninger saw Moystner's name on a bulletin board. Moystner had ten rather old copies of the *Courier-Times* and helped Pfenninger catch up on the news.

The Office of War Information gave instructions for writing to servicemen which the paper published in the middle of June.

TELL HIM: 1. How the family is doing everything possible to help in the war. 2. How anxious the family is for the boy's return. 3. How well and busy the family is. Give details. 4. How the family is getting along financially. 5. What's doing in the community: news about girls (single) he knows, doings of friends, who's marrying whom, exploits of the home team and other sports events, social doings, effects of the war on the home town. Reminisce a little about past events and places the boy used to visit. Enclose clippings from the home-town paper.

DON'T TELL HIM: 1. Your troubles. He has troubles of his own. 2. Your complaints. He can't do anything about them. 3. About things you are deprived of. He can't supply them. 4. Doleful predictions about the future. He's fighting for that future—now. 5. Unnecessary details about financial troubles. If there are things he should know about family finances, and he is in a position to do something about them, tell him. But don't string it out.

The government had rules for everything.

On June 23, with riots raging in Detroit, tragedy struck again at the Ruddell house on Park Avenue. Roy was still missing after six months, and then the Western Union boy came to their house with another wire from the War Department. Another son, twenty-seven-year-old Cyril, an Army Air Corps captain in the Pacific, had been killed in an accident. He had been home on a visit in May. He had graduated from South Bend Central High School when the Ruddells still lived there, had joined the army in March 1941, and had gone to Air Corps OCS where he received his commission as an officer.

New Castle waited anxiously for news after word came on June 30 that there had been landings on New Georgia and sur-rounding islands in the South Pacific. There had been so many casualties during the fight for Guadalcanal that took six months. Now it appeared that the United States was going to have to fight the Japanese for every island in the South Pacific, and there were many, many of them. There was a map of the place in the paper on July 5, and as usual, it was mostly a lot of odd names like Rendove, Munda, Mongo, and such. To help the war effort, tax withholding began on the same day.

There had been stories about the bombing campaigns against German-held targets in Europe, but the impression was that it was mostly the British doing it. Then the Western Union boy brought this part of the war home to New Castle, too. Mr. and Mrs. Ben Baker's wire from the War Department brought the news that their son, Lt. Thornton Baker, whom everyone at school called "Rabbit" because of his running ability, had failed to return from a bombing mission on June 25. Officially listed as missing, Baker was a bombardier who had enlisted in October 1941, and flew in the $100,000 Boeing B-17. The press reports from that day stated that American bombers hit targets in north-west Germany, and eighteen failed to return. There had been terrific opposition from as many as two hundred German fighters. Each B-17 had ten crew members. That meant that 180 wires from the War Department went out to mothers and fathers and wives all over the country for just the missing from that one raid. Baker was twenty-four years old. His family waited and hoped against hope that there might be some word that he was alive. Later in the month, Pfc. Merle Rawlings's folks received the first postcard from their son since his capture in the Philippines in December 1941. It had been mailed from Japan, and had taken seven months to arrive in New Castle. The Red Cross had reported his capture to his parents, but there had been no direct word from him for over a year and a half. Rawlings was a Spiceland boy who had enlisted in the army early in 1941. In August, word came to the Lambersons in Straughn, in the southeast part of the county, that their son, Lt. John Lamberson, a B-17 pilot, was a prisoner of the Germans.

Because of still more problems with rationing books, the Ration Board decided to reissue the A ration books to more than eleven thousand Henry County drivers. Because school was out, it was not practical to use teachers to take the applications, so the board asked service stations and tire stores to hand them out, and motorists had to mail them in to the ration office. The same week, the Red Cross announced that it would begin recruiting nurses for the army and navy in New Castle. The Indiana quota was twenty-five hundred nurses a month. For incentive, nurses received commissions as second lieutenants and drew $171.00 pay per month.

OPA authorized the local War Price and Rationing boards to establish hearing panels for violations of the gas rationing rules. The Henry County panel began to meet to hear appeals the third week in July 1943. Most of those who appeared came up on speeding violations, and the penalties were severe. A third offense of five miles over the 35 m.p.h. speed limit meant revocation of the gas ration book for the duration of the war. It only took a second offense if anyone got caught exceeding 50 m.p.h. to draw a suspension of ration privileges for the duration. Some pleaded for the replacement of books lost accidentally, but one man who had lost his book on a two-hundred-mile trip to Somerset, Kentucky, did not get much sympathy from the board members.

The big news on July 10 was the Allied invasion of Sicily by American, British, and Canadian forces. German broadcasts reported that there had been landings on both the eastern and southern coasts. Warships and B-24 bombers from the 9th Air Force pounded their targets on the islands while hundreds of Allied fighters swept Axis planes from the air. General Eisenhower, who had been in charge of American forces for the North Africa landings, headed up the whole show this time. When would the casualty counts start coming in from this one? Meanwhile, there was news of a huge battle on the Eastern Front around Orel, north of Kursk, deep inside Russia. Almost five thousand Germans were reported to have been killed on a single day in ferocious counterattacks against the attacking Russians. People in New Castle wondered what the casualty reports might be like if it were American troops engaged in that kind of battle. Would our soldiers be in similar fights in Europe soon, too?

Then on July 30, the war came home in a stunning way. The Western Union boy walked up to the door at the Kennedy home on Spring Street on the east side of town north of Broad. It was from the War Department.

DEEPLY REGRET TO INFORM YOU THAT YOUR SON, PVT. JAMES KEN-
NEDY, U.S. MARINE CORPS RESERVES, WAS KILLED IN ACTION IN THE
PERFORMANCE OF HIS DUTY IN THE SERVICE OF HIS COUNTRY. TO PRE-
VENT POSSIBLE AID TO OUR ENEMIES, PLEASE DO NOT DIVULGE THE
NAME OF HIS SHIP OR STATION. PRESENT SITUATION NECESSITATES IN-
TERMENT TEMPORARILY IN LOCALITY WHERE DEATH OCCURRED AND
YOU WILL BE NOTIFIED ACCORDINGLY. PLEASE ACCEPT MY HEARTFELT
SYMPATHY. LETTER FOLLOWS.

LT. GEN. T. HOLCOMB, COMMANDANT, UNITED STATES MARINE CORPS

Kennedy's death shook everyone. He had been one of those kids
whose face just naturally folded into a smile with narrowed eyes.
It seemed that everyone who knew him liked him. He never
seemed to make enemies. Many of his classmates of the Class of
1941 knew him because he played intramural sports, shouted
from the stands as part of Leather Lungs, or had been a member
of the Latin Club. Others remembered him as the *Courier-Times*
paperboy in their neighborhood. He worked at The Spot, the
most popular drive-in in town, and he had gone from there to the
Dudley Grocery. He was working for the Dudleys when he enlisted in the Marine Corps in December 1942 at nineteen years of
age. Everyone's best guess was that he was somewhere in the
southwest Pacific, but there were no details. The week before the
telegram arrived, his family received three letters he had written.
The news went around town very quickly as people struggled to
cope with the fact that he had been so near and so real to them
little more than six months before. His picture appeared in the
paper the next day, and everyone could see that he was even
more handsome in his marine uniform than they remembered
him. It took a while for it to sink in. Meanwhile, Associated Press
reported hand-to-hand fighting for the airstrip at Munda on New
Georgia. There must have been a great deal of fighting, because
there was talk of air strikes by Corsair fighters and bombers, as
well as ship movements.

Those who looked carefully at the front page of the *Courier-
Times* on August 27 might have noticed grim signs of what the
war was becoming in Europe. Wire reports told of a "reign of terror" in France, Poland, and Czechoslovakia, where crackdowns

on patriots resulted in one hundred or even two hundred civilians being shot for every German soldier killed by partisans. Twelve hundred Czechs were reported to have been killed for the death of Reinhard Heydrich, a high official. A Jewish group reported that only 3 million of the 8.3 million European Jews were still alive. Three million, they said, had been killed since 1939 by starvation, forced labor, pogroms, and methodical murder in death camps in Eastern Europe. The revolt in Denmark and the ferocity of the fighting in Russia could make one think that things like this could happen.

8. Together, and Alone, 1943

ED WROTE HOME to his mother and father from Camp Davis that he would appreciate it if they could help with the wedding plans. After all, he could not get away until OCS was over, and the meningitis quarantine had set back even these plans. But he was to be disappointed in the reply they sent. They liked Gemma, and they would be glad for their son to marry her, but this was not a good time, they wrote. They were too young, and with the war on, there was no telling what might happen. In their hearts, they had already lost their boy to the war, which was bad enough. Getting married would mean that he would never come home to them. He would come home to her. They wanted him back home where they could look after him and enjoy him and look at him whenever they wished. It was the only way they could reassure themselves that they had succeeded in their lives. Neither of them was very verbal, and the traditions they had been raised with ranked sitting quietly in the presence of loved ones very highly. No, they would not help with the wedding plans. They hoped that Ed and Gemma would put it off until after the war when things had settled down a little. There would be time then. They told Gemma that they would do anything for him, but they could not do this. Ed was terribly disappointed with their decision, but there was nothing he could do from camp. He told Gemma in his letters what they had said, and the two young people went ahead with plans on their own.

Gemma wrestled with the decision to marry Ed almost the entire time he was gone. She knew that this would be permanent, and that there was no backing out or changing one's mind later on. From her Nazarene upbringing, she knew that marriage was not something to be taken lightly or on a whim. It was not a test run; it was the real thing. Ed knew this too. Reverend Kinnett of the First Baptist Church in New Castle, and every other Baptist preacher he had ever heard, including his own grandfather, stressed the holiness and permanence of the marriage bond. There was no word "unless" following the phrase "until death do us part." They both worried, as everyone did, if they were doing the right thing.

The war was on, with no end in sight. Tomorrow was as remote and unknowable as the dark side of the moon. They were young and would only be young once. Many of their friends had gotten married and gone away to strange places to see what life was all about, and even with the war on, they were entitled to their dreams too. The only way to really find out what life was about was to grab for some happiness when they could. The world could pass them by, or fate could cast him down in some distant, strange land without ever knowing their love. By the time the war was over, they might not even be young anymore. Without knowing where the fates would take them or where they would end up, they both knew they must go ahead and bind their lives together. It might be their only chance at a happiness they so much wanted to believe could be theirs.

The army gave Ed two weeks leave when he left Camp Davis, and he hurried home as fast as the trains would allow. Gemma met him at the station, and they clung together with a new intensity. In the few days before the wedding, they tried the phrase "my wife," and "my husband" in their minds and studied each other with a new interest, but clouded in love. Ed's mother and father refused to attend the wedding, hoping that this would cause the young couple to put off their plans, but it did not work. Hoping to avoid friction between the future in-laws, Gemma asked her mother and father not to attend the wedding, even though it would be in New Castle. They reluctantly agreed. Gemma wanted the wedding to be in a church, and there were many friends who would have liked to attend, but she told everyone that they were just going to have a quiet wedding, without fanfare. Ed thought it would be better for the future to avoid making the wedding a big production in order to minimize his parents' hurt feelings.

When the excitement of his return had subsided, they went to the clerk's office at the courthouse and signed for their marriage license. The following Saturday, August 21, 1943, they used it. They had decided to marry each other in front of Rev. Kinnett, the Baptist minister, but not in the church. The local paper regularly carried announcements of marriages performed at the Baptist parsonage at 733 South Main Street in New Castle, just half a block south of the church. Theirs would be there, too.

Ed had borrowed his father's car, and brought Phil Perry with him. Charlie Purvis and his steady girlfriend Barbara Bunch came together, and Martha picked up Gemma and brought her the few blocks from Plum Street. It was a small wedding, without music or flowers at the altar. There were only eight people in the living room of the parsonage when the ceremony took place. Reverend Kinnett stood in front of the fireplace, with Gemma and Ed directly in front of them. Beside Gemma stood Martha Perry, her friend from Plum Street. Next to Ed stood Charlie Purvis, also a second lieutenant, who had finished OCS a week before Ed. Barbara Bunch and Phil Perry sat in chairs to one side, along with Mrs. Kinnett. Gemma wore the wool jersey dress with the fitted jacket that she had bought for the occasion. It had a pleated skirt and three-quarter-length sleeves, but the notice in the paper did not mention that it was light blue. She had bought the dress just a couple of weeks before, and fall clothes had started to come in at the stores by then. It was not terribly hot to wear, but it was not made for long-distance walking on a hot day, either. She had a small white hat surrounded with little white feathers, topped with a gauzy flounce, fastened to her hair with hatpins. Her permed hair was curled into the pompadour that so many women wore then. Ed's cousin and his wife operated a dress shop in Detroit in the 1930s, and when the war began, she saved back dozens of pairs of nylon hose. Gemma got one of these pairs to wear for the wedding. Her dark shoes were brown suede. Both she and Martha had corsages of red roses.

The engagement ring Ed had brought from Texas was a solitaire. When he came back from OCS he bought a wedding ring

Gemma beaming at her
new husband August 21,
1943, on Plum Street,
immediately after
returning from the
Baptist parsonage on
South Main. They had
decided to reach for their
chance at happiness
before it was too late.

that matched it in New Castle. It had five small diamonds set in
the narrow yellow gold band. He wore a man's ring on the third
finger of his left hand that his mother and father had given him.
For now, they felt it was all they could afford.

The ceremony seemed to go by very quickly. When they had
said, "I do," Charlie handed him the ring and he slipped it onto
her finger. Everyone smiled big smiles as they kissed each other.
They were only in the house perhaps twenty minutes, and when
they came out, they were Lt. and Mrs. Edward M. Smith. They
thanked Rev. and Mrs. Kinnett for performing the ceremony and
for the use of their house, and Ed handed over the customary
gratuity given to the minister. They walked out into the warm
August afternoon from the porch at the parsonage and Rev. and
Mrs. Kinnett waved good-bye as the wedding party got into the
cars and drove away.

August 21, 1943. L to R
Charlie Purvis, Ed Smith,
Gemma Moles Smith,
Martha Fatzinger Perry.
Charlie and Martha stood
up with Ed and Gemma at
their wedding.

They went directly to the house on Plum Street. Although it was Saturday, Jess had only reluctantly agreed to take time off from work to be there when the wedding was over. He took pictures of the newlyweds, then group shots with Martha and Phil and Charlie and Barbara. In the house, Ethel had cake and coffee to celebrate. They went down to the house where Ed had grown up and visited for a little while, then went to the passenger station to catch the train for Cincinnati.

The planning for the wedding had been somewhat last-minute because of Ed's delay at Camp Davis, and he had established in his mind where they would go for their wedding trip. They were familiar with Indianapolis, so that would not be a very exciting destination. He thought of going to Cincinnati, the next-nearest big city after Indianapolis. He bought the tickets and they boarded the train about five o'clock in the afternoon. Cincinnati was a major rail hub, with a great deal of wartime train traffic as well as vast commerce through the modern Union Terminal.

When Ed and Gemma got there, they discovered to their surprise that there was a convention in town, and that there were absolutely no hotel rooms to be had at any price. Instead of just picking a downtown hotel and checking in, they had to leave Cincinnati to find a place to stay, and they had no car. Back to the terminal they went. They waited a while, then boarded a train for the three-hour ride to Richmond. A taxi took them to the Leland Hotel, the same destination that Martha and Phil had chosen, where they found a room. It was the first time Gemma had ever stayed in a hotel. By this time it was the wee hours of the morning. Tired but happy, they went upstairs. The next day, they took a train for the thirty-minute ride back to New Castle to spend the few days that they had before they would head for Ed's new assignment. They stayed at the house on Plum Street two nights, then went out to the house in the hollow to stay until they left.

Ed and Gemma left on Monday, August 30, for their new life in the golden West. He had been assigned to Camp Haan, across the road from March Field, just outside Riverside, California. It was sixty miles or more east of Los Angeles across the desert, with Pomona the only major town in between. They were actually going to California! It boggled the mind to think that they would actually be living there. California was where movie stars lived, and where the Golden Gate Bridge had been finished just a few years before. Ed had been as far west as Kansas and had seen the Atlantic in North Carolina, but that was much farther than Gemma had ever traveled. Going to Indianapolis and down to visit relatives in Tennessee was as far as she had ever been. Neither of them had even been to Cincinnati until a week before.

Ed's orders were to report at Camp Haan on Friday, September 3. Allowing four whole days to drive out there seemed like enough. A friend named Moore from OCS agreed to provide transportation. He had the good fortune to receive the gift of a nearly new black 1941 Plymouth four-door sedan with very few miles from his grandmother. He drove from North Carolina to Cincinnati to pick up another friend, Hoff. From there the two of them drove to New Castle to pick up Ed and Gemma. Since all three of the men had been assigned to Camp Haan, it would amount to a long-distance car pool. Charlie Purvis would have gone, too, but he had finished a week ahead of Ed at Camp Davis,

August 30, 1943. Married just a week, Ed and Gemma are about to leave for his new assignment at Camp Haan, California, near Riverside. Route 66 and the golden West was just over the horizon.

and had already gone out on the train to join his new unit, the 923rd AA.

Moore and Hoff stayed the night at the Plaza Hotel in New Castle and they all left on Monday, August 30, 1943. Ed and Gemma had been married nine days. Everyone said their fare-wells at Plum Street about 7:30 in the morning, put their bags in the trunk, drove up to Broad Street, and turned westward past the courthouse and down the long grade to Highway 3. They went south, within shouting distance of the house in the hollow, to the National Road at Dunreith, where they turned west for their adventure. Gemma did not drive, so this left the three men to take turns driving while the others relaxed and enjoyed the trip. Most of that day was uneventful as they motored through Indianapolis on Washington Street, then toward Terre Haute.

They crossed the Wabash there, continuing on to Vandalia, Illinois, then to the Mississippi at St. Louis. When they crossed the river, they rolled onto U.S. Route 66, turned west, and kept going.

It was evening when they cleared the St. Louis suburbs, but they continued on into the dusk to get as far as possible. Route 66 already had a reputation as *the* way to go to southern California, and it was a treat to drive on after the gravel roads that were common in the 1930s. It ran unbroken from Chicago to St. Louis, then westward to the Pacific at Santa Monica, California. Carefully graded, with smooth concrete lanes wider than most roads and well-engineered banked curves, it was a road made for rapid travel. On the open road they could average 50 m.p.h. or even better sometimes, if the hills were not too steep. Since they were on official government business, the 35 m.p.h. speed limit did not apply. In the humid parts of the country, the highway went through an endless number of towns, many of them with a stoplight or two and speed limit signs posted on the outskirts of town. Farther west, in New Mexico and Arizona, there were fewer towns, with long stretches of country in between. As it became darker, Moore announced he was tired from the day's driving and let Hoff take over. He soon began to drift off to the side of the road from drowsiness. After this happened several times, Ed climbed behind the wheel again and took them to Rolla, Missouri, where they stopped for the night. There was a two-story hotel on the north edge of town where Route 66 crossed the main drag through Rolla, and they got rooms there. It was a little cooler at night, and with a fan in the rooms and the windows open, the air was tolerable. Worn-out from the long drive, they were all soon asleep.

It was hot in Missouri the last days of August 1943. The party agreed to get up early in order to get some breakfast and be on the road while it was still cool. Gassed up and fed, they went through the little south-central Missouri towns past Fort Leonard Wood toward Springfield and Joplin. By the time they got to Springfield, it was apparent that they had an alignment problem. A front tire had begun to wear badly and the car pulled to one side when the brakes were applied. They found a garage along the highway in Springfield, and waited while the mechanic realigned the front end. They had a spare, but tires were far too scarce to ignore such a problem. The stop in Springfield offered a break, so they had lunch and hit the road as soon as the work was done. They went through Joplin, got gas in Galena, Kansas, and started into the broad landscape of northeastern Oklahoma, but by the time they made the Oklahoma line, it was late afternoon. They began to worry as a growing concern about arriving on time in California crept over all of them. The plan had been to stay with Ed's grandfather and his wife at their home in Plainview, Texas, on the second night of the trip, but when night fell, they were only in Tulsa. They kept going. When Moore and Hoff began to get sleepy after dark again, Ed took over driving. When it got late, the three men decided that they had better try to keep going through the night. Ed could make himself stay awake, even during the wee hours of the morning, so he drove through the night while Gemma and the two others slept fitfully. When it began to grow light, they crossed into the Texas panhandle heading for Amarillo. Ed got what sleep he could during the day while Hoff and Moore drove.

It was more than two thousand miles from New Castle to Camp Haan. The trip became an exercise in endurance as they drove mile after endless mile across the blazing barren areas of New Mexico and Arizona. The car began to lose power on uphill grades in the high elevations, and Ed often had the feeling that trucks were almost pushing him up hills before coming to the summit and rolling freely down the other side. It got drier and hotter as they went, and Gemma had trouble breathing in the arid high elevations they crossed. It was like being in an oven for her, since she had never been out of the humid Ohio Valley. They stopped to eat at roadside restaurants, and often got gas then if they needed it. This presented an opportunity to use a rest room if there was one, and perhaps buy a Coca-Cola from the chest cooler in the station. Gemma was far too shy to ask to stop to go to the bathroom, so she had to wait until there was a need to stop for some other reason. She would not have dreamed of asking to make a stop for her convenience alone. The facility allowed one to take care of urgent needs, but splashing a little water on one's face and washing hands was about the extent of cleanliness. No one bathed after Rolla, Missouri. They spent most of the days hot and sweaty and not smelling very good. While Ed slept during the day, there was little for her to do except look out the window as more dreary desert came into view and passed out of sight behind them. The third day they went through Tucumcari, Albuquerque, and Gallup, New Mexico, and crossed into Arizona. It helped avoid the daytime heat to drive at night, so if the sleeping arrangements were not very comfortable, at least they were not hot. By now they were numb to it all. The dramatic views with the blue and purple mountains, the fragrant sagebrush, and the unusual birds and flowers could not be appreciated until they could get some rest. It was a little cooler when they got to Flagstaff, but the blazing sun on the black car made it hot even there. The motels in Flagstaff looked so comfortable and inviting, but they could not stop.

Lt. Moore had a C gas ration card, affording unlimited fuel for a military man traveling to an assignment. Gemma had saved $100 while Ed was at OCS, and he had saved the same amount while he was there. When they left New Castle, they had $200, a hefty sum. Hoff and Moore had their own money, too, of course. Even when gas was expensive, they could fill the tank for under $5. The trick was to make sure the tank was full for areas where there were few towns, or for driving at night when the stations would be closed. Generally speaking, they could buy gas at any filling station that was open, but few stayed open all night. Especially in New Mexico, Arizona, and California, it was very important to get fuel when it was available, not just when it was needed.

They went through Kingman, Arizona, so early in the morning that no gas stations were open, and, rather than wait for one to open, they drove on, hoping to make it to Needles. About four miles out of town, they ran out of gas, and at that time of the morning, there was no one on the highway. The road there was very narrow, so they carefully rolled downhill backward until they could find a place where the ground by the side of the road was at the same level to allow them to turn around. They coasted to the bottom, then Moore walked back into town for gas. After putting the contents of the can in the tank, they drove back into town to fill up and drop off the can. By that time they stopped for breakfast before going on. Even the coffee did not have much effect.

It was the fourth day now, grinding across the Colorado River, through Needles, California, and into the Mojave Desert in the blazing heat where the dusty black hood of the car seemed hot enough to fry an egg. They made the final 225 miles from the Arizona line in about six hours, turning south along the Mojave River at Barstow to Victorville, then on to San Bernadino. Route 66 went west toward the ocean from there, but they cut south again for the last eleven miles to Riverside, arriving early in the evening. They had made it just in time. Ed had to report the next morning.

Moore and Hoff went to a little motel in Riverside, but Ed and Gemma decided to stay at the Mission Inn, the famous and luxurious art deco hotel. Finally they could clean up and cool off and rest a little. It was very expensive, so they only stayed there two nights while they looked for a place to live. Outside, the day-time temperature reached 115 degrees, but Ed liked the dry heat. Riverside was crowded with transient army personnel assigned to Camp Haan and to the Army Air Corps base across the road, March Field. There were plenty of bachelor barracks, but Ed's second lieutenant rank meant that he could not live on the post with a spouse, so they looked for housing in Riverside. The War Department urged people who lived near military installations to make available any extra rooms they had to military personnel to help the war effort. Married servicemen went to assignments with no arrangements made for housing. While Ed went to report for duty the next morning, Gemma went to the YMCA where there was a bulletin board for available accommodations and found a place near Route 60 where it led west toward Los Angeles. It was at 4840 Rubidoux Boulevard, a road which wound around a mountain before dropping down into the Santa Ana River valley and the center of Riverside. They went out to look at it and meet the owners, Howard and Antoinette Stark. It was small, just a guest room and bath in the lower part of the house, with no kitchen, but it was furnished, so they decided they had better take it. The Starks were very kind people in their middle age, and they showed every courtesy to the young couple. It did not take long to move in.

It was a wondrous place for them. The house was older and stuccoed in the Spanish southwest style, with protruding beams from the upper part of the outside walls. There were established live oak and eucalyptus trees that shaded the house where it sat on the side of a hill. Stone steps flanked by a low stone wall topped with flowers led up the gradual slope to the guest room door which faced south toward the street, but was partially hidden by the trees and shrubbery. Upstairs where the Starks lived there were white plastered walls and cool wood floors and a Spanish-style fireplace. Thick rugs lay underneath tables and chairs, and the shade trees afforded views outside through the leaves. They had a greenhouse attached to the house where Mrs. Stark kept plants of a more tropical nature. From there the calming smell of oxygen given off by the plants wafted into the house and helped keep the humidity at comfortable levels. Further up on Rubidoux Mountain, there was a vista down into Riverside with its palm tree-lined thoroughfares and wide streets. It was possible to drive most of the way up, then there was a boulder-lined path up to the top, where the best view could be had for dozens of miles in every direction through the clear air toward the blue Santa Ana mountains to the south and Old Baldy to the north. Strange desert plants which bloomed at odd times of the year thrived in the parched, gravelly soil along the roadsides and next to sidewalks. It was so different from Indiana's cornfields and summer flowers.

The area where they lived was only sparsely populated. The Starks' house had been there twenty years or more, but there were long stretches of nothing more than wasteland between the house and Riverside. Just fifty miles away (the same distance from New Castle to Indianapolis) was Hollywood! They could just go over and see the people they had watched in the movies at home anytime they wished. When they had settled in and established a routine for a couple of weeks, they went there on a weekend and took the bus tour to the homes of the stars. There were lots of soldiers on the tour bus.

Ed reported for duty the day after their arrival, and began a daily routine almost immediately. Gemma lost no time in looking for work, as there was no point in sitting around the house all day doing nothing. She thought to go to the gas company in Riverside, and was hired instantly. She had to get a new Social Security card there because her name had changed, but she worked full-time while Ed was on duty, and that helped the time pass. Ed bought a 1939 Buick so they would have their own transportation, but Gemma had never learned to drive, so she could not use it. It was four miles into Riverside. Ed reported for duty early, and sometimes would be out in the field for days at a time, so Gemma developed the habit of walking to and from work when she needed to do so.

They were better off than they had ever hoped to be. When Ed received his officer's commission, he advanced from $78 per month sergeant's pay to $250 per month. He had a travel allowance which helped them get to California, and he could eat any meal he wished at camp. There was a housing allowance to compensate for the fact that he could not use the barracks, and Gemma was working too. She had made $18 per week at Public Service in New Castle, but she started at $25 a week in Riverside. She was twenty years old and already making $100 a month! They had their own car. As a civilian, Ed had never made more than $21 a month, but his officer's pay was as much as any foreman made at the Chrysler, and it was far more than they could spend unless they just threw money around. Neither of them believed in doing that, so they began to accumulate savings immediately.

Ed's assignment at Camp Haan was to train his own ack-ack battery to take overseas. It was one of innumerable units of all kinds that the War Department was filling with personnel as fast as they could be trained and transported. The battalion had only been at Camp Haan a few weeks when Ed arrived along with other junior officers to begin work. Ed had already been trained in all the AA weapons, so he began by getting acquainted with the enlisted personnel and non-coms whom he would be dealing with each day. He reported for duty at 7 A.M. each morning and went home at 5 P.M. There was no kitchen at the house, so he normally had breakfast at the battery mess each morning after the half-hour trip to camp. Scrambled eggs, bacon, potatoes, grits, oatmeal, coffee, and milk kept him going all day if necessary. The men attended classes, but Ed only participated with them on parade. His responsibility was to see to it that they did what they were supposed to do. They became intimately familiar with all the weapons they would use, and practiced tearing them down and reassembling them blindfolded and in the dark as Ed had done so many times. As at Fort Bliss and OCS, inspection came at noon on Saturday. After that, the men were dismissed and were free to leave camp until Sunday evening.

He concentrated the first month on getting his battery in shape for what was to come. The first week in October they went in trucks to Camp Irwin, recently established fifty miles south of Death Valley. Irwin was about as desolate as Death Valley, but not as low in elevation. Surrounded by mountains on three sides and more than twenty miles from Barstow, it was utterly barren and perfectly suited to gunnery practice. As at Fort Bliss, field training gave the men an opportunity to practice the rituals of campaigning. They camped in tents, cooked in the open, and learned to keep their weapons operating in the dusty conditions. They went out for two weeks the first time, firing the M1 Garand, the army's new main battle rifle, and machine guns. Then they went back to Camp Haan for a month. At the end of that time, they went back to Camp Irwin, this time for practice firing the 40 mm ack-ack weapons that would be the unit's mainstay. As a range officer for his battery, Ed's job was to decide when to fire on a target and when to order cease-fire. There was a great deal of calculation that went into firing the guns. The 40 mm shell casing was over a foot long, and the projectile point added another three inches. It was not prudent to open fire and just let the tracers tell whether one was close to the target. Ranges and elevations had to be carefully estimated in order to lay fire on the target quickly and accurately. Moving aircraft did not offer much calculation time. Some fighter planes could fly in excess of 350 m.p.h., and some topped 400 m.p.h. in a dive. The crews either identified a target and established an accurate pattern of fire quickly, or it was too late. If an aircraft attacked the battery itself, they could all be killed by machine-gun fire or bombs.

When Ed went to the field the second time, it was the third week in November. Gemma had gotten used to his weekly routine easily, because he was gone about the same amount of time that she was at work. His field exercises were more difficult for her. Alone in a strange town countless miles farther away from home than she had ever been, she got used to homesickness. There was a set time he would return, of course, and that helped, but he was in the field on Thanksgiving that year. The Starks knew that it would be difficult for her, so they invited her for Thanksgiving dinner and to visit during the afternoon. Gemma soon made friends at work. Minnie Krasselt became a fast friend, and she and Gemma often had lunch together or went shopping. Minnie helped with information about where things were and how to find things they needed at good prices. Yanked away from all her friends and her sisters, Gemma enjoyed having a companion for the times when Ed was gone.

Ominous Signs

The war did not stop while they went to the West Coast and got used to the dazzle there. While the newlyweds motored across the southern plains, Royal Air Force bombers hit Berlin again in what must have been large numbers, because Bomber Command reported that 47 bombers had been lost on the second night raid. Their range had increased, because Berlin had not been on the target list for very long. American bomber crews, flying in daylight, rarely flew deep into Germany. Although the American B-17 Flying Fortresses had ten .50 caliber machine guns on board, these were not enough to prevent severe losses in determined fighter attacks, as Rabbit Baker and many others had found out. When the bombers flew out of fighter escort range, losses could be severe. The numbers of aircraft and crews gradually increased, in spite of the losses, until by the fall of 1943 major raids of 250 or more planes attacked a single target. British and American bombers attacked Hamburg, the important German port city, in July 1943 in a series of raids which resulted in a firestorm, killing fifty thousand and leaving eight hundred thousand people without homes. The papers only said that there had been heavy attacks, but the air war had entered a new phase. Allied planes shot down 506 German aircraft in July 1943 while flying missions over the Continent. But there always seemed to be more German fighters and bombers where those had come from. On August 17, American crews flew one of the largest missions yet, a 230-bomber daylight raid against Schweinfurt's ball bearing plants. Sixty bombers were shot down or returned damaged beyond repair because the target was so far beyond friendly fighter range. On an extremely long-range raid from the Middle East against the important Rumanian oil facilities at Ploesti, 177 B-24s attacked the target, but German fighters shot down fifty of them. These loss rates could not be sustained, but word of them did not always find its way back to American newspapers. If there was no big announcement about the raid, the killed and missing lists could be spread over many towns and many papers.

Also on August 17, American troops under General Patton and British troops of General Montgomery completed the conquest of Sicily by taking Messina, just across from the toe of Italy. Two weeks later, the papers reported the casualty totals. There had been seventy-five hundred casualties in the Sicilian campaign, but there were no details as to how many were dead, wounded, or missing. John McCloy, the Assistant Secretary of War, reminded everyone that Sicily had been a relatively easy campaign. There had been no opposition on the beaches, followed by rapid advances once our forces had gotten ashore.

Everyone who had attended New Castle High School got a surprise when word appeared in the paper on September 1 that Miss Juanita Rucker, speech and drama teacher, had joined the Red Cross recreation service. She would be reporting for duty in Washington, D.C., on September 13. The Red Cross had previously made recruiting visits to New Castle and opened an office in town. She hoped to be working in service clubs overseas where American soldiers spent their leaves. When the 1943–1944 school year started, nineteen new teachers had to be hired to replace those who went into service or to other jobs. This would be one more.

The ration board in New Castle closed on Labor Day so that employees could catch up on their work issuing the new B and C gas ration books. More than three thousand of the five thousand new books had already gone out. Invalid S gas stamps began to show up in New Castle and the county early in September. These stamps had originally been issued for use on the East Coast only, and had never been valid in Indiana. Service station owners sold gas and accepted the stamps, then found out from the local board that they were no good.

OPA announced from Washington that butter point values

Maxine Moles in front of
1828 Plum Street in the
fall of 1943.

would be raised and meat lowered. Some canned goods went up,
too. Surveys showed shortages of butter and a dwindling supply. OPA intended that the one-point increase would slow down
shoppers' demands. There were other changes, too:

"Earlier today OPA announced changes in the blue stamp
point value of 21 processed foods—13 up and 8 down—and re-
stored dried prunes, raisins and currants to rationing. Those
changes will take effect Sunday. Increased are the ration value of
canned fruits and all frozen foods. Decreased are several types of
canned beans, beets, carrots, pumpkin and squash."

As always, it was necessary to check the ration value charts
when one arrived at the grocery.

On September 3, as Gemma and Ed awoke to their first full

day in California, the *Courier-Times* announced at home that the British had invaded Italy, encountering only light resistance. They began to advance along the toe, apparently without the assistance of American forces. The War Department offered no explanation of what our troops were doing. People in New Castle had become so accustomed to spotty news by now that there was no attempt to find out. The government announced what it wanted to when it decided it was a good time. On the same front page came the announcement that Sgt. Ralph Darling, NCHS Class of 1935, had been killed in the "North Africa area," probably in Sicily. Darling had lived in New Castle with an uncle, and had worked for over a year at the Plaza Hotel before enlisting in Indianapolis prior to Pearl Harbor.

With reports of casualties mounting day by day, there was good medical news. A new drug, penicillin, had been shown to be very effective in killing germs. The government encouraged massive production to help wounded soldiers, and soon afterward, another drug, Clavicin, also came out of university labs. A picture in the paper showed a medic administering blood plasma to a wounded GI in Sicily. Army doctors made every effort to save the lives of the wounded. It was good to know that if your loved one did get wounded, that the medics were there to help bring him back.

The Western Union boy remained busy in New Castle. News arrived on September 8 that Sgt. Robert Vannatta of East Broad Street died in the crash of his bomber in Rapid City, South Dakota, on a training mission. He had not graduated from the high school, but had attended three years, then went to work at Perfect Circle. The paper noted that seven, or about one-third, of the county men who had died in the war had lost their lives in accidents.

The rest of the front page carried good news, though. Just a few days after Allied forces invaded the peninsula, Italy had negotiated a surrender! Italian troops threw their hands up by the thousands and turned their weapons over to Allied troops. This meant that American forces could be used to strike somewhere else in Europe, now that they would not have to fight in Italy. The armistice had been arranged between Allied forces and the government of Marshal Badoglio, successor to Benito Mussolini, who had been tossed out late in July. Hostilities were to cease imme-diately. It was a great relief after the casualties that the North Africa campaign had cost. Second Lieutenant Elmer Smith came home to his parents' Park Avenue home in New Castle the second week in September to recuperate from a wound received five months earlier in North Africa. In his platoon were three home-town boys, Elmer Popejoy, Philip Morris, and Lloyd Caldwell.

Then just three days later, Allied headquarters announced that the American 5th Army had taken Salerno, part way up the coast toward Rome. This was puzzling, because the Italian sur-render should have ended resistance. German armored attacks had been pushed back, and reports had it that Germans and Ital-ians were fighting each other in the chaos in various parts of Italy. All the prisoners taken by American forces were German, so that told the tale. If the Italians would not fight in Italy, then the Germans would. Maybe it had been premature to hope that Italy would just leave the war and there would be no fighting. This appeared to be the case as there were editorials and stories about Italy being the second front that Stalin had been demanding for so long. More troops went into southern Italy to push ahead before German units could be sent there in quantity.

The first "serious" shortage to hit New Castle struck in the middle of September. Coal disappeared from dealers' yards due to a directive from the Fuel Administration giving priority to war plants, coke making, Great Lakes shipping, and domestic use, in that order. Some city dealers were thirty to forty days behind in their deliveries. When word of a looming shortage had begun to circulate two months before, people began to order their entire winter's supply, instead of just a ton or two at a time. It was possible that there might be some easing in the situation in No-vember, but it began to look like a cold winter.

Still the casualty reports trickled in. The army reported Sgt. Clarence Laboyteaux missing three weeks after his plane went down on a mission over Italy. He was one of those soldiers who, like Clay Grubbs, had qualified to receive his high school diploma while on duty in Florida. He was from the Class of 1943. Every-one hoped that he would be reported a prisoner like most of the other missing had been so far. Fighting moved toward Naples and the surrounding area to the north, and it began to look as though the Allies might have to fight all the way up the Italian peninsula after all. Sometimes sickening pictures appeared in the photo section on the last page of the paper. One showed dead GIs strewn on a beach. A couple of weeks later there was a shot of a crippled B-17, half its port wing blown away, falling over Naples. The pilot managed to hold it level long enough for at least five crew members to hit the silk. A fairly rapid advance put the Allies in control of Foggia, across the peninsula from Naples. Quick repair of the airfield there made it possible to base new air attacks from that point against German forces farther north.

A New Castle woman, Mrs. Beatrice Trout, joined the Women's Army Corps (WAC) and was one of the first to do so in the new recruiting drive launched in the fall of 1943. Plans called for a quota of two thousand women from Indiana to join in order to help fill positions needed in the army due to losses on the fighting fronts. Women had to be between the ages of twenty and fifty, but if they were under twenty-one they would have to have permission of their parents. The army required two years of high school or a high "mental alertness" score. They would not accept women with children under fourteen years of age, or women with dependants unless they could be supported without army pay.

The Army Air Corps reported more and more county boys missing as the Allies began to reach strength levels where they could increase the pressure on Germany. On October 8, 1943, SSgt. Robert Scott's wife received her wire at their home on South 21st Street; her husband had not returned from a mission on September 27. It was his eighth mission, according to a letter he wrote the day before taking off. Family members hoped for the best, but his six-month-old daughter Jan did not understand yet. It was about this time Orrin Grubbs came home from Fort Rucker, Alabama, for fifteen days furlough with his mother on B Avenue. When he left, his address was Company I, 320th Inf, APO 35, Nashville. Everyone had learned by this time the address meant he was with the 35th Infantry Division.

Every day the "Men in Service" column chronicled dozens of area men who had been transferred, promoted, assigned, or had come home on leave. A few notices of discharges appeared, as did an occasional AWOL. The discharges invariably told why the discharge had been made in order to avoid embarrassing questions from family and friends. Running into another man from New Castle or Henry County was also noteworthy, as when Harold Mitchell ran into Denby Byrnes, G. William Bailey, and K. Felkins on a South Pacific island, perhaps in the Solomons.

After renewed attacks that may have reached four hundred bombers per day, Air Corps generals hinted that these might be preliminary to an invasion of Germany "across the English Channel and North Sea." There was talk of "invasion before Christmas" but few details. The Russians still clamored for a second front, in spite of the fighting in Italy which had moved north of Naples toward Cassino in the rain and mud against stiff German defensive action. Gaining the advantage in the air was as important as destroying German factories and transport, and the report of three hundred German planes shot down in three days helped morale at home.

In mid-October, there was a press report of a new Super Bomber in production which dwarfed the B-24s and B-17s which were the mainstay of the war effort. The new plane, called the B-29, would make all "small bombers" obsolete. Designed for use over Europe, it would not be ready for combat until early in 1944. They would be needed, along with the accelerated production of other bombers and fighters.

The AP reported on October 15 that the Air Corps had raided Schweinfurt again, suffering sixty more bombers shot down. The Germans claimed 123 American aircraft were shot down. Finally, on October 16 the Air Corps brass, in the person of General Henry H. "Hap" Arnold, no less, justified the raids in the press. He admitted that 593 crewmen had been lost with the 60 aircraft, but he insisted that because 50 percent of all ball and roller bearing production took place there, and because there had been heavy damage to all three plants, this was a serious blow to the German war effort. He made no reference to the August raid that had been so costly, but there must not have been enough damage the first time, or it would not have been necessary to go back. Arnold assured everyone that we were gaining "the upper hand." The president also had something to say about it. Losses were not likely to exceed the numbers of new planes and crews arriving for duty every day, and losses like those experienced over Schweinfurt did not happen every day, anyway. General LeMay, head of the Heavy Bombardment Division, asserted that German industry would be so smashed by the spring of 1944 that the "Nazis won't be able to fight effectively on land or sea or in the air."

The bombing would go on. The boys who had been so anxious to get into the Air Corps when the war began were beginning to find out that while it might be glorious to tell about back home after training, the reality in the fighter-infested skies over Europe was different. Every bomber carried hundreds of gallons of gasoline in rubber tanks in the wings, and offered no armor protection for its crew. When Messerschmitt and Focke-Wulf fighters came at them at 350 m.p.h., there was very little that was glorious about it.

The Ration Board closed its offices on two different days the third week in October 1943 to prepare for registration and issuance of twenty thousand copies of War Ration Book #4 at the schools. Teachers again handled the task at the schools throughout the county. To get the #4 books, consumers had to turn in the #3 books. Every week, new stamps became valid and others expired in the books already issued. The Indiana Food Distribution Administration urged Hoosiers to buy bulk quantities of the bumper crop of potatoes and store them in basements. "Hoard" was the actual word they used, saying that it was justified in this situation because it would relieve pressure on storage facilities needed for Lend-Lease and other government programs. Other midwestern states also had record crops. The Michigan yield was fully one-third larger than the previous year.

On October 19, word appeared in the paper that SSgt. Clarence Laboyteaux was a prisoner of the Italian government. This was a little confusing, since the Italians had surrendered and joined the Allies, but there had been no exchange of prisoners yet. His parents had been notified by the Red Cross on October 9 that he was a prisoner, but did not know where he was being held, or by whom. Not until the end of January would they actually get word directly from him. There was also news that day that Pvt. James Kennedy had been given the Purple Heart award posthumously for his fatal wound on New Georgia. On the 27th, Mrs. Louise Bowers of Spiceland received notification that her husband, SSgt. Vaughn Bowers, had been on one of the 60 bombers that had not returned from the second Schweinfurt raid on

October 14. A graduate of the Cadiz high school in 1929, Bowers and his wife had two children, both under two years old. It was almost monotonous now. There would be a big raid or a big battle, then two weeks, three weeks, or a month later, the telegrams would start to arrive. On November 1, Mrs. J. N. Denny received a postcard dated July 11 from her husband, Pvt. Everett Denney, the first word she had had from him since he had been captured in North Africa in February. He was safe in Stammlager III in Germany. SSgt. Denver Canaday turned up missing twice on missions over France in July and August, and both times made it back to England. SSgt. Richard Scott's family learned on November 4 that he was a prisoner of the Germans, as had the family of "Rabbit" Baker. The fear of future casualties grew as talk of invading Europe increased. The Russians reported that they had caused the deaths of five million German soldiers but said nothing of their own losses.

The UMW continued its dance with the government as nearly all the 374,000 soft coal miners walked off the job again November 1, the same day that the War Department announced that American troops had invaded Bougainville. Not until November 4 did the miners start back to work. Again the bitter lesson came home to Americans that John L. Lewis cared more about taking advantage of the urgent need for coal than he did for the war effort. A coal strike in the summer was bad enough, but a coal strike as winter began meant that everyone might be cutting trees and huddling in cold rooms.

On November 1, 1943, Gemma's sister Maxine married SSgt. Kenneth Thompson of Hagerstown at the Presbyterian parsonage in Elko, Nevada. By this time, Kenny Thompson had been sent to Wendover Field, Utah, for additional training in the B-24 Liberator. Kenny had been introduced to Maxine by his friend, Orville Hammond. Orville became their sister Marie's steady date, and because he did not have access to a car, often talked Kenny into driving them to New Castle so he could see her. It was easy to introduce Kenny to Maxine, who was often at the house if she was not working at her job at the Ingersoll Steel lab. When Kenny began to date Maxine, it was much easier to talk Kenny into driving over to New Castle. By this time, Marie, although still in high school, was working at Perfect Circle in Hagerstown. She rode the bus the eleven miles to the plant after school, but when possible, she waited in Hagerstown for Orville to get off work at the theater. They then had a little time to get a Coke or something to eat before Kenny drove them back to New Castle. Maxine and Kenny continued to correspond after he went into the service in October 1942. After basic training in Texas, Kenny went to gunnery training, then to advanced training at the B-24 plant in Ypsilanti, Michigan. When this phase ended in September 1943, Kenny came home to Hagerstown for a week's leave before his next assignment. For a month before, in their letters, Kenny had pushed the idea of getting married, but the uncertainty of his assignment made them hesitate. Kenny slipped an engagement ring he bought in Ypsilanti on Maxine's finger when he was home. She was proud to wear it, but there was no telling when they might be able to make it permanent. He was not sure where he was going, but he promised Maxine he would write when he got there.

Kenny left in time to fly to his next assignment by September 13, and when he got to Wendover Field in the Utah desert, he immediately called to tell her where he was. He did not know how long he would be there, but why didn't she come on out and they would get married? It took a month to make preparations at home and in Utah, then Maxine boarded a train in New Castle for the West. When Kenny met her, he found her a place to stay for the night, then the next day, November 1, 1943, they went to a parsonage in Elko, Nevada, one hundred miles to the west, where the ceremony was performed. Another Air Corps couple stood up with them. The occasion was even less elaborate than Gemma's wedding had been. The only gift was a white lace handkerchief that Ethel had sent along with Maxine for the occasion. Similarly, there was not much of a honeymoon. Kenny had to fly again the next day. They finally found a small place to rent in Wells, sixty miles away from the base, so Maxine only saw him when he had enough time off to make the trip. The second of their four daughters had been married, and again Jess and Ethel had not been able to attend the ceremony. Military chaplains and civilian pastors in towns near army posts all over the country were busy performing marriages for couples far away from home.

Kenny's assignment was very hush-hush. Most days, small

Kenny Thompson and Maxine Moles Thompson, at Elko, Nevada, shortly after their wedding on November 1, 1943. By this time, Kenny was into advanced training on the new B-24 Liberator bombers at Wendover Field, Utah.

groups or individual aircraft practiced bombing runs or fine-tuned their routines and duties in the dry air over the desolate Nevada-Utah border. He told Maxine that if he did not return some evening, she would know that way that he had left for another assignment, probably overseas. They cherished the hours they shared during the few weeks they had together, but, just as Kenny had predicted, one morning in December, Maxine heard the entire squadron form up overhead, then fly off to the east. None of the planes returned that night or the next. It was time for Maxine to go back to New Castle. She returned there to await word from Kenny with no way to know when that word might come. If there was a crash on the way to his assignment, it might not come at all. Maxine, like everyone else, tried not to think about such a possibility. She assumed that he had gone overseas, but could not know where or when until he wrote. As it turned out, Kenny and his group had merely entered the final phase of their training, flying long, coordinated missions to various parts of the United States to sharpen their formation flying skills. He wrote that he was still officially based at Wendover but did not expect to be there long. He would have a short leave before going overseas, he thought, and he would let her know as soon as he found out when it would begin.

In New Castle, the effort to recruit women into the WAC and WAVES (Women Accepted for Volunteer Emergency Service) continued. Elizabeth Burden, who had grown up on top of the hill next to the Smith place in the hollow, enlisted as a WAVE in November 1943. She was older than Ed, having graduated with the high school's Class of 1938, then going to work in the office at the Chrysler. She left for training at Hunter College in New York. On November 16, SSgt. Keith Goar's picture appeared on the front page of the paper along with a story confirming his death in a crash in the European Theater of Operations (ETO). A 1941 Spiceland High School graduate, he enlisted in August 1942, and had been in England for only six weeks. He served as a ball turret gunner on a B-17. The same week, another New Castle family got the bad news. Sgt. Charles Brown, of North Main Street, died over East Harling, England, on November 8. He had been in England only a month. There were no details of what had happened. His wife and two-month-old daughter received his Purple Heart along with routine thanks and condolences from the government.

The last stamp in the #2 ration book expired at midnight, November 20, 1943. The ration board assured bookholders that they could discard book #2 when they used the stamp or after it expired, but it cautioned everyone not to confuse it with book #1, which still had a stamp good for a pair of shoes. Green coupons A, B, and C remained valid until December 20 for canned and processed goods. Brown stamps G, H, J, and K for meats and fats still could be used until December 4. OPA issued a new point scale for meats early in December, reducing the point values for most cuts by two. One other practice began in December and soon became standard across the country. OPA began issuing red ration points, the ration coupon "change" when purchasing cuts, for used cooking fats. Every household began to save drippings to turn in at the meat counter at the grocery store. These fats were needed to produce glycerine for gunpowder, medicines, and for other wartime uses. A pound of used fat could be exchanged for two red points plus 4¢. The government wanted it in cans which could be melted down, not in glass.

News of new fighting came in from the Pacific. The navy announced that Americans had invaded beaches in the Gilbert Islands, including Makin and Tarawa. But it was progress. It was the first invasion north of the equator, according to the press. Was this the first sign of a new drive in the central Pacific? In Italy, American and British forces still moved forward, but progress there had slowed to a crawl in the terrible mud and storms of the fall. It was a little ominous that there had been so few New Castle casualties from Italy. Maybe it would stay that way. Elmer Pfenninger of 18th and Plum Streets arrived safely in England according to his wife Florence. His brother, Sgt. Alvis Pfenninger, got the good conduct medal at his B-17 base in England where he served as a carburetor and ignition specialist on a bomber crew. On November 30, a message arrived for the mother of Sgt. Charles Loer reporting that he had been killed in New Guinea on November 26. There were no details of his death. He was another member of the NCHS Class of 1940, and was an air crew gunner. He also had been a *Courier-Times* paperboy.

When December began, the armchair generals had undertaken the analysis of the attack on Tarawa. There had been heavy loss of life, we now knew. Marine General Smith compared it to Pickett's Charge at Gettysburg, except that this one succeeded. Even the generals admitted that the losses had been heavier than any other American force had suffered in the war so far. No one released any official numbers until December 15. Then, on the back page, the numbers were listed: fifty-two hundred Japanese casualties, more than one thousand dead and twenty-five hundred wounded Americans on Tarawa, and 65 dead and 121 wounded on Makin. The battle for Guadalcanal, which went on for six months, cost fewer casualties. This struggle lasted seventy-six hours. Practically all the casualties had been marines. New assault techniques would come out of the lessons learned at Tarawa, military officials assured the public. There had been the usual fanatical Japanese resistance, requiring flamethrowers to clear some of the log and concrete bunkers. There was open talk of an assault on the Marshall Islands, 250 miles to the northwest.

There was a long way to go before the war could be won. The two Henry County draft boards selected the first men who had been married prior to Pearl Harbor in their calls for the first week in December. In the same December 8 paper appeared a photo of the first New Castle man to complete the required twenty-five combat missions over occupied Europe. SSgt. Donald Ellis, tail and waist gunner on a B-17, was shown at the waist position aiming his .50 caliber machine gun.

As the year waned, President Roosevelt announced that General Dwight Eisenhower would be the Allied leader of the invasion of Europe. British naval vessels sank the German battleship *Scharnhorst,* and Sgt. Argil Doyle of Walnut Street in New Castle died of a brain abcess in San Antonio. Sgt. Canaday came home on leave after his two narrow escapes. Eisenhower predicted that the Allies would win the European war in 1944. Predictions of record casualties in the first three months of the new year led many to speculate that the invasion would come then. It was clear to many observers that although fighting continued in Italy it was no longer considered a major operation and would not be the place to strike the final blow at Germany. There were soon reports of invasion rehearsals by American troops in England.

Home Again

Ed's AA battery had begun to work well together by December. After trips back and forth to Camp Irwin, they smoothed the rough edges and became comfortable with field operations. Ed was flattered when a new officer, 1Lt. Shafer, arrived at Camp Haan and was assigned to him. Shafer was fresh out of West Point, but he was new to the army. He asked Ed's advice the next morning when the men went out to hike. His shoes bothered him that first day, so Ed showed him how to wear them in the shower to shape them to his feet. There were the usual tricks of carrying empty cans, toughening the feet in cold water after a hike, and changing socks often. Even though Shafer's rank was the same as Ed's, he drew a less desirable assignment because he lacked the seniority and experience that Ed had. There was no rivalry. The men of all ranks helped each other get along. When they went into action, they would all help each other survive.

Ed got leave to go home over the Christmas holiday. It was a long trip, but they both wanted to go, so they made preparations. They were unable to book a train with a sleeping berth from Riverside, so they decided to drive home in the '39 Buick. They only made it to about Ludlow, east of Barstow on Route 66, when they blew a tire. This left them with no spare, and the problem which led to the blowout would certainly lead to more trouble on the long trip home. Dejected, they made repairs and drove back to Riverside. They tried one more time to get train tickets, and this time, due to a cancellation, there were two sleeper seats on the Southern Pacific's famous *Chief* from Riverside to St. Louis. They were expensive, but they took them, went to the station, and boarded the next day. This train was one of many famous for speed and luxury in its day. They were coming home from California on the *Chief*! This was another of the undreamed-of adventures that had happened to them since they had been married just four months before. In St. Louis they made connections for Indianapolis, and from there took the bus along the National Road to Dunreith and then up State Road 3 to New Castle. As they approached Riley Road on the south side of town, they asked the driver to stop. The two of them stepped out into the crisp white snow that had been falling heavily the last half-hour. They each took a small bag and held on to each other as they walked the quarter mile to the crest of the hill in front of the Burden's house and down into the hollow. The snow made Gemma's feet cold in her open-toed shoes as they walked silently along, but she did not care. When they turned into the drive at the house it was approaching 10:00 P.M. that Christmas Eve, and they could see that all the lights were out and his folks were already in bed. There was no sound from the cow in the barn or the chickens in the henhouse as they crossed the last fifty yards to the house. They quietly climbed up the snow-covered front steps and tried the door. It was locked. When they knocked, Fred came to the door and to his great delight, discovered their only son and his wife at the door. Their boy had come home for Christmas 1943.

9. Despair and Bitter Hope, 1944

Assignment: ETO

THE HOLIDAY SURPRISE Ed and Gemma brought to their families and friends did not last long. Jess, Ethel, Marie, and Wanda were just as surprised to see them on Christmas Day as Fred and Lillian had been on Christmas Eve. It was a joyous but restrained Christmas, because there were not many things that a serviceman needed as gifts, and they did not spend much money on such things anyway. Gemma caught up on the news from Martha and from Sarah, but most of the time they spent together at the two houses they had left when they got married. They stayed at the hollow the first night, then went to Plum Street. Their reception at the little farm was warm, but the arrangements were less so. The only really comfortable room was the kitchen. At night the stoves there and upstairs died down and the house was always cold in the morning. Going to the outhouse first thing in the morning was a necessary, but not a very good, way to start the day. The bone-chilling cold and unpleasant odors had to be tolerated, and Gemma was glad when they went to stay in town the next day.

Fred took his son aside just before he was to leave and told him that he had something for him. He had asked around and located an army model 1911 .45 caliber semi-automatic pistol that someone was willing to sell, and he had bought it. He wanted

Ed to take it with him when he went overseas. Officers were authorized to wear sidearms, but they were not provided unless they were considered necessary. Fred, from his experience in the Great War and from reading the papers, must have thought it might come in handy. Ed wrapped it up and took it with him.

Ed went to the plant on another day with his father to look around at the home front production efforts and to say hello to people they knew. He saw steel blocks in the forge room and similar ones down in the machine shop where they were being precision-ground to specifications. He asked the men working on them what they were, but they didn't know. Ed told them that they were the firing blocks for the 40 mm anti-aircraft guns he had learned to fire at Fort Bliss. His own father and father-in-law might have worked on any of the guns he and his crew would be using.

On January 3, they said their good-byes again and headed back west. Train stations and trains everywhere they went were invariably packed with soldiers, sailors, and marines and their loved ones going to or from assignments just as Ed and Gemma were. Ed had just returned to Camp Haan when he learned that he had been selected to help fill a new unit (the 23rd Replacement Battalion) that would be going overseas. He had had a vague notion for some time that he had gotten on the bad side of his executive officer, a first lieutenant, but had never been able to put his finger on a specific incident that might have caused it. They never quite hit it off, somehow, and this was the only reason Ed could figure that he was being shipped out. The AA platoon that he had worked with was in good shape and performing well, and there had been no confrontations. It was a mystery. Strangest of all was his assignment. He was not going to another AA unit; he was assigned to a replacement battalion whose job would be to receive, process, and ship replacement soldiers for other units to their destinations. These units would be needed, of course, but why him? Why had the army spent all this time training him for ack-ack if a lieutenant could place him in a completely different unit out of mysterious personal pique?

He was to go to Camp Cooke, just north of Lompoc, California. Camp Cooke was preliminary to his being shipped overseas, so Gemma could not go. Ed sold the Buick. What little there was

Kenny Thompson came home on leave the end of February 1944, just before his crew flew their B-24 to England to join the 8th Air Force. Maxine had already come back to Plum Street. In the background, the morale-boosting poster reads "AMERICANS DON'T QUIT." No one knew how long the war would last, or if a farewell might be forever.

in the way of linens and belongings Gemma either gave away or stowed in her suitcases. The third week in February they said good-bye in California, knowing that there was no telling when, if ever, they might see each other again, and Gemma got on the train to make the journey to New Castle. They gave up their little apartment in glamorous California and went separate ways. It was a long, sad trip for her. She had grown up in adversity and she knew how to handle it, but this was different. Sometimes the desert landscape blurred with tears as the train huffed and clicked eastward and she thought of the wonderful days and nights they had spent together. By the time she arrived in New Castle, she had cried herself out and had resolved to make the best of it for him. Only if they both got through what lay ahead could there be a golden day of reunion. That day quickly faded away into the future as only the dimmest of hopes. It could be years before she saw him again, and for now even an hour was an agony.

Maxine had been back at the house on Plum Street for a little over a month when Gemma arrived. Maxine had just spent a few bittersweet days with Kenny, who had gotten a furlough from his flying duties before going overseas. He arrived in New Castle from Utah on January 4, and had to report back on January 11. They both knew that he would be leaving soon, but the need to visit his family in Hagerstown and hers in New Castle left them little time to themselves. They stayed with Kenny's brother Bert and his wife because there was a spare room at their house in Hagerstown. There was a little privacy there, at least. They visited at Plum Street during the daytime. After four days, he was gone again. Maxine got by very well on his sergeant's pay of $114 a month plus 20 percent for service overseas. He received 50 percent additional pay when he flew frequently. Most of this went home to Maxine to save for their future.

The best thing for Gemma to do was to stay busy. She got her old job back at Public Service which would help pass the time. She wrote letters nearly every day when she got home from work, and she learned every detail of the mail service in New Castle. With Ed gone overseas, letters were her lifeline. The mail came twice a day on weekdays, so she often called to see if anything had arrived for her in the morning delivery. If it had not, she checked for mail first thing upon her arrival back at the house on Plum Street after work. She could have the satisfaction of writing and sending letters every day. But she was at the mercy of the wartime mail for receiving any. Ed could not write every day because of his duties, and even if he had, that would not assure a steady, daily stream of arrivals on Plum Street.

He was at Camp Cooke for only about two weeks. The army shipped his new unit to Camp Kilmer, New Jersey, for transfer to England. When he arrived in New Jersey he called Gemma to tell her where he was and to guess that he might be there two or three days. While at Camp Kilmer, he did one thing that thousands of GIs did just before going overseas. He had a portrait done at a photo studio on the post, and paid for it in advance so that the prints could be sent home to Gemma and his mother and father. There was no way to tell who would come home and who would fall. This was a way to preserve forever the twenty-two-year-old son in his army officer's uniform. If something happened, they would always be able to remember him strong, proud, and whole. When these prints got home, they went proudly into frames in prominent places on the mantels.

They took trains to the docks in New York City, another place Ed had never expected to go. He was expecting a troopship, and he got one. It was the liner *Queen Mary.* Luxury ocean travel was something that the Vanderbilts and Rockefellers could afford, but not many people he knew from New Castle. Of course, in wartime, Uncle Sam could afford it. Ed received his stateroom assignment then he boarded and began the long wait. To lose a troopship the size of this one to hostile action would be the equivalent to losing a major battle on land. A submarine could fire a pattern of two or three torpedoes, costing only a few thousand dollars, which could sink such a ship in a matter of minutes. It would be a very cheap victory, and one that was much sought. "Wolf Packs" of German submarines patrolled the stormy waters of the North Atlantic throughout the war seeking merchant vessels and troopships that were keeping England alive and transporting the men and materiel of war that would be needed in an invasion some day. The more ships that could be sunk, the longer such an invasion could be put off. During the worst of the U-boat depredations in 1942, the Allies lost as much as five hundred thousand tons of shipping per month. Emergency construction programs to build basic "Liberty Ships" attempted to replace the vessels faster than they could be sunk. By the time Ed boarded the *Queen Mary,* shipping losses had fallen to under two hundred thousand tons per month, still a serious problem, but considered within endurable limits. The most telling statistic of this struggle on the water was the number of missing members of the merchant marine. At the middle of October 1943, there were forty-one hundred missing already, one-sixth of what the army reported missing, and half that of the navy. Whereas many army missing eventually became prisoners, only one hundred merchant sailors were known to be prisoners at that time.

To protect a large liner full of soldiers, the War Department took extraordinary precautions. Typically, they left at night so that vessels could not be silhouetted against city lights. Once at sea, engines turned at maximum speed for the shortest possible trip. Screens of destroyers, Coast Guard cutters, and sometimes larger warships such as cruisers and battleships escorted the convoy. By the time Ed crossed the Atlantic, escort carriers had begun to accompany convoys to supplement long-range patrol bombers. Cruisers and battleships could launch seaplanes from catapults on their sterns and recover them, which helped maintain vigilance and direct fire if submarines or hostile surface vessels came near. All of these efforts helped provide an uneventful crossing for the soldiers who sailed with Ed. They arrived in Scotland early in March 1944, after a crossing of five days.

This did not mean that the folks back home had no worries. On February 18, the army reported that one thousand soldiers had lost their lives in the sinking of a troopship in European waters. As many as one thousand had been saved, but the report did not say where the ship had been bound. There was great secrecy about sailing dates. Ed was still in California then, Gemma thought, but there was no way to know for sure.

Kenny Thompson avoided the danger of submarines on his way to his new assignment. He was going to the ETO also, and his bomb group would be taking their aircraft with them. Flying the Lindbergh route was considered too long and too risky to send entire formations of bombers that way, and besides, there were not many bases that could handle scores of heavy bombers should they be held up by storms. Particularly in February and March, the Atlantic was a forbidding place for an aircraft. They took a longer but safer route south to Central America, then to the east coast of South America, across to Dakar in French Senegal, to Marrakech in Morocco, then around Spain to England. Kenny and his crew left on March 1, and arrived at their base at Rackheath, England, on March 19 after many hours of flying time. Rackheath was in East Anglia, the flat farming area east and north of London where so many bomber and fighter squadrons made their homes. By the time his first letter to Maxine telling her where he was stationed arrived in New Castle a month later, he had already flown his first two missions.

Building Up to the Big Show

An unprecedented operation was clearly under way. Nearly every day in the first months of 1944, the *Courier-Times* printed notices that soldiers had arrived safely in England or in North Africa, the staging area for the Italian campaign. In January, Earl Spears arrived in North Africa. Harry Ridout, Ed's high school friend, arrived in England the end of January after completing his training as a medic. Harry's buddy Robert Pitts, also a medic, got there in February. Sarah notified the paper early in February that Clay Grubbs had arrived safely somewhere in the Pacific. Miss Rucker's picture, showing her in her Red Cross uniform, appeared in the paper on March 15 to announce that she had arrived safely in England. Fred Walker arrived there about the same time.

It was winter in Europe, and the going was difficult for everyone. The Russians made some headway against the Germans in the snow, but warm weather brought big gains in the Ukraine and into Rumania. The Russians also reported discovering the graves of ten thousand Polish Army officers in the Katyn Forest, near Smolensk. Evidence pointed, they said, to the Germans because of documents dated to the time the Germans had occupied the area in 1941. The Germans said the officers had been shot in 1940, when the Russians held the area.

The British and Americans made very little progress in Italy during the winter, battering German positions along the Gustav Line south of Rome. The third week in January Allied troops made an amphibious landing at Anzio, just a few miles south of Rome, in a flanking move that would, it was hoped, cause the Germans to abandon the Gustav Line. At the same time they launched new attacks at Cassino, but they failed to prevent the Germans from moving several divisions south to oppose the Allied forces in the Anzio area. Although their landing was unopposed and they put fifty thousand troops ashore in the first two days, there was no effort to effect a major advance until the Germans had reinforced their positions. They were only thirty miles from Rome, but the going was tough again in the January mud and cold. New Castle boys were there. Cpl. Philip Morris of New Castle stepped on a mine in Italy on January 16. He lost his foot below the ankle, but considered himself lucky. He wrote home from the hospital in South Carolina that of the original members of his infantry company who had fought with him in North Africa and Italy, he was the only one left alive. He had healed rapidly and the artificial foot would allow him to walk, and even run, without a limp. For the next four months, the Allies tried to break out of the Anzio area against strong opposition.

Then there came news of atrocities against American soldiers captured in the Philippines. Three officers who experienced the brutality and escaped brought stories of brutal treatment of sick and wounded prisoners in Japanese camps. Deliberate starvation, beatings, and beheadings had been the daily routine for some thirty-six thousand Allied prisoners after their capture on Bataan and Corregidor. More than twenty-two hundred American prisoners had died in one camp alone in April and May 1942, immediately after their capture. Those who had fallen during the forced march to the camp were bayoneted or shot. It made the gas shortage at home seem pretty trivial by comparison. To add insult to injury, the local postmaster announced that there could be no endorsements or slogans promoting the war effort on envelopes going to prisoners of war. They would not be allowed through. This included the cancellations put on by post offices. There could be no V for Victory, Buy War Bonds and Stamps, or any other slogan so common here at home.

The first news of action in the Pacific often came from the Japanese. Such was the case on February 1, when first word of the attack on the Marshall Islands came via the Associated Press from Japanese broadcasts. Sure enough, the next day the War Department confirmed that a large task force had attacked Kwajalein atoll. AP reported that more than two million tons of Allied warships made up the fleet which had attacked the islands and supported the assault. A map in the paper that day showed that we were moving west. The Marshalls were north of the Solomons, twenty-three hundred miles west and a little south of Hawaii, and twenty-six hundred miles from Japan. This time navy ships and bombers pounded the islands for four days in what one reporter called the heaviest bombardment of the war. Tiny Kwajalein cost 370 American dead and 1,500 wounded. Roi and Namur, other atolls in the area, cost 740 casualties. On Kwajalein, only 265 of the 8,700-man Japanese garrison surrendered. The rest were killed. On Roi and Namur, nearly every one of the thirty-seven hundred Japanese died.

The pace of the bombing continued to pick up in Europe. B-17s went to Schweinfurt again and blasted major cities in raids of as many as eight hundred bombers. Gemma's cousin Glenn Cowan came home on leave after his promotion to corporal, and went to the dance after the basketball tourney late that winter in New Castle. Marie Moles, Judy Capshaw, and Jean Linebeck from Plum Street also went. Several other soldiers and sailors home on leave showed up, too. Two days after the dance, a War Department telegram arrived in New Castle for the wife and family of Pfc. James Spitler. He was dead on a Pacific island that the Marine Corps would not reveal. Once he reported for duty in October 1942, he had never been able to come home on leave.

Better news arrived on March 4, 1944. The first American bombers hammered Berlin in force in daylight raids. American fighter planes flew with them all the way, a change, since they had not had the range to get that far for all of 1943. These fighter planes included the new Mustang fighters, a secret design whose pictures had not yet appeared in the papers. Now American heavy bombers faced better odds of reaching their targets and being able to concentrate on delivering their bombs accurately. On March 8 they went back for the fourth raid in eight days, this time with incendiary bombs along with the high explosive types. The newspaper reports spoke of two thousand fighters and bombers over the capital and 176 German fighters shot down. This was really applying the one-two punch. The next day they were at it again, but listed the American losses for the four previous raids at 130 bombers and 55 fighters, which meant as many as 1,355 men lost over Berlin. It was a fearsome price to pay, but the London *Daily Mail*, familiar with bombing raids on cities, remarked that the failure of the Germans to prevent the bombers from reaching Berlin day after day might "herald the downfall of the German air force." Family members hoped it was true. Men were still being trained as fast as possible to replace the crews that were being lost every day. In the same day's paper was the picture of newly commissioned Lt. Earl Chandler, of the Class of 1940, who had arrived home on leave to visit his parents on P Avenue. He had just completed bombardier training in New Mexico. Just a few days later, the paper carried a picture of a white puff of smoke that was all that remained of a B-17 that had exploded over Berlin.

The same day came the announcement of New Castle's first woman casualty of the war. Second Lt. Elizabeth Howren of A Avenue in New Castle, an army nurse, died in the crash of a medical evacuation plane in Italy. She had been in the Nurse

Corps just a year, and had only been in the ETO for nine weeks. Howren was a little older, from the Class of 1933, than many of the men in service because she had done her nurse's training as a civilian at Methodist Hospital in Indianapolis and then served as a surgery nurse at the hospital in New Castle.

On March 14, 1944, OPA cut the A ration allotment for gasoline from three gallons to two in the Midwest and West. This equalized the allotment across the country, since the East Coast had been on a two-gallon A coupon rule for some time. A squadron of four-engined bombers burned a thousand gallons of gasoline every few minutes while it was in the air. Every jeep, armored car, aircraft, and most trucks burned it every day. The people at home would just have to do with less. The Indiana OPA estimated the number of counterfeit gas ration stamps in state ration banks at three percent, considerably better than the 18 percent estimate just a few weeks before.

Headlines trumpeted the GREATEST CONCENTRATED BOMBING ATTACK IN HISTORY against Cassino on March 15, as Allied aircraft dumped fourteen hundred tons of bombs in an area less than one square mile. German troops had taken up strong defensive positions in the ruined town and abbey, barring the way for advance up the Italian peninsula for more than five months. The Anzio landings were supposed to flank this position and allow the armies to push northward, but the Germans had stopped both. Casualties mounted as the weeks went by and fruitless attacks failed to reduce the positions. This saturation bombing, dangerous to those who inflicted it and devastating to the Germans, might do the trick, but it failed too. With the cost mounting a week later, the Allies stopped the attack and consolidated. They could not seem to break the Cassino line. The Italian campaign was a mess. There had been little progress for almost six months when confirmation came from the War Department that American and German anti-aircraft units had joined together to shoot down twenty-three American transport planes full of paratroopers after the Allied units mistook them for Germans. This took place in July 1943, but the news had only just come out. The 410 crewmen and paratroopers were with the 82nd Airborne Division, part of a flight of 170 aircraft supporting the Allied landings at Gela, in Sicily.

Invasion speculation continued in the barbershops and on the street corners, but it abated in papers because the government asked that it stop. Enemy agents would be on the lookout for all such information and might learn vital secrets about where the landings would actually take place. It was obvious that this was the year that the invasion, somewhere along the northwest European coast, would take place. Our bombers and fighters continued to pound the Germans, and the casualty rate, even in New Castle, showed it. Second Lieutenant Dale Wilkinson, 15th Air Force B-17 bombardier, was reported missing over Italy. He had already been wounded on a previous mission. Wilkinson was another New Castle boy who had signed up to serve with the National Guard like Clay Grubbs, but had taken an opportunity to go to bombardier school and become an officer in the Air Corps. He was also a member of the Class of 1940 who had been sent his diploma while he was away on duty. He ended up in a German prison camp, too. Pfc. William Brewer was lost over Italy January 22 and declared missing. A post card from him reached his home the end of March.

The same front page carried the picture and story of SSgt. George Woods, who had been awarded the Distinguished Flying Cross after fifteen missions over Europe from his base in England. Woods had shot down two German fighters as they attacked his formation on a mission to Schweinfurt. Woods completed twenty-six missions in early May and came home to New Castle for three weeks leave before going to his next assignment. Just a couple of days later, Cpl. James Moystner appeared in a front-page photo showing him working on one of the engines of a B-17 at a base in England. People in New Castle knew him as a Coca-Cola plant employee. The bombing increased. Between 1,250 and 1,750 bombers and fighters raided Berlin again. More missing and wounded appeared in the *Courier-Times*. With this evidence of activity, Britain banned civilians from a ten-mile-wide strip along seven hundred miles of coastline after April 1 due to invasion preparations. This included the entire southern coast of England and a third of the eastern coast as far north as the Wash. When would it begin and where would it strike?

An agonizing tale unfolded in the paper over several weeks for the family of SSgt. George Kessel, missing after a bombing raid to Germany. The War Department reported him missing February 4. A crew member from another aircraft reported that the plane went down on fire but under control after being hit by flak over France. A few days later letters arrived from other crewmen's families that two of the crew were safe and in German prison camps. There was a report that seven parachutes had been seen to open as the bomber went down. Finally, on March 30, the Adjutant General wired his parents that the Red Cross had reported Kessel a prisoner of the Germans. After seven weeks of suspense, they could relax a little, but there was no mention of the three crewmen who had not been seen to escape.

On April 10, after three weeks of briefings and practice formations, Kenny Thompson flew his first combat mission with the Eighth Air Force. The 467th Bomb Group attacked a German aircraft factory at Bourges, France, on a seven-hour mission which met no opposition and suffered no losses. P-47s escorted them all the way. The bombardier reported that their six one-thousand-pound bombs were right on target. The B-24 had been specifically designed to carry a larger bomb load than the B-17, and at long last, growing numbers of the awkward-looking aircraft were taking the war to a growing list of Nazi-occupied cities. A week later, the day before his letter reached Maxine, they flew again, this time to Brandenburg in eastern Germany, with a load of fifty-two incendiary bombs for another aircraft factory. This time there was flak, but his plane suffered only a single hole in a wing. In clouds on the way back to England, Kenny's plane and four others lost their formation and came home alone. He was relieved that the fighter planes that approached them after they lost the protection of the other bombers were little friends, Army Air Corps P-38s.

It was dangerous in the air, but it could be dangerous on the ground, too. On April 21, German fighter-bombers raided the Rackheath base, killing two bomber crews and a ground crewman in their quarters. Their missions continued when weather permitted. Low clouds sometimes forced them to bring bombs back, but usually the primary target or a target of opportunity could be hit. Sometimes even with heavy flak they returned without damage, but a peppering of holes in the fuselage was a common occurrence. The thin metal outer skin slowed the hot shrapnel down just enough, sometimes. Their bombardier was hit on the arm on a mission over Belgium on May 1, but was not hurt.

On their ninth mission on May 9, Kenny distinguished himself in a ticklish situation. On the way to Belgium again, Kenny's plane sustained flak damage to an engine and had to turn back. To reduce weight, they dropped their load of forty one-hundred-pound bombs on the coast, but ten of them caught on control cables in the bomb bay. Kenny and two other crew members crawled carefully along the catwalk between the bomb racks and lifted each of the bombs off the entangling cables and dropped them out by hand. Below them was nothing but air. Their plane, dubbed the "Palace Meat Market," landed safely with twenty-seven holes in it. Kenny flew only sporadically in May and June, then resumed regular missions in July.

This Place Is About to Sink!

Not until the third week of April did Gemma finally receive a letter from Ed assuring her that he had arrived safely in England. The troopship sinking she had read about in the paper had been in February, and surely she would have been notified before the end of March if he had been among the lost. When day after day went by without word from the War Department, her spirits rose, and finally, in the afternoon mail, the letter came. Everyone kept telling her that "no news is good news," and she learned that it was true, at least this time.

Assault troops trained in England and Scotland for the invasion, while other units went about their tasks of preparing to support them once they went ashore. The army wanted the camp for Ed's unit near Bath, England, and that's where they put it. As in the desert, it took time to establish field operations that ran smoothly. Latrines had to be dug, wires had to be run, trucks and jeeps had to be parked and maintained, offices had to be set up, and supplies located. Ed was with a new outfit now, so he had to begin learning who did what best and finding his way around. The job of a Replacement Depot (in GI jargon they were known as "repple-depples") was to shuttle men to the place they had been assigned. Until the invasion came off, there was not too much to do. Ed's unit did process and send forward the few men who came through, but most of the units preparing for the invasion had trained together at home and stayed together once they arrived in England. They were not losing men because they had not gone into action yet.

Once Ed's repple-depple had a place to establish camp, he had an address, and he soon received a wire from home. Like a wire from the War Department, it could be good news or bad news. Often it meant the loss of a loved one or news of a brother or sister in the service. This wire for Ed was news he had not expected. A few weeks after Gemma had returned to Plum Street, she began to wonder if she was pregnant. The doctor confirmed that she was. The baby was due sometime in the first week of August, the doctor guessed. This was big enough news to warrant the expense of a telegram. Ed had an APO, or Army Post Office address, when he went overseas, as did every GI. There could be no actual locations given in England or Italy or the Pacific, of course, because spies in the post office would be able to figure out where certain units were located, how many of them there were, and when they arrived at their positions. Soldiers posted to England or Italy usually had APO New York or APO Baltimore addresses. Sailors, marines, and army personnel in the Pacific, wherever they were, usually had APO San Francisco addresses. The army sent the mail where it went without telling anyone. Gemma sent her wire as soon as she learned of her condition, but Ed had already left for Europe. The wire waited until his unit had an address, and then he got it. He might be a father in August! Like thousands of other GIs, Ed had gotten married in wartime because there was no way to be sure that there would be a time called "after the war." That could be too late, and the chance for happiness for them might have been lost. Now, back home, there was a new life unique to the two of them. If all went well with Gemma when her time came, something of Ed would live on, even if the worst happened and he was killed. There was a new reason to get the war over as quickly as possible. He wrote back to her as soon as he found out, but the first letter that he had written when he arrived in Bath got there first. Their letters soon filled with news about how Gemma felt and how big she was getting.

Ed, like all GIs, could not say much about what he was doing, and nothing about where he was, beyond "somewhere in England." Everyone could at least say what country they were in. Ed usually wrote his reactions to what Gemma had written, limiting characterizations of his own circumstances to cheery generalizations. That was the safest thing to do. The papers had long ago quit divulging the unit identifications of the men from New Castle. There was no mention of unit, only vague references to duties and branches once a GI had finished training as a gunner or bombardier. As in the typical case of Kenny Thompson, there was no indication that he was in the 467th Bomb Group in Rackheath, East Anglia in England.

It was not long before Ed began to chafe at the minimal routine. From time to time, an opportunity would come up to travel in the countryside. A convoy officer was needed to take responsibility for reaching the destination with all the equipment and trucks intact, and when he could get away, Ed volunteered for this duty. He had never been one to visit the local pubs or seek excitement, so this gave him an opportunity to see the countryside and get to know England a little better. What struck him everywhere he went was the quantity of war materiel. He saw thousands of trucks, half-tracks, tanks, jeeps, steel drums, bridge trusses, boats, gas cans, Quonset huts, barrage balloons, and every other item in the army's equipment list placed, parked, and piled everywhere he went. There was so much of it that he wondered what kept England from sinking. Fields everywhere that were not planted in crops had sprouted acres of tents. MPs were thick, directing traffic and restricting access to air bases and headquarters units. Overhead, the drone of aircraft might be heard at any hour of the day or night. England was an army base, staggering under its load of Uncle Sam's property.

He began to look around. He was close to the Salisbury plain, and one day drove past Stonehenge. There was no one about, so he stopped and had a look. The countryside was already bright green with spring color, and the soft atmosphere made the war seem far away for a few minutes. Everything was so much older here. These stones were old when the Romans arrived in the first century. He also got to see a piece of Victorian England when he took a load of prisoners to the old circular prison at Cheltenham, where German prisoners of war (PWs) repaired shoes. When a jailer shut the great iron door behind Ed, the echoing boom scared him and renewed his determination not to earn a long-term stay at such a place. He went to Wells and looked around the famous cathedral and saw other towns in the south of England.

He often took convoys to Southampton, a major southern coastal port and major base of the Royal Navy. While there, he saw his first German aircraft, a jet-powered V-1 "Buzz bomb." He also saw what could happen when excited, inexperienced pilots were pushed into action. As the air raid sirens sounded, Ed spotted the pilotless V-1 as it approached from France. A Royal Air Force Spitfire pilot on patrol picked up the pursuit and made a furious effort to catch up with it. When the pilot began to get close, he opened fire with his wing-mounted machine guns. He kept firing as he approached, and just as he was about to lift fire and peel away, the buzz bomb exploded, destroying the Spitfire and killing the pilot. The debris fell over the docks below. It was easy to get killed in a plane.

One of Ed's duties as an officer was to censor the mail of the men under him. No word was supposed to leak out that might give the Germans any useful information about troop positions or plans. Much of the mail went back and forth on ships. Bags of mail floated off a freighter sunk by submarines in the Atlantic could be picked up by the Germans or intercepted in other ways. Early in the war, letters sometimes arrived home with words or sentences razored out by censors, but the task became too big for the post office, so the burden fell on lower-level officers. Postal censors did spot checks after that. Once the men learned the rules about what could and could not be written, there was little need to cut anything. Ed continued these duties the entire time that he was in Europe. Ed followed the same rules when he censored his own mail, so there was not much of importance to be discovered in a letter gone astray. Ed did not fancy himself much of a letter writer anyhow, so they tended to be short and sweet. Back on Plum Street, they were treasured. It was a very long lifeline.

Back home, it was a waiting game for Gemma. Days and even weeks sometimes went by without a letter from Ed, even though he wrote faithfully and regularly. Then she might get a handful all on the same day. The mail became even more important now.

The mail, the child she carried, and a few pictures were the only ways she could keep her hopes alive for his safe return.

Also back home, the government made it clear it would brook no opposition from any company that dared to defy the rules. The Attorney General, with the help of soldiers, took over the Montgomery Ward Company when its board chairman refused to acknowledge a labor order from the government. Sewell Avery, head of the huge mail-order company, refused to extend a contract to a CIO union until it could be confirmed that it represented a majority of the workers it claimed to represent. The government ordered the contract extended and, when Avery refused, he was arrested and hauled bodily from his Chicago office. Administration officials decided what was a fair way to operate a business and what was not, and would continue to do so for the duration.

The first of May brought more casualty reports in the *Courier-Times*. This time it was two dead, one wounded. One had been killed in Australia, probably in a plane crash, one had been killed in action on Bougainville, and the wounded man had been hit in Italy. There were some signs that the war was going well. The military governor of Hawaii announced the lifting of the nightly blackout that had been observed since the attack on Pearl Harbor. Since trials of the initial blackout plan in New Castle the whole notion had quietly been put aside. There was not much chance of German planes bombing New Castle when they did not bother England much any more. Then the OPA lifted ration restrictions at midnight, May 3, 1944, on all meats except beefsteaks and roasts. Ration administrators explained that Lend-Lease purchasing had slacked off, that the army and navy were buying less, and that government warehouses were full. That one about the army and navy was a little hard to believe, since more men went into the service every day, but at least it would be easier to buy meat now. Price controls still applied, of course.

It was a time of building anticipation for everyone about the coming invasion of Europe. For weeks the headlines told of the "air invasion" sweeps by every kind of aircraft to prepare for the landings. References to the "invasion coast" of France appeared, and reports monitored the levels of German fighter resistance, since Eisenhower had said that control of the air must come before the invasion could begin. By the first of May, there were days when no German fighter planes rose to meet the onslaught. Sometimes there were no losses among the attackers, even from flak, and this seemed even more miraculous after the terrible losses of the previous ten or twelve months. When the bombers went over now, they were usually escorted by numbers of P-51 Mustangs and P-47 Thunderbolts eager for Germans to engage. There were fewer and fewer who wanted to try it. The fighters began "fighter sweep" tactics flying low over the countryside looking for German troops and trains to attack.

Miss Rucker wrote of her visit to an American bomber base, offering something rare in the pages of the hometown paper, a local woman's view of what it was like for the men there. She told of a "tiny America" at the base in the English countryside with American GIs, jeeps, and Boeing B-17 bombers. She discovered that aircrews got up at 3:30 A.M. for a day's mission, had breakfast, warmed up their planes, and got into the air by 6 A.M. They circled the field until everyone had taken off, then assembled and headed off for their rendezvous and target points. The crews returned exhausted about 7 P.M. after flying, dropping their bombs, and watching for fighters all day. Miss Rucker got the opportunity to go up herself the next day, riding up in the Plexiglas nose where the bombardier sat. She could not say where the base was or which air division or bomb group flew out of it, but the many families in New Castle who had loved ones stationed at bomber bases in England felt a little closer to the war.

The invasion of Europe was just a matter of time now, and everyone knew it. Newspaper articles noted that Indiana towns and cities had decided to hold prayer services instead of celebrations when news of the invasion arrived, after parents of servicemen who would likely be involved objected. Front-page stories reminded everyone of what they already knew, that the big event could come at any moment. Headlines repeatedly called attention to the "air invasion" and anxious families back home hoped that the fighters and the flak spared the fliers they prayed for. The weather along the invasion coast was fine, the AP reported on May 20. Clear skies, a steady barometer, and cool temperatures over the Dover strait meant that another favorable day had come and gone. A thousand American bombers and twelve hundred fighter planes pounded targets almost daily by the end of the month, but there was still no invasion.

In Italy, Allied troops battered at the German defense line and struggled to link the forces that had landed at Anzio with the main elements of the American Fifth Army and the British Eighth Army southeast of Rome. Progress was spotty, and casualties continued to mount. Some days the Allies advanced, and some days the Germans pushed them back. British troops finally captured Cassino. By May 29, the AP reported that the Fifth Army was only seventeen miles from Rome. Progress was measured in captured villages and hills, much like on the Eastern Front, or in the Great War. The Germans fought bitterly and launched flame-thrower counterattacks all along the front, often bringing Allied advances to a standstill, and always extracting a heavy toll in blood and lives.

In New Castle, everyone waited for the big day of the invasion, but they did not have much to go on beyond what there was in the papers. Gemma had learned that the fastest letter from Ed in England took two to three weeks, and on the last day of May 1944, she had received nothing from him for about that long. The last letter she had received had been written in the middle of April, and with the anxiety over the imminent invasion, she worried constantly. Other wives she knew were in the same predicament. The mail seemed to have stopped since around the last week of April, and no one had received a letter in over two weeks. The Allies were probably worried about spies or submarines picking up hints in soldier mail, but everyone knew that there was very little of substance to be learned about the goings-on of the troops until long after the action had ended. From home, the assumption was that when the invasion took place, practically every soldier in England would cross over to France or Belgium. Every effort went toward delivering the maximum punch on the fighting front, and that's what the whole war effort was about. Everyone had to assume that if a loved one was in England, he was bound to be in the invasion.

While those on the home front waited those last days of May 1944, the time came once again for graduation from New Castle's high school and the commencement dance. Miss Rucker was absent from the guest list this time, of course, as were the other teachers who had enlisted, like Herbert Heller, the social studies teacher who had gone into the navy. Mrs. Heller attended, and Orrin and Clay's sister Erma enjoyed being named part of Queen Wanda Phillips's court of attendants for the evening. Barbara Bunch, who had gone to Gemma and Ed's wedding with Charlie Purvis, was there, as were Jean Linebeck and Roseann Poston from the days when the Moles girls were growing up. Marie Moles, a senior now, and her friend Rosemary Mitchell from Hagerstown went, but Orville was away in the navy, so she did not have a date. From further east on Plum Street, James Capshaw attended just three days after going to Fort Harrison at Indianapolis for his army physical. Monday's paper announced that he and fifty-five other boys, twenty-one of them from the Class of 1944, had passed and would be inducted immediately. The paper said that Capshaw would go to the navy, but he went to the Commencement Dance the following Thursday first. There was a sprinkling of servicemen there, too, including SSgt. George Woods, home from Eighth Air Force bombers in England. For the baccalaureate, Reverend Thompson of the New Castle First Christian Church called on the seniors to take part in the creation of a brave new world of the future.

A few weeks before graduation, Gemma and Sarah drove out to The Spot, one of New Castle's favorite teen locations, to get a Coke and visit. In the adjacent car, some high school boys whistled and tried to flirt with them. Sarah, eight months pregnant, and without cracking a smile, asked Gemma, six months pregnant, if she thought they should get out of the car to show them how big their bellies were. When the mothers-to-be erupted in gales of laughter, the humiliated and bewildered boys could only wonder at the mystery of women. There was just no understanding them.

10. Invasion, 1944

THE WEEKEND AFTER commencement for the Class of '44 was quiet, and Monday was the same. The Allies took Rome that Sunday and Monday when German forces decided to evacuate and fight farther to the north. Gemma had a small radio on the table next to her bed in the house on Plum Street, and in the early morning hours of Tuesday morning, June 6, 1944, she sleepily turned over and switched on the set. It took thirty seconds or so to warm up, and she had almost fallen asleep again when she heard General Eisenhower's plain Kansas accent come through the air suddenly. Allied troops had landed that morning on the coast of France, embarking on a great crusade to liberate captive Europe from Nazi oppression. Soon, paperboys were walking neighborhood streets shouting "Extra!" and offering the invasion news in print for three cents. The headlines read

ALLIES BEGIN INVASION OF EUROPE;
TROOPS SWARM FRENCH BEACHES

Reports placed Allied forces all along the coast from Brest to Le Havre, which included much of Brittany and Normandy. Allied battlewagons, cruisers, and aircraft of every sort smashed, shelled, and bombed targets everywhere in the vicinity of the landings, and naval gunfire was reported by Allied reporters landing as far as eleven miles inland.

Toward midday, a second extra edition of the paper came out, announcing that American, British, and Canadian forces had actually secured beachheads in Normandy and Brittany and were digging in for expected counterattacks by the Germans. Churchill told the House of Commons that four thousand ships had taken part. Among these had been hundreds of minesweepers which had gone ahead of the landing craft to clear channels through the floating obstacles which ringed the coast. Waves of aircraft followed one after another, looking for an opportunity to strike at anything flying with a German cross on it. Parachute and glider infantry landed in many areas behind the beaches, disrupting German deployments and creating havoc in rear areas. Entire divisions were reported ashore and pushing inland.

A third edition of the *Courier-Times* came out that evening at the usual time. INVASION PROGRESSING RAPIDLY, the headline shouted, with fighting reported at Rouen, forty-one miles inland, and Caen, nine miles inland. As many as eleven thousand available Allied bombers and fighters filled the air all day with the drone of their engines and the crash of bombs. There was already a New Castle connection in the invasion. Lt. Col. Mike Murphy, a stunt flier who had run a flying service on the old Carpenter farm south of the city in 1929 and 1930, had been among the first glider pilots to land in France with airborne troopers aboard. Murphy was also among the first casualties returned to the states. He broke both of his legs when his glider skidded into a tree on D-Day. Gemma prayed that if Ed was involved, he would be safe. She knew it could still be weeks before she would receive any mail from him.

Gemma had other worries, too. Her best friend Sarah was very pregnant and due the first week of June. Clay was gone overseas, and Sarah was on her own as Gemma would be sometime in August when her own time would come. Sarah finally went into a long labor on the fifth of June, and gave birth on D-Day to a baby son they named James. Clay, unaware in Hawaii of what was transpiring in New Castle with Sarah, developed serious abdominal pains which persisted for several days. They suddenly stopped on June 6. When they compared notes in their letters later, they discovered that Clay's pains had stopped at the moment that Sarah had given birth to their son. Gemma visited Sarah when she came home after her week-long stay in the Clinic, but there was not much she could do for her. The new arrival did not help the unhappy atmosphere that Sarah's mother maintained in the house.

Pictures began to come in from England showing chipper soldiers embarking on ships and pulling away from the docks, headed for France. LSTs (landing ship tanks) jammed with tanks, trucks, jeeps, supplies, and men labored toward the beaches in a front-page photo. The Allied Command would not say exactly where the invasion beaches were, but the Germans could, and maps based on their reports began to appear by June 8. Eastern Brittany and western Normandy seemed to be the places where the landings had begun. One photo showed the first American casualties being evacuated by air back to hospitals in England. Progress was being made linking the invasion beaches and pushing inland, but there was stiffening resistance as German ground forces began to consolidate. Better maps appeared as reports of towns captured by the Allies began to come in. Bayeux, Ste. Mere Eglise, and Cherbourg soon told everyone that the initial German reports had been correct, and that the invasion centered in Normandy and the Bay of the Seine area. On June 13, the first photo of the dead appeared, rows of bodies covered with white sheets lying in a French field. They would be buried soon, and the bad news would be sent home. Always there were pictures of the anonymous dead from a big battle before the wires from the War Department began to arrive at front doors in faraway little towns.

On June 14, the British announced at least a partial description of the units engaged, including the American 1st, 2nd, 4th, and 29th Divisions, and 101st and 82nd Airborne Divisions. Gemma did not know anyone in those units except Stanley Winegarden with the 101st, whom they had met in California, but of course Ed could be assigned anywhere and attached to any division. Still there was no word from him.

Ed's repple-depple moved down to Southhampton as troop movements and massive convoys told him the last two weeks in May that the big show was about to start. The quantities of equipment he had seen before had amazed him, but now it all seemed to be moving to the south of England. He volunteered for convoy duty again and made several runs to the coast area where ships of all kinds blackened the shore and barrage balloons floated serenely in the gray skies overhead. The closer one got to the coast the more frantic the traffic and the heavier the congestion on the roads. On the morning of the invasion, he and his unit were up early, as aircraft filled the skies, but there was only routine business for them, and he chafed at his situation. This continued for two more days. On June 8, his replacement depot processed its first batch of replacement troops, which made for some work, but he wanted to do more. On that same day, his brother-in-law, Kenny Thompson, after getting lost on a mission to France, picked up some friendly fighter planes heading back to England and headed for home. As they approached the French channel coast, they saw the invasion fleet spread across the water below. They were glad to be high and dry.

Ed's unit was surrounded by transportation parks and air bases. This was how it happened that on D-Day+3, June 9, a friend from the quartermaster corps asked him if he wanted to fly over to the beach area. "Sure, when do we go?" was the reply. A few hours later, Ed was approaching the coast of Normandy in a C-47 Dakota cargo plane, its floor tightly packed with five-gallon jerry cans each filled with gasoline. On the plane's wings and around the fuselage near the tail were the broad black-and-white invasion stripes which, it was hoped, would help identify Allied planes in the confusion of the invasion and protect them from friendly attack. Through the cargo door window, he could see stretched below him the biggest invasion fleet in history lying off the coast in the dull water. Hundreds of supply ships clustered off shore, loading smaller craft and sending them into the shallow water to deliver their goods to the beach and return for more. Warships patrolled just beyond, searching for submarines and lobbing shells inland. The beach he saw was dark with trucks, piles of supplies, and men. He did not know where he was, of course, but it was one of the two American beaches, Omaha or Utah. As Ed neared the coast on the way in, it occurred to him that even a small piece of shrapnel or a stray rifle bullet could easily come through the thin metal sides of the plane and with all the gasoline on board, make a spectacular pyrotechnic display for the troops below. Of course, it was already too late to think of such things. The pilot banked sharply once he had passed over the beaches and headed steeply down toward a road on the high ground a mile or two inland. The Dakota sat down stiffly on the road which was a temporary runway and taxied to a stop at one end. The doors opened and Ed helped carry out the cans and line them up on the ground where quartermaster personnel loaded them into jeeps and trucks. They took aboard a batch of German prisoners and bounced down the road again to take off. The flight back was uneventful and less nerve-racking than going the other way. The POWs gave no trouble and rode quietly, hoping as Ed did that no German fighters would appear looking for an easy target like a slow transport plane. England's green fields and dark fencerows were a welcome sight just as they always were for the flight crews who made it back.

Ed made three or four such trips, taking responsibility for seeing to it that the correct quantities of supplies reached the drop point, and making sure that no one smoked around the gas cans when they carried them. Sometimes he would stay for two or three days at a time before heading back to England. He continued to write home regularly, and about a week after the invasion the backed-up letters began to arrive in New Castle again.

Big news arrived in New Castle on June 15, when headlines shouted ARMY B-29S BOMB JAPAN TODAY! It was the first time since the Doolittle raid in 1942 that American bombers had dumped bombs on the Japanese homeland. These were the new, secret planes which had been rumored recently: not Fortresses, but Superfortresses. Their wingspan was almost forty feet wider than the B-17s, and they had far greater range and bomb load than anything else that flew. The 20th Bomber Command raid came from bases somewhere in the China-Burma-India (CBI) theater. A picture appeared in the next day's paper, the first anyone had seen of the new bomber. The first strike was against Japanese steel plants at Yawata, home of 20 percent of their production.

The same day, marines invaded Saipan in the Marianas group, farther out in the Pacific, but still fifteen hundred miles short of Japan itself. The initial reports mentioned the islands as a potential base for the new B-29s. Good progress was reported. There had been reports of carrier actions in the Marianas recently, but no one at home knew where the next blow would come. It seemed there were carrier attacks all over the Pacific now. American manufacturing and shipbuilding strength had begun to be felt. The navy even announced it hoped the Japanese would come out and fight. Word was that Japan's navy was hard-pressed to defend the islands it had already taken. Could it save itself for later battles while letting the Americans take islands without at least a preliminary naval battle? An editorial cartoon pictured a Japanese warlord at the theater looking at the previews. On the screen was "INVASION, coming soon!"

In France, American divisions drove to within six miles of Normandy's west coast in their effort to cut off the entire peninsula and isolate the port of Cherbourg. German counterattacks struck hard against the Allied line, but gains had been made near Carentan in spite of them. The news of the advances was good, but the pictures of more casualties appearing in the paper were always the harbinger of bad news. On June 17, the Associated Press reported 3,283 killed and 12,600 wounded in the first eleven days of the invasion of France. That was a rate of almost three hundred dead per day. The same day there appeared a photo of rows of holes dug for their bodies in World War II's first American cemetery in France. Once again, they were planting crosses, row on row, just as they had done so many times in the Great War.

The Germans had a new weapon, too. The reports were sketchy, but press reports called them radio-controlled robot planes which spat fire on their way to targets in England. British civilians were being killed. They could be launched in bad weather, making Allied interception difficult, but they appeared to be aimed randomly, rather than at specific targets. What would they come up with next?

From Plum Street, Maxine sent Kenny's picture to the *Courier-Times* along with notification that he had been awarded the air medal at his base in England for having completed ten missions over Nazi-occupied Europe. Kenny, handsome as always in his leather bomber jacket and overseas cap with his wings pinned on it, did not say much about the missions in his letters. To hear "we've been flying a lot" was unusual. Like most GIs, it was safer to say nothing. When he wrote, he told of his love for Maxine, and sent ideas and plans for their future after the war. She could tell him to be careful, but that was about all. In the air over France and Germany, Kenny, as crew chief, was in charge of the crew while the pilot and copilot concentrated on flying the plane. What there was of the atmosphere at twenty thousand feet was unforgiving with the temperature sixty degrees below zero and hostile territory below. From his Plexiglas rotating top turret, Kenny had the best view of any crew member, and as a result had the greatest responsibility for spotting enemy fighters. When the opportunity came, he had two .50 caliber machine guns to use on them. He often directed the fire of other crew members. His view of the top surfaces of the plane and all four engines also surpassed anyone else's. His job included seeing to it that the ground crew kept everything in perfect working order. It was for this reason that he had been assigned to Ypsilanti to learn how the aircraft worked and went together. Serious, sometimes gruff, and well trained at Perfect Circle and at home to understand complex machinery, he got along well with his officers and crew. So far they had the habit of coming back in one piece.

People could be cruel and unthinking at home. Kenny Thompson, on duty in England, heard from someone in New Castle or Hagerstown that Maxine sometimes met a man after work who picked her up in a car and drove off. Maxine was horrified to think that rumors like that had troubled her husband, who had too much on his mind to have to worry about such things. But it was true that a man picked her up sometimes. It was her father. When he could, he drove her home to save her the walk across town. No one else had done so.

Charlie Purvis and Barbara Bunch took advantage of a leave he got from Camp Cooke to get married in New Castle on June 22. Charlie had stayed in California training ack-ack crews when Ed left for England. Although he finished OCS a week ahead of Ed, Charlie was still in the States. They waited for Barbara to finish high school with the Class of 1944 before getting married. They took a brief wedding trip, then Barbara stayed home with her parents on North Main Street while Charlie went back to California.

By the end of June, Americans had reached Cherbourg and cleared the entire Brittany peninsula. They now had a major seaport on the French coast to use for unloading the equipment that the growing armies never seemed to get enough of. It seemed odd that with all the invasion casualty reports, it had been some days since there had been any bad news for families in the county.

The lull ended June 27 when the parents of Pfc. Robert Pitts, Jr. received the wire at their home in Kennard announcing he had been killed on D-Day. Pitts played varsity basketball and baseball at the Kennard High School, graduating with the Class of 1940. Kennard, seven miles west of New Castle, had its own schools, but when older students learned to drive they often went to social events and dances in New Castle. Harry Ridout met Pitts this way, and by chance, Uncle Sam sent them both to medic school at Camp Butner, North Carolina, two weeks after Ed went to Fort Bliss. When the two men were assigned their units, Harry went to the 59th Medical Company, and Pitts went to the 60th. Pitts landed in England January 11, 1944, about the same time as Harry. On D-Day, Pitts went in with the first wave on Omaha Beach, ready to serve the expected casualties. Instead of helping others survive, he became a casualty himself when he suffered a direct hit from a German shell. The newspaper reports listed him as killed, but there was no body recovered. Harry Ridout went ashore immediately behind his friend, with the second wave. Harry survived. Pfc. Robert Pitts, Jr. was his mother and father's only child. It had taken exactly three weeks for the news to reach home.

Another county boy, Sgt. Douglas Gorman of Knightstown died in France on June 11. A paratrooper, he left a wife and daughter near camp in North Carolina. In the June 30 paper, yet another piece of bad news appeared. Lt. Milton Kellum of Cadiz, northwest of New Castle, failed to return from a mission in the southwest Pacific on June 17. He was a bomber pilot who graduated from Cadiz High School and went on to Indiana University. In his senior year there he enlisted in the Army Air Corps and was based in New Guinea. There was a chance that he might be found, so his family, which included a six-month-old son he had never seen, kept their hopes alive. Other Henry County boys met their fates in France on June 12 and 13. These events took three weeks to get back to relatives in Mooreland, where Pfc. Willie Nichols had worked on a farm before going into the army. Pvt. Charles Cranor, Jr. died in France on the 12th, but the War Department failed to give details. The Zetterberg boys, of the family who owned the rolling mill, were moving up in the service. Stephen, a Coast Guard Academy graduate, made executive officer on his cutter, the USS *Tiger,* and Pierre, infantry OCS candidate and a classmate of Gemma's in 1940, was named aide-de-camp to Brig. General Rice.

The government had changed the ration rules at home. Lamb and soft cheeses went back on the ration list the last of June and the points for beefsteaks and roasts went up. The new limit was thirty points per month for meats. Before that, the allocation had been sixty points per month. Butter required twelve ration points per pound as July began, while margarine cost only two. A porterhouse steak cost fourteen points a pound, while a standing rib roast took eight to ten points per pound. Cheaper cuts of beef, pork, and lamb remained unrationed.

While marines continued to push forward on Saipan, in Normandy the British Army under Montgomery began to push toward Caen, an objective that was supposed to have been taken early in the invasion. By then, in spite of massive Allied air attacks, the Germans had begun to mount counterattacks at various points, especially in the Caen area. The last days of June even some German fighters took to the air to help Rommel push the British back but lost twenty-seven in the process. The Germans continued to retreat in White Russia along the route Napoleon followed to disaster. One thousand B-17s and B-24s attacked German targets, escorted by one thousand Allied fighters. The Germans sent up a few fighters against this onslaught, pounced upon eagerly by fighter pilots hoping for something to shoot at in the air for a change. Photos of long lines of German prisoners marching out of Cherbourg helped morale a little, but new attacks by the American First Army southward from the beaches toward St. Lo promised more casualties in the days ahead.

The "robot bombs" which began falling in England hit mostly in London, where the toll began to mount. Press reports called them rockets, like the science fiction rockets, people guessed. More than twenty-seven hundred people, including American soldiers, had died in the attacks, and more than eight thousand had been wounded. The British began sending children out of the city as they had done during the Blitz. It was no wonder, since each of the bombs carried more than a ton of explosive charge. Churchill admitted that more people had been killed in England by the rockets than there were British soldiers killed in the first two weeks of the invasion. London's emergency shelters had gone back into daily use. Allied bombers hit back at the launch sites in several raids, but weather hampered their effectiveness. Two more fliers from New Castle, Lt. William Barnard and Lt. John Lindsey, failed to return from missions in Europe, the paper reported on July 7. There was another B-29 raid on Japan. With Saipan almost mopped up, Japanese radio reported activity in the vicinity of Guam, also in the Marianas. President Roosevelt, with enough delegates to assure his renomination, agreed to serve another term if elected. It would be his fourth.

Chrysler announced in an ad in the paper that it was a big part of the Superfortress project, contributing engines, the cabin unit, and other parts of the giant bombers. The war products produced by the efforts of New Castle workers were going to all fronts of the war to supply New Castle's sons and daughters there.

A Family Milestone on Plum Street

On July 11, 1944, Marie Moles married Orville Hammond. The boy she had met and dated for three years had grown up, joined the navy, and come back from camp in North Carolina for her. Marie liked him almost from the moment a friend had introduced them when she was fifteen and a sophomore and Orville was beginning his senior year at Hagerstown High School. Urgency was in the air for thousands of couples like Marie and Orville, just as it had been for Maxine and Kenny. Orville went into the navy soon after he graduated with the Hagerstown Class of 1942 and had few opportunities to come home. Marie and Orville had a little falling out when he had been in the service a year. His mother was not crazy about Orville dating a girl still in high school, and refused to cooperate with or acknowledge her. Orville did not want to worry his mother any more than she already was, but he was far away and could do little to smooth the situation. Marie liked to go out with friends and have fun. Her carefree reputation and sense of humor assured her a full social calendar, and she took advantage of it, often staying out late and sneaking in the front door, hoping that Jess did not hear her. Jess's paranoia about the behavior of adolescent boys and girls, based on his experiences in the navy, drove him to make life difficult for the suitors the girls brought home. He had shoved a boy off the porch at Plum Street and sent him home for having the audacity to light a cigar in front of the girls without permission.

Marie missed Orville, but did not want to forfeit all social occasions her senior year when they had only dated. They had not made plans to marry or even talked about it. Neither knew what the war would bring, and neither had definite plans for jobs after it was over. From camp, Orville did not press her to stay at home or make plans for an engagement or wedding. Marie dated Bob Cronk and considered his suggestion that Marie marry him. Bob was at home because of a bad eye that kept him out of service, but she drifted back to Orville as her senior year got under way.

Orville took flight training at Banana River, Florida, learning his duties in the patrol bombers (PBMs) built by the Martin Aircraft Corporation. Patrol bombers, capable of landing on water if necessary, flew antisubmarine, reconnaissance, and rescue missions providing eyes and ears over the vast expanses of the Atlantic and Pacific. They carried bombs for use against submarines, which could make greater speed traveling on the surface. When spotted by a patrol bomber, submarines often could not submerge before the aircraft could make a pass. A bomb which exploded even close to a submarine often succeeded in sinking it, making patrol bombers potent weapons in the battle against German and Japanese subs. Orville and his crewmates sharpened their skills on long flights from North Carolina to Guantanamo Bay, on Cuba's southern coast. Orville served as radioman and rear gunner. Vigilance was needed, because a patrol bomber was a sitting duck for an enemy fighter plane.

Orville came home on leave from radio school at Albemarle Sound, North Carolina. When he came to see Marie, their love blossomed again instantly. They went to Memorial Park to the little seat made of stones that was built into a hillside and decided then and there that they could not live without each other. The next day they went to the courthouse for a marriage license, but did not tell his mother. They knew that no girl could secure her approval to marry Orville, and thought it best to notify her after the wedding was over.

They arranged for Rev. Kinnett to marry them at the Baptist

Orville Hammond and Marie Moles, February 1944. Orville briefly came home on leave before reporting for advanced training.

parsonage on Tuesday, July 11, 1944 at noon. Jess and Ethel could attend a daughter's nuptials at last, but it was a small wedding party that entered the same front room that Gemma and Ed had gone to eleven months before. Jess, Ethel, Wanda, and Gemma made up the audience, while Maxine served as Marie's attendant. Again it was a single-ring ceremony, with the bride dressed in powder blue with brown purse and shoes. Orville, tall and handsome with his chiseled features, sandy hair, and standard enlisted uniform of navy blue blouse and broad-fly bell-bottoms, stood quietly as the words that bound them together sounded in the air. Dale Weintraut, a friend from Hagerstown, stood with him as best man. They all drove the few blocks back to the house on Plum Street for pictures and a small lunch, then the newlyweds went to the Pennsylvania station to catch a train at 2:00 P.M. Marie changed into a white dress for the trip which would take them to Washington, D.C., then to Norfolk, Virginia, on the way back to North Carolina. July is always hot in Indiana, and the trip across Ohio, West Virginia, and Virginia to the nation's capital was a long one, so the passengers opened the car windows to allow the moving air to cool them. Marie sat by the window, protected from the aisle by her new husband, but as the train labored over the Ohio hills and West Virginia mountains, through tunnels and across bridges, the smoke and dust from the steam engine that pulled them turned her dress from white to gray. Small cinders and dirt coated them both well before they arrived at Union Station in Washington.

They washed the grit from their eyes and faces in Washington, then caught another train for the great naval base at Norfolk, Virginia. From there a navy bus took them south another hour to Hertford, North Carolina, adjacent to the naval air station there. They rented a room from a couple who had added two attic rooms to the rooms their two sons had given up when they grew up and moved away. Another navy couple rented the other upstairs room, and all the renters got their meals at a boardinghouse down the street. Marie walked or rode a bicycle down to the boardinghouse every morning while Orville went to the base for breakfast. The window looked out over the main street of the tiny town a block from the business district. Marie cleaned up every afternoon and waited on the porch for Orville to come home on the navy bus with other naval airmen who lived in town. This was her daily routine for the five weeks that they had together before Orville shipped out to the Pacific. It was not quite as abrupt a departure as Maxine had experienced in Nevada, but they did not have much warning, either. Only two days before his departure did Orville learn that he was about to leave. Marie made plans to gather their few belongings and return, on the train as her two older sisters had done, to the family home on Plum Street. As had been the case with Gemma when she came back, Marie was pregnant also.

The house on Plum Street was a busy place when Marie returned. It was like the old days before the war, because all four sisters and Jess and Ethel were living under one roof again. Jess continued to work long wartime hours at the Chrysler, and Ethel now worked steadily as a cook at the Clinic, next door to the police station on Indiana Avenue in New Castle. Maxine had been rehired at her old job in the lab at Ingersoll Steel, the rolling mill on the west side of town. Wanda was a junior at the high school, or would be when the school term began in September. Gemma discovered she was expecting soon after she got back to New Castle in February, and had worked at Public Service for a little while, but then had to quit and stay home. She could be alone that way now, because no one was at home on weekdays, except Wanda in the summertime.

There was a new resident on Plum Street when Marie arrived, too. Gemma's time had finally come on August 10, and at the Clinic where her mother worked she gave birth to a dark-haired son they had agreed to name James Edward after Ed's grandfather. Gemma had taken advantage of the pregnancies of her friends Martha and Sarah to observe the process and ask some questions. She learned a lot from Martha's experience because she was the first. Mothers usually did not talk to their daughters in detail about such things, and no mention of the process took place in a school classroom, of course. Gemma remembered that Marie had been slapped for just saying the word "pregnant." Childbirth was something that women endured when it was time because that was the way things were. Martha's mother had never even mentioned what it was like or what to expect. When it was time for the baby to come, the process would begin, and Martha would be the first to know. Martha's time was close at hand when she discovered to her horror that she had suddenly soaked her clothes and a chair with what seemed a very large quantity of clear liquid, like water. When she called the doctor's office to ask what it was, she was told to come in. Only when she had been examined did the doctor tell her not to worry, that her water had broken, and that it was perfectly normal. In fact, it had to happen in order to begin the birthing process. Martha gave birth to their son John on April 26, 1943.

Martha told Gemma a little about the labor, but preferred to talk about her baby. Sarah's experience was about the same. At least as Gemma approached her due date she had the benefit of some knowledge about the event. She knew not to panic when her own water broke, or when the light contractions began.

Ed was in France now, and he had written often enough for a few letters to begin to reach Gemma on Plum Street. He knew that the baby was due in the first half of August, but had no way of knowing when Gemma went into serious labor about 4 A.M. on the tenth of August. The doctor had told her to go to the Clinic when it began, and Jess drove her over there, complaining as usual. He did not think Ethel should go with them or be with her at the Clinic. It would interfere with the morning routine at the house and, besides, there were nurses and doctors at the Clinic who did not need any help. Ethel went anyway, and began working at her regular starting time, occasionally checking in on Gemma in her room. Jess left them there and went back to get ready for work. Her water did not break at home but did later in the course of a normal labor which ended at one o'clock in the afternoon when she delivered an eight-pound, two-ounce baby boy. A little ether at the end of the process had helped her finish, but there had been no other anesthesia, the same as had been done for Martha and Sarah.

When Gemma delivered, Jess went to the Western Union office and sent Ed a wire to let him know that he was the father of a baby son. This reached him in about three days. Like Clay, Ed had been sick for a week with abdominal cramps and nausea that had come on suddenly without apparent cause. When he received the telegram, he was finally beginning to feel a little better. The other GIs he worked with toasted him with some brandy. Ed celebrated with a glass of water.

Gemma was at the Clinic a week while she recovered from the strain of her ordeal and waited until she could go back to Plum Street. She already knew how to take care of the baby because she had helped her mother with Wanda and the other girls, and had maintained her skills with her babysitting jobs. She nursed him as most women did, and followed the doctor's orders to lie still and rest as much as possible while there. Back at the house there was a feeling of a little more crowding since Gemma and little Jimmy had a room to themselves. Gemma stayed in bed

Wanda Moles with newborn nephew Jimmy in the back yard at 1828 Plum Street, August 1944. About this time, the casualty reports from the Normandy breakout began to hit closer and closer to the house on Plum Street.

for the most part and got up to take care of her baby and for meals. Ethel had been through the process of taking care of babies four times, so Gemma had a ready source of helpful advice when she needed it.

There was another advantage to having a new baby as well. Every person, regardless of age, was entitled to a ration book. Soon after Jimmy was born, Gemma went down to the local ration board and applied for his ration book. It doubled the quantities of foods and other rationed goods that Gemma could buy. Some things like shoes had to be purchased for the baby, but food items could be used by anyone.

Many people traded rationed goods, in violation of the rules, with friends. Trading the coupons themselves was difficult, because they were not to be torn out of the book before the purchase. The store clerk was supposed to do it or watch the customer do it. Once the rationed goods had been taken home, however, they could be traded. Coffee was a favorite barter item because not everyone drank it, but to those who did it was considered essential. Sugar, needed for practically every baking recipe and with hundreds of other uses, was always in demand. Many people traded sugar for coffee, and there were dozens of other goods that found ready barter customers. This was generally not done among strangers, because the danger of being reported to the local ration board was always there. Among friends and relatives, however, it was commonplace.

Grim Days in France

By the middle of July 1944, enough ground had been captured and enough time had elapsed to permit a large Allied buildup of supplies and troops in Normandy. American, British, French, Canadian, and Polish divisions had come over from their training areas in Britain, equipped and assembled for action when needed. A severe storm hit the invasion beaches just a few days after the Allies landed, inflicting considerable damage on the artificial ports constructed by the engineers to off-load supplies. One was completely destroyed. Even after capturing Cherbourg the last week of June, there was much repair work to be done before it became fully functional as an Allied port. British forces made only slow progress moving up the coast toward Le Havre, blocked for weeks by German defensive positions around Caen, still only ten miles from the beach. There were sixty-two thousand Allied dead and wounded by the end of June.

By July 11, American forces smashed their way to within two miles of St. Lo, but less than twenty miles from the nearest American beach. After nine weeks of heavy fighting, the Allies did not have much to show for it. The Germans had rushed reinforcements to the area in spite of furious air attacks. In the beautiful hedgerow country of Normandy, tough earth-and-root-bound fencerows five to seven feet tall surrounded nearly every field, making natural defensive positions that tanks could penetrate only with great difficulty. Here German infantry extracted a heavy price for real estate in the weeks that followed the invasion. Fears of a reestablishment of the murderous static warfare of the First World War reemerged among Allied military planners as they fretted away the days with steady losses but no major gains.

By July 15, sufficient force had been gathered to attempt a major advance. On the eastern end of the fighting front, a British battleship shelled German positions around Caen, and the weight of the Eighth Air Force was thrown into the battle. Heavy bombers began saturation bombing of German positions, and Caen suffered nearly complete destruction from thousands of tons of Allied bombs. To the southwest, American troops pushed toward and then into St. Lo on the 17th at great cost, knocking out tanks and dug-in Germans.

On July 20, St. Lo was firmly in American hands when word came in the paper that Hitler had narrowly escaped assassination by his own officers. Most Americans regretted the fact that he had escaped, apparently suffering only burns and a concussion. The next day, the navy announced that American forces had landed on Guam, the first American territory to be retaken by American troops. Soon marines landed on nearby Tinian, last of the larger island group which included Saipan.

It was a busy week for the reporters. On Friday, the 21st, delegates at the Democratic convention in Chicago took the sitting vice president, Henry Wallace, off the presidential ticket with Roosevelt and replaced him with Senator Harry Truman of Missouri. Truman's name was practically a household word after he became famous as chairman of the senate's war corruption investigating committee. Wallace, the left-wing former agriculture secretary from Iowa, gamely endorsed the change.

A month after he was killed in France, T/5 William E. Rector's family in New Castle learned he had died in action of wounds received a week after the invasion. He was a medical assistant probably hit by a shell. He graduated with New Castle's Class of 1938.

On July 25, headlines announced the start of a big Allied drive in Normandy, but gave few details. Thundering artillery and massive air strikes marked the beginning of the push, including one mission of fifteen hundred heavy bombers. British and

American forces at "both ends of the 100-mile Normandy front" broke loose and advanced southward. Newly arrived American armored divisions went in to widen the gap, and rumors reported in the papers had it that General Patton might be the break-out commander. Infantry units followed the tanks, mopping up strong points and clearing scattered pockets of resistance. Shelling, snipers, and dug-in Germans took a toll even after the heaviest fighting ended in an area. To the east, the Russians were in Poland at the Vistula and close to the East Prussian frontier, 335 miles from Berlin.

In New Castle, the Western Union boy rode up to the house at 1702 Indiana Avenue, less than three blocks from the house on Plum Street, on August 1. In this way the parents of Pvt. Earl Spears, nineteen, learned he had given his life in Italy. An infantry medic, he had left high school before graduating to enter the service in March 1943. His survivors included his parents and a sister, Jean, whom Ed had dated while in high school. Gemma sent the news to Ed in France. Sgt. Warren Younce, Class of 1940, died in France on July 6. He was another only child of a New Castle couple. Gemma's cousin Glenn Cowan came home on seventeen days furlough August 6 after finishing aerial gunnery training in Texas. Gemma and Ruth Cowan maintained a friendship from their childhood and shared their sorrows during the war.

Ed's 23rd Replacement Depot shipped to France on August 1, 1944. They set up tents a few miles inland on a hilltop near Carentan, just inland from Utah beach, for about ten days. They did not like the exposed position because of the possibility of attack from the air, but it was better than the swampy low areas that flanked the sluggish rivers nearby. As they arrived, the great Allied push known as Operation Cobra succeeded in allowing American forces to break out of Normandy and begin the rush toward Paris. Ed's replacement processing work was a continuation of the daily routine which had begun shortly after the invasion. Battlefronts consume troops, and replacements must be sent up continuously when there is fighting. Moving to Normandy meant a change in the location only. For all of July casualties had been heavy and new units freshly arrived from home came up to be sent to their forward assignments. The processing duties went on day after day.

Orrin Grubbs came home on leave from duty with the 320th Infantry, 35th Infantry Division, Ft. Rucker, Alabama in October 1943. The 320th arrived in England in May 1944, and crossed to France on July 7, 1944. His mother Erma took his picture just before he left New Castle.

In New Castle, papers carried Eisenhower's prediction of a great victory for the coming week on Monday, August 14. Allied troops landed in southern France the next day, and DeGaulle called for a general uprising by the French people. The Allies hesitated, then closed the Falaise Gap after many of the German divisions in it escaped to the east. Gemma's friend and classmate in the Class of 1940, Esta Belle Morris Austin, called her parents on August 16 to tell them that her husband's plane was missing on a flight in South Carolina. Esta Belle and several of her friends from high school had decided to heed the call of adventure for war production workers in California, and moved to Long Beach in 1942, renting an apartment together. There she met and married Lt. Robert Austin, the Army Air Corps pilot. He and his crew died in the crash.

On August 21, 1944, the war struck very close to Plum Street. On B Avenue, Clay and Orrin's mother Erma had often seen her boys ride home on their bicycles wearing their Western Union uniforms when they worked for the company. That day, though, Clay was in New Guinea with the 38th Infantry Division and Orrin was with the 35th Infantry Division in France. Just three days before, Erma had received a letter from Orrin at the front in Normandy telling her that he was receiving the *Courier-Times* on a regular basis and was doing fine, but hadn't bathed or shaved in 25 days. "I wish all the people of New Castle could see what war means," he wrote to her. This time it was a different Western Union boy who rode his bike onto the grass and walked to the door. Mrs. Vitatoe, ashen-faced, took the envelope and opened it. Orrin had been missing in action since July 30. Looking back through the papers, it had happened about the time of the big push around St. Lo. Erma held out hope for Orrin's safety, but Sarah had to write to Clay to tell him the news. They knew that with the Allies advancing in the sector where Orrin had disappeared, there was only a slim chance of his being captured. In North Africa and Italy, those listed as missing sometimes turned up later as POWs because the advances were not always in one direction. German counterattacks often succeeded in making gains in which prisoners could be taken. Erma kept hoping she would hear from him, but Clay wrote to Sarah that it did not look good. Throughout this time and for long afterward, Sarah mourned for Orrin and regretted treating him callously to get close to Clay. Orrin had been delighted to receive a picture of Clay and Sarah's son James, and had written to Sarah almost as though the child had been his. He had never given up his fondness for her, even after she had married his brother. Gemma comforted her and tried to help distract her thoughts, but Sarah wondered if God might punish her in some terrible way for treating Orrin as she had done, and Gemma feared that the war might come to Plum Street in a way that was even worse.

Operation Cobra and the breakout from the Normandy killing ground proved to be the advance the Allies had tried to pull off all summer. German defenders, outflanked, pulled back as Patton's armored spearheads poured into Brittany and the rolling country between Normandy and the Loire Valley. Behind the stubborn German lines of June and July was open country, and the new Third Army, with Patton at its head, flowed out to seize the area before the Germans could form a new line to defend.

They dashed to Angers, Le Mans, Chartres, and Orleans, then to the Seine south of Paris, tank crews driving off the maps they had been given. Ed's 23rd moved to the vicinity of Viers for two weeks, then on to Fontainebleau southeast of Paris on August 25, just five days after its capture. The previous day, triumphant Allied troops, led by the French 2nd Armored Division, entered Paris while Free French radio called Parisians to the barricades. American units joined them on the 25th and helped clear the remaining Germans as celebrations began. Newspaper reports in New Castle placed General De Gaulle in the Paris suburbs, poised to enter the city.

Orrin paid with his life part of the price of the breathtaking Allied advance that now began to unfold in the papers back home. By August 29 American armies reached and crossed the Marne to take Chateau-Thierry, where Ed's father had served in the first great American campaign of the summer of 1918. The Germans appeared to be giving up the old battlefields without a fight as the armored columns kept rolling eastward. Some forces drove fifty-five miles northeast of Paris, only one hundred miles from the German frontier. On the 30th, they had taken Rheims and Chalons-sur-Marne, and forced the evacuation of Rouen. The British captured Amiens as they moved into the "rocket coast" of France near Calais, source of the ongoing attacks against London.

The war came to Plum Street again while Allied forces pushed to within 30 miles of the Reich. On Friday evening, September 1, the Western Union boy knocked on the door at the Pfenninger house, on the corner of 18th and Plum, just around the corner from the Moles house. It was for Florence, the Pfenningers' daughter-in-law. Her husband, Lt. Elmer Pfenninger, had been killed in France on August 13. Florence had married Elmer, the oldest son, and had given the Pfenningers a grandson who was four months old. Elmer, thirty-one years old, had been a familiar figure in New Castle, running a taxi service out of the garage behind their house on Plum Street, and working at the Chrysler. An Eagle Scout, he had been scoutmaster for the troop at the Methodist church before entering the service in September 1942. An OCS infantry officer, he arrived in England in November 1943, and went to France on D-Day. Only a week before the telegram arrived, Florence had a letter from Elmer in France telling her that except for one week's rest, he had been in the front-lines continuously since the invasion. On that Sunday, a German sniper spotted his officer's insignia through his scope and shot him in the head. Besides his wife and son, he left four sisters and four brothers, three of whom were also in the service.

Better news followed on September 4th as Allied troops rolled into Belgium and took Brussels while the Eighth Army in Italy, largely forgotten in the excitement over the news from France, broke through a German defensive line and moved forward twelve miles in north-central Italy. On September 12, American columns pushed into Germany. The American Seventh Army, moving north from the French Mediterranean coast, linked up with Third Army units, cutting off any German forces in southwest France. New Castle's Chief of Police announced that plans were nearly completed for the V-day celebration when and if Germany surrendered.

In New Castle, citizens could get their new A gas ration books, to go into effect September 22, at just five places in the county. The ration board, acting on a new rule, allowed distribution of the ten thousand books only if a ration board official was present. Due to the small number of officials, the books went to only five locations, making headaches for school officials handing them out and for those trying to get them. The OPA suddenly raised blue point values for canned goods soon after eliminating other foods from the ration list. Points needed for many items doubled overnight because of a "change in the supply picture," according to ration officials in Washington. Blue points were to be phased out and replaced with higher-denomination red points for making ration coupon "change."

Then the news began to turn sour. British troops joined the American advance toward Belgium by going around some of the port cities and pushing into Holland. In the delta of the Rhine in western Holland, water was a major obstacle to the Allied advance and military planners, faced with the unexpected opportunity to leap across the Rhine there, decided to try to seize the bridges intact. If the Germans succeeded in destroying them, the rapid advance by tanks and trucks would be slowed down considerably. British airborne troops parachuted into key areas around the bridges at Nijmegen and Arnhem, then were cut off by German armored attacks. The British discovered they had miscalculated, sending their lightly armed airborne troops too far ahead to be supported by the heavier ground forces. For nine days, frantic German attempts to destroy them made headway as Allied units fought their way toward the site. When they finally got there, all that could be done was to withdraw those who had survived. The British failure and the worsening weather helped halt the entire Allied advance. Just two weeks before, victory celebrations were being planned back home and Eisenhower was predicting the end of the war in six weeks. Now all bets were off. Churchill on September 27 stated before the House of Commons that the war against Germany might last until well into 1945. Allied troop strength was approaching three million in northwestern Europe, he reported, but the British had suffered 90,000 casualties in France and the Americans had reported 145,000.

It was time to catch up and consolidate. As the supply lines to the front from the Channel ports became regularized and stray pockets of Germans were eliminated, the fighting units could sort themselves out and report on events of the amazing dash from Normandy to the German border and Holland. There had been steady casualty reports from the Normandy fighting that had taken Orrin Grubbs and from the beginning of the rapid advance which had claimed Elmer Pfenninger. Then the news had lagged because most units had been too busy fighting, advancing, or supplying those who were. The progress slowed and nearly stopped at the end of September after Arnhem. Consequently, the New Castle paper was filled with reports of casualties in October as the forward units found time to report their losses, and most of them were from Europe.

Cpl. Philip Morris of the Class of 1940 left New Castle on Monday, October 2 to return to Percy Jones Hospital for Amputees in Battle Creek after spending a month at home with his mother and father on North 20th Street. Allied armies had attacked the German Gothic Line in Italy and made partial breakthroughs by September 4. Heavy fighting continued day after day in Italy with little notice in the papers because the main focus of attention continued to be on the activity in France and Belgium. On September 17, the day the Arnhem operation began in Holland, Pvt. James Stiers died in the Italian fighting, leaving a wife and two-year-old daughter with her parents just a few doors from where the Smiths had lived on Grand Avenue. The telegram reached New Castle two and a half weeks later. Kenneth Gwinn's family received notice on October 4 that he was missing in action in the Pacific. He had earlier been awarded the Silver Star for action on his submarine and had been in the navy for seventeen years.

On the same day that Ray Frost's parents at 1815 Plum Street reported that he had begun training for the Merchant Marine in New York, another family learned of the death of their son, this time in the Pacific. Pfc. Emmit Neal, a marine who had graduated from Sulphur Springs High School northwest of New Castle in 1941, died somewhere in the southwest Pacific. He lived with his sister and her family on P Avenue and worked at the Kroger store before he left for service.

There were three more deaths in the paper on October 7. SSgt. Richard Rutherford died in Corsica after being wounded on a mission in his B-26 Marauder medium bomber. Another marine, Pfc. George Roach, died in the southwest Pacific, but the Marine Corps, as usual, declined to say just where. T/4 Edgar Hicks died in France September 29 after being seriously wounded on July 7. Another county boy, Pfc. Louis Beal, was reported killed in the October 10 paper, but such things had become so common now that they no longer commanded the attention they had previously. News of the election of the new president of the Tuberculosis Association got a bigger headline than Beal's death or the four reported wounded.

Patton's tanks approached and attacked the Siegfried defensive line early in October and attacked the forts surrounding the city of Metz. British and Canadian troops captured Dunkerque. Pictures in the *Courier-Times* began to show another enemy, the weather. Mud was a growing concern as the fall rains began to slow every movement. Advances grew more difficult and harder to sustain because fuel and supply convoys bogged down more often. The U.S. First Army surrounded Aachen while Canadian forces moved toward Antwerp, the big port city in Belgium which, if captured, would greatly shorten the Allied supply lines which ran across most of France. Naval action continued in the

Pacific and marines attacked another of the Palau Islands east of the Philippines.

At home, Indiana native son Wendell Willkie, Republican nominee for president in 1940 against FDR, died in New York on October 8. His family brought the body home to Rushville for burial. Almost forgotten in all the war news was the presidential campaign of 1944. The Republican ticket of Dewey and Bricker hoped to retire Roosevelt, but the Democrat slogan was "Don't change horses in the middle of the stream." FDR was the heavy favorite and won easily in the November elections.

Another county soldier, Pfc. James Stubbs, died on September 19 of wounds received in fighting in Germany. About the same time, expectations of an invasion of the Philippines began to grow during the third week in October following air attacks on the island group. Japanese reports confirmed that such an assault had taken place in radio broadcasts reported on October 19. MacArthur went ashore on Leyte Island announcing that he had returned as he promised more than two years before. Fighting spread over Leyte and onto other islands as sea and land forces committed to the offensive grew.

After a volunteer convoy run to an area near the front in October, Ed had a couple of days to wait until he could head back to Fontainebleau. He had a knack for friendly banter and struck up a conversation with an artillery forward observation officer from New York City named Murphy, a 2nd Lieutenant like himself. Murphy wondered if Ed wanted to go with him on a little reconnaissance mission. They took two jeeps, each with an officer, a driver, and a machine gunner, and headed east. They drove for some time, with Murphy checking his map now and then before driving on through the quiet countryside. They eventually came to a small river with low banks where they stopped. In the distance could be heard the rumble of artillery fire, which made everyone nervous. They drove up and down the bank a quarter mile or so, then Murphy decided to go across. Murphy produced the remnants of a bottle of cognac, took a pull, and handed it to his driver, who finished it. Ed's jeep waited on the riverbank to offer covering fire should it be necessary while Murphy forded the river in the other one and disappeared. He returned after perhaps twenty minutes, crossed back, and they headed back westward. He had driven two or three miles to the east looking for any sign of Germans. Weeks later, Murphy wrote to Ed telling him that the river they had reached was the Moselle, that he had been able to establish the important news that the Germans had pulled back from the river at that point, and that he had been given the Bronze Star for it. Ed realized that had the Germans not pulled back, they all might have been killed.

American units continued to move eastward toward and into Germany as November began, trying to keep the forward momentum going against the Germans under deteriorating conditions. They fought in the passes of the Vosges Mountains the first week of November, then began a bitter assault, with much hand-to-hand fighting in the gloom of the Huertgen Forest between Cologne and Aachen. Patton's Third Army approached the fortress of Metz and began probing its defenses.

Maxine Learns of Kenny's DFC

Maxine received word November 10 that Kenny had been awarded the Distinguished Flying Cross (DFC), and a notice appeared in the paper the following week. The letter from General Doolittle cited his performance on "numerous special operational missions over enemy-occupied Europe." The vagueness, repeated in every official release, told Maxine on Plum Street and his brother Bert in Hagerstown nothing about what he had actually done. By this time the original tour of twenty-five missions expected of a bomber crew member had long since been extended to thirty, then to thirty-five. At the end of the required missions, an airman could return to the States, usually to serve as an instructor.

In May, Kenny transferred from the 467th's Nissen huts to less comfortable tents on the flat farm fields of the 492nd Bomb Group at Harrington. He and his new eight-man crew began flying solo "Carpetbagger" night missions in special B-24s painted flat black so they would be difficult to spot from the ground. A very few special crews had been selected for their experience and their ability to work together, and Kenny had been asked to serve as crew chief for these missions. Beginning in late May, they took off after 10:00 P.M., returning to base before 6:00 A.M. Alone and unescorted over France, they homed in on special radio signals from the ground before dropping supplies and agents to resistance forces behind German lines in the interior.

In many ways the secret night missions were less risky than bombing in daylight with the rest of the Eighth Air Force. If the weather was favorable and there was no moon, they only gave away their presence with the sound of the Liberator's four big engines, but they avoided cities and known military installations where spotlights might find and follow them, exposing them to night fighter attacks and flak. A betrayal of the mission might bring ground fire over the drop site, but this never happened to his crew. All sources of light had to be suppressed, including engine exhaust and gun muzzles, which were altered. Needed light from within the aircraft was carefully used to avoid giving away the plane's location.

But there were many dangers. All of the ship's guns were removed except Kenny's two .50 caliber machine guns in the top turret and the two in the tail gunner's turret. The oxygen lines and tanks were removed because the missions were all low-level. Rather than use the bomb bay doors, the ball turret opening became a drop hole for packages and those who parachuted into the night. The navigator held everyone's life in his hands, and instruments indicating altitude and position could fail. Enemy aircraft did not know they were approaching, so a collision might occur. Worse, the Royal Air Force filled the night sky with its bombers on the way to targets in Europe, creating countless opportunities for friendly collisions. Observing strict radio silence, the crew would have little opportunity to call for help or give a position should the plane be damaged or downed. On one early training mission in May, they suffered damage from flak and attacks by night fighters over Belgium. Their pilot, Captain William F. Dillon, managed to baby the plane home to England with little fuel left. That particular aircraft was so badly damaged it never flew again.

As a rule, the navigator only had coordinate points to aim for, so that the rest of the crew knew practically nothing about their destination. Should they have to abandon the aircraft, there would be little information to give to enemy troops who might capture them. Sometimes their "bomb" load was supplies and equipment, and at other times they dropped agents. The missions, mostly over France, were restricted to the summertime hours of darkness and usually lasted less than six hours.

In October, Captain Grace, Ed's CO, became sick and needed to go to an army hospital in Paris. Ed had been serving as his executive officer, so he arranged the paperwork to have Ed promoted to 1st Lieutenant so he could take over in his absence. Ed practiced signing the captain's name so that he could complete any paperwork needed while he was gone. In this way, Ed advanced in rank and had the opportunity to command the unit in the CO's absence.

Late Fall and Early Winter of 1944

Heavy fighting continued in Belgium, Luxembourg, and against the German lines west of the Rhine throughout November. This was the beginning of the push against the fortified "West Wall" defenses constructed by Hitler to protect Germany itself. Miles of trenches, concrete tank obstacles called "dragons' teeth," and carefully placed pillboxes offered endless opportunities for German troops to extract a high price for each objective the Allies gained. Metz fell to Patton's forces November 22 as Allied armies drove to Strasbourg, which fell before month's end. In the Pacific large numbers of ground troops and the largest American naval force assembled so far battered its way into the Philippines against heavy resistance. The big B-29s began to hit Tokyo in a series of raids the last days of November, lifting spirits in New Castle and across the country.

Early in December, the Third Army crossed the Saar River in several places and the British finally reached the Arnhem-Nijmegen area on the ground. On December 8, the dreaded telegram arrived at the Don and Mary Ridgway residence on South 21st Street in New Castle, informing them that their son Billy had become a casualty in the fighting along the Siegfried line on November 19. He had died a private in the 16th Infantry, 1st Division, in the assault on the fortified German lines in the gloomy Huertgen Forest south of Aachen. The Ridgways had moved to New Castle from rural Mooreland, northeast of the city, about three blocks from where the Moles girls lived on Plum Street. Don worked in the defense plants during the war. Billy had been born in Mooreland and went to high school there, then he had joined the army reserve and enrolled at Purdue but was called up in February 1943. Billy had gone overseas in September as a replacement and had not been in the lines long when he was killed. He was the Ridgways' only child.

On December 12, three days after the notice about Billy Ridgway's death appeared in the paper, the 1st Division broke out of the Huertgen Forest and reached the Roer River pushing toward Cologne. The "West Wall" defensive line loomed ahead, unbroken in many areas, but on December 16 the Germans launched a major counterattack through the Ardennes Forest into Luxembourg and Belgium in an attempt to retake the port of Antwerp. For over a week this break in the American lines grew wider as German armor and infantry poured into it. The army news summary that had become a front-page feature in the *Courier-Times* suddenly became vague as the War Department suspended releasing the locations of individual divisions. Weather conditions improved just before Christmas to allow air reconnaissance and fighter-bomber attacks. Wire reports began to call the offensive a "bulge" in the Allied lines after about ten days of fighting. It became clear back home by December 26 that the town of Bastogne had been cut off and surrounded with a significant American force trapped inside. With a thirty-six-hour news delay imposed on dispatches from the front, it was December 29 before anyone in New Castle found out that it was the 101st Airborne Division that had been isolated there. It would be the end of March before the folks at home learned that two county boys, Pvt. Charles Horn of Knightstown and Pfc. Francis Snell of New Castle, were there with them. An armored column broke through to relieve the besieged town after Christmas.

As word of the American recovery from the counterattack came in, the news that Cpl. Otto Stephens had been killed arrived at his mother's home south of New Castle. Stephens, a Ranger, had been among the soldiers who had scaled the cliff at Pointe du Hoc on D-Day, receiving a sniper wound in the process. He had recovered and returned to his unit in October, only to be killed on

December 6. Another member of Ed's Class of 1941, 2Lt. Chet Curry, arrived in northeast India at the same time, where his weather unit began their support efforts for the Chinese army on the other side of the Himalayas.

With fighting raging in the Bulge in Belgium, OPA released new rules for rationed food. Dozens of coupons previously valid were cancelled, and a long list of foods went back on the restricted list or had their point values raised. Red points given as ration stamp "change" remained valid. Meats added to the ration list made a total of 85 percent of all cuts subject to new rules. All but one sugar coupon became invalid, along with all canning sugar certificates. Sheets and pillowcases, towels, and men's underwear became scarce, and candy bars disappeared by the first of the new year because of increased demand by soldiers, the reports in the paper said.

Heavy fighting always meant casualty reports later, and the winter months were no exception. Vernie Griffin was in the little egg and milk stand she ran in front of her house on South 18th Street when the Western Union boy rode up, stopped, and handed her an envelope. Her son Owen was dead. He went into the service early in 1943, but he had been in France only since late November. He had been home the previous January on leave from his artillery unit and all his letters indicated he was doing well. Because Owen was Kenny Thompson's cousin and they had all known who he was, Gemma sent the paper reporting his death to Ed in France. He was shocked to get the news because he had seen Owen about two weeks before his death. Going through the lists of replacements one day, Ed noticed that someone listed his hometown as New Castle. It turned out to be Owen Griffin. Ed had made a point to look him up when he came through and visited with him briefly one afternoon. Soon after going into the lines two weeks later, Owen was dead. In their yearbook, only Clay Grubbs and Doris Grose separated the pictures of Owen Griffin and Orrin Grubbs.

The irony of actually encountering someone from his hometown only to hear that he had been killed stayed with Ed for a long time. Griffin was the only soldier from New Castle he saw while he was in Europe. Ed's replacement unit had remained at Fontainebleau where it had arrived in August, still in the drafty cavalry barracks and stables that Napoleon's troops had used. He decided that sitting around a repple-depple 150 miles behind the lines or taking convoys back and forth to supply dumps was no way to fight a war. His commanding officer was in a position to assign soldiers to units coming through the depot at Fontaine-bleau, so Ed asked him to transfer him when a unit came through that needed an officer. He asked for tanks at first, but when he saw one that had been hit soon after making his request, he decided he probably should ask for an ack-ack unit, since that was what he was trained to do.

While Ed waited for his transfer, he continued to take a convoy now and then. On one of these excursions he had occasion to meet a very famous figure in the war. Convoy instructions, like other orders, contained only the minimum amount of information needed to obtain the desired result. An officer would meet the convoy at point A and conduct it to point B, a certain number of miles beyond any one of the countless little towns and villages to be found all over Europe. The destination was usually a supply dump away from larger cities but near a road that could handle heavy truck traffic. On one of these missions, Ed had been entrusted with a truck convoy consisting of quantities of gasoline and overcoats. He was northeast of Paris at night headed north, perhaps between Soissons and St. Quentin, when he pulled to one side in his jeep to allow the convoy to pass in order to count the trucks to make sure that no one had fallen behind. As he completed the checklist and began to return to the front of the column, he noticed that the lead trucks had begun to slow down, then stop. This was strictly against orders, of course, because a stopped convoy became a sitting duck for attack. Word had already circulated about the German troops dressed in American uniforms who had created havoc in the early hours of the Ardennes counteroffensive just a little over two weeks before. As Ed and his driver approached the lead truck, they could see a green sedan, perhaps a Packard, pulled off to one side of the junction of two roads. On its side was the white star indicating that it belonged to an American staff officer. The car's driver had gotten out and flagged the convoy to a stop. Fearing the worst, Ed told his driver to cover him and got out of the jeep and approached the other GI, ordering him to stand aside so the convoy could pass.

The staff car's driver, an enlisted man, said that he had orders to take over the convoy. Now Ed became more alarmed. This was a story that was too much of a stretch. Ed told the driver that he had better just wake up whoever was in the car and prove it or the convoy was going to roll over him and anyone else. As the unhappy driver went toward the car, the truck drivers began shifting into gear to prepare to move in case there was trouble. The driver opened a back door and reached inside, then stepped back. Out came a white-haired officer wrapped in an overcoat, growling and cursing about being awakened in the middle of the night. It was General George S. Patton, Jr., respected and feared even more than most general officers among the ranks of the army. Ed explained that his orders were to take the convoy somewhere else. The general signed off on the order papers relieving him of the responsibility, and ordered him and his driver to return to their point of origin. Glad to be out of the situation, they did so. Patton was scrounging gasoline wherever he could find it to keep his tanks and trucks running.

When Patton struck north to relieve Bastogne and hit the German bulge in the flank, he had to halt his attack against the Siegfried fortifications. This meant that much of the front stabilized for a while during several weeks of the worst winter weather to hit Europe in many years. By the time the Bulge had been completely reduced, it was mid-January.

11. Will It Never End?
1945

More Casualties

THREE FULL YEARS of war had passed since Pearl Harbor, and there was still no end in sight. The Allies were closing in on Germany, but as the December fighting along the bulge in the western front had shown, the Germans still had plenty of fight left in them and there was no predicting when the end might come. If the Russians got closer to Berlin, or if the Allied armies on the western front could get there, then it might not last long, but who knew when that might be? Even if Germany were beaten, there was still Japan to be dealt with. It was hard going in the Philippines just now, and the Japanese islands were a long way off. B-29s kept hammering the factories and cities there, but the British and Americans had pounded Germany from the air for more than three years without being able to avoid massive invasions of France and Italy and much bloody fighting. And even with that, the Allies were only barely into German territory in the west, with most of the Siegfried Line fortifications intact and filled with Germans. It seemed like a long way to the Rhine just now. The Russians were still only in Poland after coming back so many miles from the tank ditches in front of Moscow.

Little had changed in the daily routine on Plum Street. Gemma's primary concern was with baby Jimmy, who was nearly five months old. She had sent a picture of herself and the baby, taken in the back yard, to Ed so he could be reminded of both of them. They wrote steadily, reminding each other of their love and trying not to talk about the war. Everyone tried not to dwell on that too much, wherever they were. They exchanged dreams about a house after the war and shared information and questions about what the little one was doing. Marie was about five months pregnant, due sometime in May. Maxine had left for Miami Beach late in December to be with Kenny, who had finally completed enough missions to come home. They were posted to a resort hotel along with hundreds of other airmen where Kenny began preparing to become a gunnery instructor. It was like a honeymoon for them this time, with opportunities to walk on the beach and savor the fact that he had made it home safely. The war had already made so many reunions impossible. Wanda was still in high school and once again crowded in her room, with two of her sisters back home again and a baby in the house. Gemma took an upstairs room for herself, leaving Wanda to share a room with Marie. Jess went on working long wartime hours, usually seven days a week, and Ethel continued to cook at the Clinic.

The news from the fighting fronts came back to New Castle steadily that January. The deaths of three city boys, all in France and Germany, appeared in the paper early in January. The father of one of these soldiers worked with Fred at the Chrysler. When Fred offered condolences at work, they were accepted, but the boy's father commented that with their remaining children to support, they were just happy that they had the GI insurance of $10,000. Outraged, but unwilling to confront the man for making such a comment, he walked away. Fred, with his one living child in the army, would not have considered any sum adequate compensation for such a loss. The two men never had much to say to each other after that.

The war's toll mounted on Ed's mother and father. Natural worriers, they dealt with their fears in different ways. Lillian fretted silently, keeping her own counsel alone at home every day, poring over the papers to glean any news about how the war was going in Europe. Ed wrote to her and she cherished the letters, but as with so much of the wartime mail, there was not much of substance except confirmation that, a certain number of days before, he had been well and sound. She always let Gemma

In the fall of 1944, Maxine and Wanda Moles posed with their new nephew Jimmy, on the steps at Plum Street, so Jess could snap the picture. All of the Moles girls were back home again while Ed, Kenny Thompson, and Orville Hammond were overseas or soon to go.

know that they had heard from him, and Gemma did the same for them. Her teeth bothered her a great deal during the war now that she was in her forties because she had never thought much of going to a dentist. Toothaches bothered her often, to the point that she lost a considerable amount of weight, especially in 1944 and 1945.

Fred worked long hours during the war as all the defense workers did at the Chrysler and other war plants in New Castle. When his ride dropped him back at the house in the hollow in the late afternoon, he had his usual chicken, pig, and cow chores to tend to, then a short evening in the house before the usual early bedtime. In the summer there was field work to be done. Crops would help win the war, too. But the gnawing fear he felt about the dangers his son faced in Europe caused him great concern. He, too, worried quietly. For a time, he drank some. He was never one to linger at a tavern, so he kept a bottle hidden in the basement of the house where Lillian would not be likely to find it. Usually it was distillery-bottled Kentucky bourbon, but on occasion there was the homemade stuff he remembered when he was younger: crystal clear with a kick like an old mule. Someone at the shop always knew where to find the genuine Clinton County article. Others in the family knew he did this, but never saw any effects from it.

The first week in January, Japanese radio reported that 450 American ships were headed for an invasion of Luzon in the Philippines. Days later, the War Department confirmed that the invasion had occurred in the Lingayen Gulf on the west side of the island. This brought extra worries for people back home in Henry County. Sarah Grubbs received word from Clay the first week of January that he had arrived in the Philippines and she sent it on to the *Courier-Times*. This meant that everyone in New Castle knew that the 38th Division, including the companies from New Castle, was there. With this invasion, there was a good chance that the division was involved. Everyone hoped and prayed that the casualties would be light.

At the same time reports of missing and casualties began to filter in from the fighting in the Bulge in the lines in Europe in December. Two more killed, two wounded, and six missing appeared in the paper by January 25. The War Department announced that there had been over seventy-four thousand killed, wounded, and missing in December on the Western Front, with more than ten thousand of those killed. This figure was higher than the casualty total had been for the month of the invasion.

In early January Ed took a convoy north with an enlisted man from the battery, Lewis Morin from Mississippi. Ed had learned to respect him for unflagging devotion to his duty no matter what it was. When packages of food and treats came in from home, Ed shared them with Morin. On the trip north, Ed noticed that Morin did not eat much and did not keep down much of what he ate. When they returned to Fontainebleau, although Lewis did not want to go, Ed took him to the army hospital nearby to have him looked at. The army doctors decided that he had a serious stomach ulcer that could best be treated back home. Although Morin did not want to return until the war was over, Ed regretfully ordered him back to the States to recuperate. When he arrived, he wrote to Gemma to tell her about how Ed was getting along. Morin was able to tell her much more in mail written in the United States than Ed had been able to do writing from France. At last, she at least knew where he was and that he was well when Morin had left.

Morin's digestive troubles illustrated a larger problem with GI diets. In England, even when living in tents, field kitchens and the availability of coal for fuel made for regular hot meals for most soldiers. This might be suspended when some units moved about for their training, but Ed's replacement outfit had been regularly supplied with an almost daily routine of hot meals featuring endless quantities of pork. This reflected a glut of pork produced by farmers back home in response to government policies guaranteeing low feed prices and high returns for every pig. GI food in England was plentiful and loaded with the calories active soldiers needed. Once they transferred to the Continent, this changed somewhat. If located near a unit which had established field kitchens, a steady supply of good food, and good army cooks, the fare was much like it had been in England, except that there was more dried chipped beef made with gravy, served on toast and known fondly among GIs as "shit on a shingle," or SOS. At Fontainebleau, cooks prepared food in kitchens in the buildings, and there was even a mess hall. This was like living at an army post back home.

Soldiers on the fighting fronts or those on the move made do with field rations. K rations were the most common fare for Ed and his men. These rations followed a pattern. There was a can about the size of a tuna can, which contained sausage, Spam, or cheese. This provided concentrated protein preserved in fat so that it would not spoil. A larger can held the pork and beans, sometimes mixed with wieners. Several crackers, sealed in waxed paper, accompanied by a packet of butter that was usually too hard to spread on anything came next. Sometimes there was a packet of powder that, mixed with a little water, made into something resembling pudding. Finally, for dessert, there was a small cake of chocolate not unlike the baker's chocolate Ed's mother bought at the store to melt for making frosting. This bar was always hard as a rock, and to be eaten had to be gnawed with the side teeth. Ed thought this was more trouble than it was worth and usually gave it away. The French or the Belgiques were always glad to get some of it.

The canned meat or cheese could be cut into chunks and mixed with other canned food, roasted on a stick, fried in the pan that was part of the GI mess kit, or masqueraded in other ways. For convenience, most soldiers punched a hole in the top of the cans of meat and beans and heated them in whatever way was available to them. Ed's battery usually had a vehicle nearby, so the men put their cans on the hot exhaust manifold of the engine to heat the food. It could be eaten cold, of course, and often was, but heating it up made it much more palatable. Every meal in the field was eaten with the big GI spoon which each man carried. Each K ration included three cigarettes and a packet of ground coffee.

They occasionally had C rations, which most thought were better. There was often more variety, including, sometimes, a portion of chicken in the meat can instead of the usual sausage, Spam, or cheese. They used the mess kit only when there was more variety or there was actually something to cook. It was less work to eat rations out of the containers and throw them away than it was to clean up a mess kit afterward.

When they could, cooks farther to the rear made hot meals and took them to the units in their areas in insulated containers which kept the food hot for several hours. These meals offered a change from the monotony of rations and made an approaching chow wagon a welcome sight.

Uncle Sam assumed that all his soldiers liked coffee, and made it available when possible. In camp conditions when there were no cooks about, ground coffee had to be boiled in a pan of water over a fire. This made for a brew that warmed one up inside, but had few other redeeming qualities except providing caffeine. Ed had learned to drink and enjoy coffee with his mother at home, and kept up the habit in the army. As a result of this diet, he had heartburn on a regular basis, and there were only two remedies, drinking bicarbonate of soda dissolved in water or trying to find the little green rolls of Tums. In other words, the GI diet was often hard on the stomach, in spite of providing the calories and nutrients soldiers needed. Soldiers like Morin whose digestive systems did not handle such rations as well suffered even more than most, and sometimes had to be sent home because of it.

Soldiers had to be careful where they got their water. Most depended on supplies trucked to rear areas where the cooks set up kitchens. From these trucks it was transferred to five-gallon GI cans or canvas bags in which it moved forward to the men who needed it. Drinking contaminated water usually did not happen more than once. The result of drinking bad water tended to leave a memory most did not wish to repeat.

Ack-Ack Duty in Belgium

It was late in January 1945 when an AA unit came through Fontainebleau in need of a battery officer. Ed took his transfer and headed out. His new outfit, the 788th AAA Auto-Weapons Battery, arrived in France in September and was being moved up just behind the front. They set up camp east of Liege and south of Aachen at Verviers in eastern Belgium, next to the Huertgen Forest and only a few miles from the German frontier. Nearby were old lead mines with large tailing piles all about. In the 788th Ed met and took on as his assistant Sgt. Milner from Arkansas. They quickly became friends and learned to depend on each other. Ed was unable to tell Gemma where he was, of course, but he made it clear that he had moved. That would have to be good enough.

Moving about as he had for the last six months over many parts of northern France, Ed had discovered a pattern in the damage to cities and towns. In Normandy and as far inland as Orleans there was considerable damage from the fighting that had been concentrated there until the end of July 1944. From there to the areas in eastern France and the Rhineland that had been overrun very quickly after the breakout there was only scattered damage, usually where the Germans had stopped to fight. The towns and villages got worse as he moved across the area of the Bulge fighting toward Germany.

It did not take them long to discover why they had been

moved to this particular place in the rolling Belgian countryside. They soon became aware of the noise overhead of something new to warfare. The 788th had set up under one of the routes the new German rockets flew on their way to Britain and the port of Antwerp. Ed had seen what V-1s could do in England, but the new V-2s were much larger and faster. The attacks became so menacing that by the fall of 1944 Kenny Thompson's crew took their furloughs in Scotland or the north of England to avoid the danger of rocket attack in London. Thousands of civilians in London and the south of England died and were injured in the last half of 1944 in the growing missile attacks.

The Germans fired their rockets sporadically, so there was no way to tell when the next one might come over. The AA crews on duty had to be vigilant for any opportunity, ready to adjust for altitude and speed. The V-1s were slow enough to get a decent shot at them if everyone was ready to go. The V-2s were much faster and usually much higher, so the odds of hitting one of them was considerably less. But the 40 mm guns had an effective range of five thousand yards, over 2.8 miles. They had to be careful to fire only so many degrees up from the horizon, then stop to avoid being hit by debris if they were on target. Higher up they could resume firing until the target went out of range. They usually had an opportunity to fire at least once per day, and occasionally they hit one. When this happened there would be a flash and a concussion wave from the fuel and explosives detonating. The debris might land anywhere.

It was in this way that Ed learned why it was important to wear a helmet. His battery was on duty one day when a target appeared and he gave the order to commence firing. While the crew raised the barrel to keep a V-1 under fire, Ed through his binoculars observed the trajectory and watched for evidence of a hit. Suddenly, the lights went out. For three days, he lay unconscious in a field hospital. When he woke up, he had a bad headache and a souvenir helmet that looked as though someone had hit it with a sledgehammer. A spent 40 mm projectile or a piece of shrapnel from somewhere had struck him on top of his head. Without the helmet, he would have been killed instantly. After taking it easy for a few days, he was good as new and back with his outfit. While he was unconscious in the hospital, he had been given a Purple Heart. He knew he was lucky that it was not given posthumously.

At Verviers, the 788th kept up the routine of watching for and shooting at buzz bombs and missiles, and tried to keep warm as February turned into March. The men chewed their K rations and hoped for the war to end soon. Keeping warm could be difficult. Any kind of shelter from the wind helped, and sometimes the heat from a truck engine or a fire made of branches or anything else that would burn helped a little.

In New Castle, the encouraging news that a local boy, Sgt. Floyd Cooney, had been among the 513 Allied prisoners liberated in a raid by the Rangers against a Japanese prison camp 23 miles behind the fighting front on Luzon brought hope to many families. Cooney had been a prisoner since the fall of Corregidor in April 1942. First word was that many of the prisoners suffered from malnutrition and wounds that would not heal.

On the other hand, the government announced on February 1 that when Germany was defeated, there would be a quick transfer of troops from Europe to the Pacific. Much of the equipment presently in Europe would be left there to speed up the transfer process and aid in rebuilding the European countries devastated in the war. Civilian production efforts would have to remain high in the United States to supply the equipment being stockpiled in the Pacific for the invasion of Japan. The War Department confirmed that fifteen infantry divisions, including Indiana's 38th, were in the Pacific, along with marine and airborne divisions, Rangers, and others. The government was showing some boldness in announcing such information, but most people suspected that either the Japanese already knew about these units, or the government was not releasing a full list.

The Germans reported that the Russians were only forty miles from Berlin along the banks of the Oder River, meaning that it was almost certain they would reach Berlin before the Allied armies. The British and Americans were still three hundred miles to the west. The Russians probably had an advantage of more than two to one in troops, while the Allied advantage in the west was estimated at roughly one and one-half to one. German resistance stiffened as the Russians neared the Reich capital, so they slowed down and dug in along the river. American and

French troops cleared sections of the west bank of the Rhine around Strasbourg by early in February.

After months of hoping for a miracle, Erma Vitatoe received a letter on January 6 from SSgt. Fred Carnahan of Nashville, Tennessee, a buddy of Orrin's, telling her he had witnessed Orrin's death. Not until January 30 did confirmation come from the War Department that this was true. Carnahan wrote that he and Orrin had surprised a group of Germans while on patrol. After an exchange of grenades, Orrin stood up to heave another and was shot through the arm with the bullet lodging in his chest, probably in his heart. Orrin died on the spot as the Germans beat a retreat. There had been a mix-up involving Orrin's body after his death resulting in a report that he was missing which Carnahan could not explain. "This is a letter that I have been putting off for some time, not because I didn't want to write to you, but I hoped this war would soon end and I would be able to tell you the truth in person. It would be a lot easier that way. Hope you understand why I couldn't write and tell you the bad news at first. It was just a little more than I could do. Orrin was one of the best friends I ever had. We were more like brothers than friends and his death was very hard for me to take. That was way back when we first started in this thing and before I realized what war was. Since then there have been many to go and I have gotten hard, but it still hurts me deeply to think of Orrin. . . . In closing, I wish there was something I could say to make it easier on you, but the words just aren't there. . . . His braveness is one of the reasons I have been able to keep going in the long months since his death." The letter did not help. Erma did not want to believe that Orrin was dead. As February wore on, a steady stream of notices of the other wounded, missing, and killed appeared in the paper nearly every day.

There were stories of a meeting in the Black Sea area between Roosevelt, Churchill, and Stalin early in February, then a report on what they had accomplished. The meeting, which took place at the resort city of Yalta, settled issues concerning the defeat of Germany, how the country was to be occupied, and assuring that the liberated countries could choose their own forms of government. The headline actually mentioned the end of Nazism! Maybe it would be over in Europe soon. But at home the selective service was still giving pre-induction physicals for young men. Forty-one, including Ed's school chum Harold Rothrock, qualified in February, ready for induction when they were needed.

There was no letup in Europe. With land and air forces reaching new record strength levels every day, over twenty-two hundred American aircraft attacked German targets on February 13, following heavy night raids by the British. To assist the Russians, the raids included a series of devastating attacks on Dresden, about sixty-five miles ahead of the advancing Red Army. Dresden had been left burning. Names of classmates Gemma and Ed had known appeared frequently in the paper. Pierre Zetterberg of the Class of 1940, son of the Ingersoll rolling mill family in town, received a promotion after participating in the capture of two German towns and a dam. In this way it became known that he was in the 310th Infantry, 78th Division.

Initial Japanese reports again turned out to be true when Pacific Fleet headquarters announced officially February 19 that marines had invaded Iwo Jima, an island 750 miles south of Japan and 1,500 miles northeast of the Philippines. Resistance was even more fanatical than usual, according to the reports, but the marines had made progress. Casualties mounted even faster than before. In the first forty-eight hours of the operation, there had already been a sickening toll of over thirty-six hundred dead and wounded marines.

More Bad News

The war came home to Plum Street in a double blow when the paper arrived at the Moles house on February 20. Pierre Zetterberg, recently featured in the paper for his promotion, was dead, killed February 7 before the letter about his promotion reached New Castle. Word of the death of a Plum Street boy traveled faster. Pvt. James Capshaw, from just a few houses up the street, was killed February 11, also in Germany. He had been in New Castle on leave the week before Christmas, and had only arrived in France on January 15. His family received his first letter sent from overseas just the day before. James's sister Judy had been Wanda's close friend since the Capshaws moved to Plum Street about the same time the Moles girls moved down the street to the house at 1828 Plum.

Judy was at school the morning the telegram arrived at the house at 2008 Plum Street reporting that Jim had been killed at Olzheim in Germany. Both parents were home because Jack worked the second shift, and they immediately called Rev. Kinnett at the Baptist parsonage. They then called the high school to relay instructions to Judy to get ready to be picked up. Judy suspected that her mother or father was ill, and it was Rev. Kinnett who told her that her brother was dead as he took her home. His mother took the news especially hard. Jim, nineteen years old, had graduated from high school only the previous May, and had never been away from home until he went to Texas for training. In accordance with the usual practice in New Castle, friends and neighbors brought food, stopped by to express sympathy, or sent cards. There was no funeral service because, like practically all those killed overseas, he was buried near the spot he had fallen. Judy stayed out of school for several days before going back. Her friends there did not say much about it when she came back. Everyone tried to keep a stiff upper lip and get on with their lives. It would not help win the war to go on dwelling about his loss indefinitely. But his mother just could not get over it. She hung the cardboard square with the gold star on it in the living room window that indicated that a member of their family had been killed in the war, and attended the meetings of the Gold Star Mothers. Talking about her loss with others who knew the same experience seemed to help a little.

How much longer could Germany hold out? Reports from London indicated that nearly seven thousand planes had attacked targets in one day on February 22, concentrating on the German rail system. The next day, the phenomenon of learning of the deaths of three servicemen in the same day happened in New Castle again. Two of them died on the ground in France and Luxembourg, and one in the air on a bombing raid to the oil refineries at Ploesti in Rumania. The flier, 2nd Lt. John Lindsey, had been missing since the previous June. There were bound to be more to come. The headlines that day announced a "Big Push" by the Allies toward the Rhine and the Ruhr industrial area. Yanks cleared Japanese troops from Manila in mop-up operations while even the headlines called the struggle on Iwo Jima a "bitter fight" as casualties lists continued to swell. B-29s wrecked 650 acres of the industrial area of Tokyo, more than a square mile, in a raid by more than 200 bombers.

By March 1, 1945, checking the list of killed, wounded, and missing had become a daily routine for most people in New Castle. That day, Sgt. Willard Porter of Knightstown was reported killed in Europe, and SSgt. Denzil Keith Pope of Route 4 was declared missing in Germany since February 16. Porter left two children with his wife, and Pope's wife Cora was caring for their two-year-old daughter Karen Jane. Everyone knew that, like the case of Orrin Grubbs, missing could mean anything, or everything.

Opportunity Knocks for the First Army

Americans pushed forward to secure all the areas on the west bank of the Rhine, but news reports made it clear that the Germans allowed the bridges to stand only until their own troops had crossed before they were blown up one after another. Some portions of the German army in the west were cut off and surrounded. American troops entered Cologne, on the Rhine, and began clearing Germans out of it. More Americans closed in on Bonn and Koblenz, where Fred Smith had served occupation duty after the Great War.

Then a tremendous break fell the Allies' way. On March 8, the Associated Press reported that the First Army had found a way across the Rhine somewhere south of Cologne. The river, deep and fast flowing, was a major barrier that would be very difficult and costly to cross when the time came. There had been a press blackout for twenty-four hours until the opportunity could be exploited. The bridge had been seized on the afternoon of the 7th, in spite of partially successful attempts to blow it up. Troops of the 9th Armored Division fought through roadblocks into the small town of Remagen on the west bank and rushed for the bridge. As foot soldiers from an armored infantry regiment braced themselves for the assault, wires, apparently cut by shellfire, failed to carry the current to the charges set along the bridge. A hole blew in the approach ramp, but when smoke cleared, the bridge still stood. GIs ran for the other side, expecting the bridge to be blown from underneath them at any second. Dodging a gaping hole in the floor part way across, they made it. They cleared the remaining Germans from the tunnel mouth on the other side and held on.

First Army command expected a German counterattack as soon as it could be mounted, so every available motorized unit in the area west of Remagen was sent toward the bridgehead immediately. Armored units, including nine tanks and some tank destroyers, crossed that evening and more followed the next day. These forces repulsed the German counterattacks that night. Engineer battalions began to build pontoon bridges across the river in case the strain of the traffic caused it to collapse. By the next afternoon, eight thousand troops had gotten across.

Among the nearby units in position west of the Cologne-Bonn-Koblenz sector was the 788th AAA. Ed and his battery were ordered to pack up immediately and board trucks to bolster the toehold at Remagen. German air attacks, including sorties by the new German ME-262 jets, had already been launched against the bridge the first day, but had failed to destroy it, and ack-ack batteries were needed immediately. They convoyed through Aachen and Cologne, then turned south along the river toward Remagen. They left Verviers early in the morning, but by the time they had gotten through Bonn and forded various creeks where bridges had been damaged along the route south, it was past noon.

They arrived early in the afternoon of March 10, as the first pontoon bridge was being extended to the eastern shore toward the little German town of Erpel below the bridge. Half the men of the battery, including Ed, immediately went across the steel bridge, towing two of their single-barrel 40 mm guns to the far side, and began to dig them in next to the towers that anchored the bridge. Ed positioned one on the downriver side just north of the bridge and one on the south. He had ordered the other two guns in the battery set up on the west side of the bridge before the rest of them had gone across. They would have to be vigilant for attacks from either direction. Searchlight battalions pulled up nearby to spot aircraft or floating objects at night. They crossed back and forth as needed the next few days, staying in tents when they were not on duty. After a couple of days, Ed found a building that offered some shelter and slept there with a few others in the battery. This became his home for the month the battery was at Remagen.

The 788th got a few chances to shoot at German aircraft that tried to knock out the bridge, but they were fleeting opportunities. Two attacking aircraft, both fighters, made their runs from the south at top speed, in excess of 350 m.p.h., dropped their bombs without hitting the bridge, and fled. There was one attack the morning after the 788th arrived, and one the next day. There was little time to shoot and neither plane was shot down. No other pilots made the attempt, at any rate. Allied fighters swarmed the area when the weather was fit to fly, and other ack-ack units were in the area, too. They occasionally fired a few rounds at suspicious objects in the water, but few targets appeared.

Ten days after the bridge had been seized, it groaned and fell into the river, killing twenty-eight engineers and injuring sixty-three others who were working to strengthen it. By then two pontoon bridges were carrying a steady flow across the Rhine to the Allied sector spreading into Germany. Ed was away from the river at the time and heard nothing. While Ed and his battery were there, it was cold and gray most of the time, and they were glad they had their winter clothes and caps and boots to keep them warm. It was getting a little warmer, but the constant cloudiness seemed to help the cold seep into every bone and joint.

In New Castle, people read about the Remagen news hoping it would shorten the war. On the day Ed crossed the Rhine bridge the first time, a picture of much more interest to most people in New Castle appeared in the paper. It showed men of the 38th Division, including Pfc. Paul Cleek of East Broad Street, taking a rest during fighting in Zigzag Pass on Bataan in the Philippines. This confirmed that the hometown boys were engaged with the Japanese. All of them looked tired and obviously had not shaved for several days. While marines continued to push northward on Iwo Jima, the 21st Bomber Command in the Marianas announced a new tactic. In a night raid on March 10, more than 250 B-29 Superfortresses concentrated a massive attack using incendiary bombs on the heart of Tokyo. In a city whose homes were built largely of wood and paper because of the danger of earthquakes, the sixteen hundred tons of gasoline bombs started fires which burned most of the city, nearly fifteen square miles, to ashes. Kobe, Nagoya, and others soon followed. It was good news for the home front.

Other news counterbalanced it. The war came to the Moles house on Plum Street yet again on March 12 when they learned in the paper that Sgt. Glen Cowan, a B-24 gunner, had been killed in Europe on February 23. Like Orrin and Clay, he was part of the Class of 1942 at the high school and was the brother of Gemma's cousin Ruth Cowan. Glen had been home in New Castle the end of November 1944 on a furlough before shipping overseas. Nearly all enlisted fliers were sergeants because men of that rank received better treatment if shot down and captured. Glen received his third stripe January 30, 1945, just three weeks before going down. More casualties came in every day, and they were getting closer now. Was there any hope that the war might end before Ed or Kenny or Orville was lost? Would it never end? The War Department announced that thirty B-29 crews had already been saved by the use of the airfields at Iwo Jima, mostly secure now at the price of almost four thousand dead marines. Among the marine casualties there was Cpl. Fred Haynes of the little northern Henry County village of Middletown, killed on Iwo Jima February 28.

Moving through the war-shattered towns in Belgium and along the Rhine, particularly in the winter, left very little time for good grooming. What remained of the civilian population concentrated on finding food and surviving. When GIs crossed over into Germany, civilian attitudes changed considerably and people were more sullen. General Eisenhower announced early in the year that the army did not consider feeding the civilian population a top priority. There was a war to fight and finish and the men who were doing the work were his first consideration. If the army's food left something to be desired, at least it was available.

The soldiers were fed, but keeping clean was another matter. Finding drinking water was sometimes difficult, and locating enough to wash in was nearly impossible. When furloughed back to rear areas or to cities for rest, soldiers cleaned up in baths, hotels, or in camps with shower facilities set up by the army. Out in the field, these were rarely available. Always on the lookout, enterprising GIs sometimes found them, however. After Ed had been at Verviers for six weeks, and then at Remagen for about three, everything he wore was filthy. His pant legs and sleeves were black with grime and dirt from working and sleeping in the same clothes day after day. Socks and underwear he could rotate and hang up to dry, but they rarely got washed. Socks could be dried and rubbed together to knock some of the dust out of them. Putting them back on dry was the next best thing to clean and dry. Like most GIs, Ed had but one pair of boots which he water-proofed with grease and tried to keep dry.

Everything else got dirtier every day. About the first of April Ed learned that there was a place downriver where baths were available, and he went to see about it. It was a house in a village about a mile and a half north of Remagen that had a hot water furnace, which meant that if fuel could be found, hot running water could be produced! When he arrived there was already a long line, but the wait was worth it. The house was cold, but there was abundant warm water. Except for being wrapped up in a wool blanket at night, it had been quite a while since he had been warm on both sides at the same time. It seemed as though he washed off pounds of dirt with the GI soap in the well-used shower, and it felt wonderful. He climbed into dirty but dry socks and underwear afterward, put on his dirty uniform and coat and boots, and felt like a new man. He might look gritty and smell the same on the outside, but he was clean underneath, at least for a while.

GIs scouted for anything to imitate the comforts of home or provide a diversion. Food, shelter, and drink usually headed the list, of course. Most GIs would drink nearly anything alcoholic they could lay their hands on. An enlisted man in Ed's battery approached him with secret information one day late in March. A place in Erpel, across the Rhine from Remagen, had been located with three enormous wine barrels badly in need of liberation. Ed agreed to investigate with them. When they went inside, they discovered that the first two barrels, each even on their sides taller than a man, were empty. But the third one seemed to have something in it. A sample all around proved to be white wine!

They had brought GI water cans along with them in the personnel carrier, so they began to fill them one at a time. Ed stood watch in front while the others filled the cans in the back of the long house and brought them out. Because the level in the barrel was low, the wine did not run fast enough to fill a can very quickly. Finally, the first can came out, eventually another. It seemed to take longer to fill the third, and even longer for the fourth one. After waiting for some time for the fifth can without result, Ed went back to see what had happened. The men were all drunk, having kept their cups full while they were filling the cans. He rounded them all up and took them back to their quarters to sleep it off, and they did not liberate any more Rhine wine.

There were food shortages and rationing chaos back home, too. The sudden new restrictions on meat announced while the Battle of the Bulge raged in December came as a shock to most people because American farmers had produced more meat than could be consumed by the civilian population at home, soldiers and sailors in training and overseas, America's allies, and those getting food under Lend-Lease. As a result, most meat had been removed from the ration list or had its ration point requirements drastically reduced in the summer and fall of 1944. When OPA announced the new, more severe restrictions in December 1944, Americans at home were forced onto the skimpiest diets they had faced so far in the war.

Not until the following March 20 and 21, however, did the government get around to explaining what had happened. Put simply, government food planners believed that the war would end in 1944 and planned for food production to peak that year, then decline. There was every indication this might actually happen in Europe when Allied forces raced from Normandy to Germany in just six weeks, arriving on German soil September 12. At that time, even General Eisenhower predicted publicly that the war would be over in Europe in six more weeks, recalling the way Germany had sought an armistice in 1918 when Allied troops appeared poised to enter Germany. Most people hoped that, rather than fight a town-by-town battle all the way across the German countryside, Hitler would sue for terms. These assumptions proved wrong.

When the government encouraged stock farmers to expand

using huge surpluses of feed grains available when the war began, production, especially of meat, rose so rapidly in 1942 and 1943 that slaughterhouses could not handle it. The government ordered farmers to hold fat cattle and hogs using a permit system which was like taking a number at the delicatessen. When the animals could be processed and the meat used, they could be sold and shipped.

Complicating the picture was the soaring demand for American food overseas. The Russians scorched their own earth when retreating, and fighting destroyed much of what was left when the Germans conducted a savage series of fighting retreats across the same areas in 1943 and 1944. As demand for war materiel leveled off, demand for food kept rising. The first pinch at home came in December 1944, when the German counteroffensive in Belgium proved that the war would not be over for some time. With production of sugar and high-protein items such as meat, chicken, cheese, and eggs declining and livestock feed stocks way down, the only way the War Food Administration (this new organization seemed to have power over the OPA, in a way mysterious to most people) could respond was to use rationing requirements to cut consumption of items no longer plentiful. From record meat consumption levels in 1944, Americans had no choice but to cut their intake to per capita quantities lower than in the depression years of the 1930s. Because it takes two years to feed a steer, the reductions in the national beef herd in 1944 could not be made up quickly. Similarly, hog production went down for the same reason as slaughter hogs and many of the sows that produced them went to market in 1944. Although it only takes six months to feed a hog to market weight, it takes longer than that to expand the national herd. The earliest hope for increased production would not come until late in 1945.

Similarly, egg production peaked early in 1944 and there were more eggs than could be eaten, shipped, or stored. The glut produced a collapse of prices for eggs, prompting the government to step in and guarantee egg prices to "prevent waste." Consequently, the government bought huge quantities of eggs at a time when demand was down because meat was plentiful. Egg production declined. When the meat shortage appeared late in 1944, egg production was also down and the eggs stored by the govern-

ment had been used or had spoiled. Demand for eggs as a sub-
stitute for meat shot up just when egg production had fallen off. It
took five to six months to raise a laying hen to full production
from a baby chick. At best, it would be some time in the middle of
1945 before this shortage could begin to be addressed. Soon rent
control came to New Castle in the form of an order from the OPA
freezing rents at the October 1943 rates. In the meantime, civilians on Plum Street used their ration coupons carefully and
cleaned up their plates as they waited for the next day's papers
and another chance at the lottery of sorrow and dashed dreams.

They would not have long to wait. The next day's paper notified New Castle that Lt. Earl Chandler, a 1940 classmate of
Gemma's, was missing after a bombing mission in the Pacific. One
of the seven Leisure boys of Knightstown in the service, Mellis,
died in action in Germany on March 5, while two of his brothers,
Robert and Max, were missing in action there. New opportunities
would appear soon. The Japanese reported that American forces
had begun an invasion of Okinawa, south of Japan, which turned
out to be false for a few days, then true on April 2, and Eisenhower confirmed reports that American and British armor had
broken German defensive lines about 225 miles from Berlin.
Nearly a thousand bombers escorted by 350 fighters bombed
Berlin and Hannover as the German high command declared its
intention to evacuate unnecessary people from what was left of
Berlin. By the end of March, American units were only 175 miles
from the capital, having cut off 21 German divisions in a sweep
around the Ruhr. By April 4, only 150 miles separated advance
elements of Patton's 3rd Army moving toward the Czech border
and the Russians advancing from the east.

In New Castle on the evening of April 4, Sgt. Floyd Cooney,
the GI rescued from a Japanese prison camp earlier in the year,
told a crowd of over four hundred people about his experiences.
He said that six thousand prisoners went into the camp in 1942,
and only 511 survived the skimpy rations, disease, and harsh
treatment, including mandatory work eight to eighteen hours a
day. Cooney weighed 174 pounds when he was captured, 111
when freed. He received three letters and one package during the
nearly three years he was a prisoner. The crowd applauded its
approval when he announced that the day after his liberation he

had said good-bye to a diet of rice and rice soup by eating seventeen eggs for his first breakfast. Cooney added his contribution to a fund to build an honor roll of the names of everyone from Henry County who had served. As Cooney finished speaking and went outside, he spotted a youth about eighteen years old running from his car as he approached it to go home. His gasoline ration book was missing.

Moving Again

As April began, the weather started to warm up a little and the Allied push first into the Ruhr and then into central Germany generated a flood of German refugees on the roads. This tide began to impede troop and transport movement behind the front, and news of the problem even appeared in the papers back home. With the danger gone at Remagen and regular traffic crossing the river there on two pontoon bridges, Ed and the 788th were ordered down river, north to Cologne. They set up their trailer-mounted 40 mm guns again and assisted with the crush of civilian traffic trying to cross the river there. Ed drew the duty of monitoring the flow of refugees across the only pontoon bridge during the day and keeping it clear and secure at night.

Here at a floating bridge connecting two parts of a shattered city the war came home to Ed in a way he had not experienced before. French and German workers moved forcibly into the industrial centers of the Reich, and people whose families had lived west of the Rhine, walked for days and weeks to reach the bridges at Cologne. Thousands of civilians bombed or shelled out of their homes as the fighting moved east began walking to find a safe place to stay for a while. As the fighting approached the Rhine and the Germans withdrew from the area, they drove much of the civilian population, which hoped to escape the danger, ahead of them. With this threat passed, these people flooded back to the west. All hoped to find intact their towns and relatives. They sometimes carried a little money or concealed some hoarded food to share with the people still alive when they reached home.

When Ed reached Cologne, this column of refugees mixed with army trucks and jeeps and tanks in a never-ending stream in both directions, but mostly moving westward. Cologne, one of the most bombed cities of the war, looked to Ed as though it had been made of sand before a heavy rain. The pockmarked twin towers of the medieval Gothic cathedral, miraculously intact, stood towering above him and the utter destruction below. Behind it the three long pairs of bowstring-truss spans of the Hohenzollern steel bridge lay partially submerged in the waters of the Rhine. Alongside it on the downstream side ran the pontoon bridge, lashed to the ruined bridge's pilings with cables to keep it from floating away.

Ed's job, besides keeping track of his battery, was to monitor the flow of refugees and keep them moving. Nearly all were women and children and old people. The bridge closed at 6 P.M. and remained closed until 6 A.M. next morning. One of the most difficult tasks he had to perform in the entire war was to close the gate to this bridge at 6 P.M. every day. Many of the refugees begged to be allowed across, having come so far, but his orders were to allow no one on the bridge after it closed. They cried and pleaded and sometimes offered him some of the miserable belongings they carried, but orders were orders. Each night when the bridge closed, he and some of the men in the battery handed out rations to those who were going to spend the night in whatever bits of shelter they could find nearby in the ruined buildings and partially cleared streets and alleyways, or out in the open. The line was sometimes half a mile long or more when they handed out food. It was heartbreaking to see them straggle through day after day, all day long while he was there, especially when it rained.

As Ed waited at Cologne and watched the flow of displaced persons (DPs), a story reached the *Courier-Times* which provided another reason it might have been necessary for the United States to get into the war against Hitler. The AP reported that Bela Fabian, leader of a Hungarian political party dissolved under the Nazis, had announced that five million Jews had been gassed and cremated at a "murder factory" at Auschwitz, in upper Silesia in the eastern part of Germany. Fabian was aware of this because he had been one of five hundred thousand Hungarian Jews taken there in June 1944. Over four hundred thousand of those had been killed in the first two months there, and only one thousand remained alive when the guards left as the Russians approached in 1945. Fabian had made it to the American lines where he told his tale, "so horrible as to be almost unbelievable," to American translators. The commander of one tank unit which discovered another death camp at Ohrdruf ordered civilians living nearby to be marched through it to see for themselves. The next morning the mayor of the town and his wife were found hanged. Fighting on Okinawa, in Italy, and the end of a miners' dispute in which the government took over 235 mines from strikers competed for news that day, April 11. The next day President Roosevelt died.

The nation plunged into mourning as the armies in Europe went on with the business of finishing off the Germans. Clergy timed their memorial services in many churches in New Castle and all across the nation to coincide with the services in Washington or the burial formalities at Hyde Park. At home, Jess, almost disbelieving, mourned with the rest of the country, because even those who hated FDR's politics respected his political skill. Loyalty to Roosevelt was such a pillar of the orthodoxy at the Moles house that it would take time to adjust to having Truman from Missouri as president, and never would the luster disappear from the halo FDR wore in Jess's memory.

The 788th was at Cologne for most of April, then went upriver to Godesberg. They moved east to the front along the Elbe River about April 25, shortly after advance tank units reached it. They were only seventy miles from Berlin. But there were no German aircraft left flying, at least not in their sector. After keeping watch on the Elbe for a week, they motored back to Godesberg on the Rhine.

While his battery was posted on the Elbe, Ed decided that his uniform was just too dirty to tolerate any longer. Poking around in the ruins of a building, he found two cooking kettles and decided to do something about it. Back home his mother had always done the laundry, but he had watched. He filled the kettles with water, brought them to a boil on a fire of wood debris, and added some shaved GI soap to the first one, just like his mother did with the Fels naphtha bar. The most offensive things he owned were his olive drab wool pants and tunic, so badly soaked with sweat and dirt that they reeked so that even he could not

escape the odor. These went into the pot along with some underwear while he wore a less dirty pair of pants with holes in them
and his jacket and overcoat. He stirred the pot with a stick until
the dirt in the water indicated something was working, moved
them into the hot rinse water, then lifted them out to drip and
cool. He noticed something right away that made him a little
anxious. The pants legs did not seem as long as they had been
when he took them off, but he assumed it was because they were
a little wadded and soaking wet. They steamed in the cool air
until they reached a temperature at which he could wring them
out. When he untwisted them and held them up in front of him,
the legs were about eight inches shorter than the pants he had on.
The wool tunic looked as though it had been made for a twelve-
year-old boy. A pair of wool socks would have held only a little
change. In this manner Ed learned the hard way that his mother
had never washed anything made of wool in boiling water. He
had a clean uniform that he could no longer wear. After returning
to the Rhine a few days later he was able to find an army supply
depot that would issue him replacements.

Fighting continued on Okinawa and in the Philippines while
two more New Castle soldiers' deaths came home from Germany.
Ernie Pyle's death was in the same paper. He was killed on Ie
Jima, near Okinawa. Pyle, a native Hoosier and graduate of Indiana University, was a war correspondent loved by millions across
the country for his down-to-earth reports on the average GI Joe
in every theater of the war, and he would be missed by the soldiers whose life and hardships he had shared.

As the Russians entered Berlin the last week of April and
American armies pushed up to the Elbe and headed into Bavaria,
fighting raged on Okinawa and in the Philippines. The death toll
climbed steadily in April, as did the list of wounded and missing.
A day or two might go by with no deaths, but it also was common
to have one or two every day for three or four days. The town was
almost numb to it now, reading the notices but not reacting to
them as they had done when they first began to come in.

The rationing toll also rose. All meats except mutton were on
the ration list, with point increases for margarine, oils, beefsteaks
and roasts, and lamb. A meat thief got caught outside the Rose
City Packing Company where he worked after hiding two hams

and three slabs of bacon in a barrel. When he returned after work to pick up his loot, police, who had been told of disappearing meat, nabbed him. In the back pages of the paper, AP stories about V-E cutbacks that had already begun or were on the horizon began to appear. Production would be reduced under the cutbacks to materiel needed for the Pacific theater.

12. We'll Meet Again, 1945

As May began, the headlines in the hometown paper got larger and longer. President Truman announced on the 2nd that all the German forces in Italy and southern Austria, totaling nearly a million men, had surrendered unconditionally to the Allies. Hostilities came to a conclusion in these areas, ending the bloodbath for Allied forces that had continued every day of the campaign up the Italian peninsula. Italian partisan forces found Mussolini and shot him, then hanged his body upside down in a public square in a northern Italian town square where residents could pay their respects. Most spat on the body. Reports and rumors flew that Hitler was dead but could not be confirmed.

On Friday, May 4, banner headlines announced the surrender of the German forces in Denmark, Holland, and northwestern Germany. The U.S. Fifth Army, marching north into the Alps, linked up with Patch's Seventh Army at the Brenner Pass south of Innsbruck as the remaining resistance began to collapse. Hundreds of thousands of prisoners staggered the capacity of the military police and guard units to cope with them.

Finally on Tuesday, May 8, the paper proclaimed what had been on the radio for hours: The Germans had surrendered unconditionally and the last hostilities in Europe were to end at 5 p.m. that day, with an afternoon V-E parade in New Castle beginning at the courthouse and church services to follow. On the same front page was the news that Pvt. Max Leisure, one of the seven Leisure sons in the service, had been killed in Germany, making him the second of the Leisure boys killed there in hostile action. Many New Castle businesses placed ads in the paper over the next days celebrating the victory, but calling for continued all-out effort on the home front to finish the Japanese. On that day there were sons and daughters of Henry County scattered across every theater and battlefield of the war.

Another Cause for Celebration on Plum Street

With partial euphoria in season in New Castle, Marie sensed that it was time for her to deliver. As with Gemma, Ethel was at the Clinic to keep an eye on Marie and work at the same time. After laboring with some difficulty for thirty-six hours, Marie gave birth to a baby son she named David on May 9, 1945. Jess sent a wire to Orville, stationed in the Philippines, that he was a father. When Marie came home a week later, both she and Gemma knew it was time to begin looking for another place to live. Neither knew when her husband would be home, but even the larger house at 1828 Plum Street was crowded now. Housing was scarce everywhere, and New Castle was no exception. Gemma began looking early in the summer, and Marie did the same as soon as she was able to be out and about. The ration books for the two babies helped at the dinner table.

On May 10, the War Department announced its discharge point system for determining the order in which men could return home from the European theater. Soldiers who had fought in North Africa and Europe were exempted from service in the Pacific, but the ones who had served only in Europe, no matter how long, were eligible for shipment to the Pacific if needed. Any soldier with eighty-five points was to be shipped home immediately. Soldiers received a point for each month of service, an additional point for each month of service overseas, five points for each award of combat decorations, and twelve points for each child under the age of eighteen (limit of three). Those who attained eighty-five points would be released unless their presence was considered vital. Officers would be released at a slower rate than enlisted men because of their responsibilities and duties.

The army expected two million men to be released in the coming twelve months. This good news did not extend to the men already headed for the Pacific theater or expected to go there. Among these was Ed's friend Harry Ridout, a medic who had seen wounds and death all across Europe. Ed learned that after some rest and relaxation Harry would be going to the Pacific for duty in the invasion of Japan. The War Department announced on May 22 that the First U.S. Army in Europe would go to the Pacific via the United States, but with many unit changes. From this, no one could tell if he would be going to the Pacific or not. The end of the war in Europe brought to the fore the plight of an estimated ten million refugees and DPs. Ed had been shocked and saddened by the plight of those he had seen as they crossed the Rhine.

Some frightening moments came to New Castle homes in the next couple of weeks when the Western Union boy rode up with telegrams. One, for Mr. and Mrs. R. H. Baker of North 17th street, informed them that their son, Lt. Thornton "Rabbit" Baker, had been freed from a German prison camp. Other similar announcements followed. Soldiers who returned home in May were noted in the paper.

On Okinawa, the bitterness of the Japanese resistance increased. Suicide plane attacks launched from the home islands became common, with serious losses among ships in the fleet supporting the operation and in other areas. Outrage spread rapidly when a kamikaze plane hit a hospital ship south of Okinawa late in May. Reports from early in May had pegged casualties very high in the Okinawa operation. They continued to go up. Every family with a marine or sailor in the Pacific prayed for their own and others to be spared. In the air over Japan, incendiary raids by growing numbers of B-29s torched more Japanese cities, and they returned to burn areas previously missed. In the Philippines, a Sulphur Springs medic died while evacuating wounded men from the fighting as American troops continued to push into areas still under Japanese control. A steady stream of liberated prisoners of war began to appear in the paper, sometimes as many as three or four in a day. But the paper listed ninety-nine from Henry County who had died in the war so far, more than fifty of them in just the previous twelve months.

Peace in Europe, at Last

Now it was all over in Europe. There would be no more danger of German planes, counterattacks, snipers, or shelling. But for those there, the daily routine did not change much. GIs still stood duty, kept their weapons clean, and wondered what was for chow. They could relax a little now, though, and spend more time watching for news of the fighting in the Pacific.

All soldiers look for souvenirs, and certain things are prized above others. Insignia and flags of the enemy always ranked highly, as did weapons. While the 788th sat at Godesberg after the German surrender, one enlisted man in the battery came across a German pistol for a trophy. While he cleaned it, he moved the trigger not knowing there was a round in the chamber. The bullet hit him underneath his jaw and went up into his brain, killing him. He was the first soldier lost out of the battery. There was nothing to do but notify his family that he had died as a result of an accident, a job officers were expected to perform. The irony of surviving World War II in Europe only to be killed in a senseless accident was lost on no one there or back home.

That May the leaves broke out of their buds in northern Europe and brought color to the landscape in a way few had noticed the previous several years. Ed noticed the pale spring colors turn darker green as warm days finally arrived and it was possible to be comfortable without being huddled against a wall or a truck. Without the urgency of keeping the pressure on the Germans, more time might be spent in finding a way to wash clothes and clean up a little, but it was not easy. At least it was not such a struggle to keep warm. The laundry would wait a while longer.

South of Remagen in those spring days was another sight that Ed would never forget. The bag of prisoners taken in the months of March, April, and May had been huge, and the army set up temporary camps for them until decisions could be made about what to do with them. One of these camps sprawled along a flat area beside the Rhine south of Remagen about five miles. Ed drove past it several times, seeing the thousands of German soldiers in their gray-and-green uniforms looking out through the double barbed wire enclosure. Most huddled in coats and boots because it was still chilly and damp. There could have been one hundred thousand in the area of seventy-five acres or more, sitting, standing, passing time. MPs were everywhere. There was some smell, but it was not too bad. Army tents stood row on row for housing. Ed thought to himself that it was better for a lot of reasons to be on the winning side.

President Truman announced June 1 that troop strength in the Pacific would be doubled, and would be larger than the armies had been in Europe. He called for civilians to abstain from travel during the time the soldiers would be moving to the West Coast to reduce the burden on the railroads.

Good news continued to arrive in New Castle for families of prisoners of war. On June 4, Cora Pope received a letter from her husband, SSgt. Denzil Pope, missing since February 16, saying that he had been liberated April 28 deep in Germany. For the first time his outfit, the 94th Infantry Division, was identified in the paper. When he wrote, he was already at Le Havre, awaiting transportation back to the States. For the first time, Cora learned that Keith had been captured in the attempt to break through positions built during the war for defense of the German homeland. His 302nd Infantry unit had attacked and taken a machine gun position in the Siegfried Line fortifications as part of Patton's effort to break out into central Germany. A German counterattack overran his position. Because of the changing military situation by that time, the prisoners he was with had been moved frequently. There was no opportunity to try to send word home, as so many of the fliers who had been captured earlier in the war had been able to do. The Germans were short of everything, including food for prisoners. Pope had very little food during his seventy-three days of captivity, and some of the prisoners with him died. Rabbit Baker arrived home in New Castle the same day for sixty days leave after being a prisoner for twenty-two months.

Some news was not so good, however. The parents of Pfc. Flossie Flannery, of Springport in the northern part of the county, learned that she had been missing since May 30 on a flight in Africa. She had been serving as a WAC on the African Gold Coast with the Air Transport Command. Except for some WACs injured in bombing in London, none had been lost overseas during the war. June was nearly over when the War Department confirmed Pfc. Flannery's death in a crash in the Atlantic. Her WAC unit was being transferred to another duty station on the African coast when her plane went down.

With only thirteen square miles of the island left in their control on June 14, the Japanese conceded that Okinawa was lost and announced preparations for the next Allied blow. They did not know whether it would come against China or Japan itself, but in the months before it took place, they intended to have 2.5 to 5 million soldiers ready to defend the home islands. They claimed to be confident that they could repel an invasion. This was grim news, considering that the conquest of Okinawa had cost more than 12,000 American lives and 120,000 Japanese, in addition to more than 40,000 civilians. All resistance ended on Okinawa June 22.

The War Department announced that the 3rd and 7th Armies would occupy Germany, while the 9th Army would be headed home as of July 1, only two weeks away. Ed's unit had been in the First Army's sector when the war ended, but the lines of authority changed from time to time, especially with entire armies being pulled out of the line to go home. The announcement specified certain units which would go to the Pacific, including the 97th, 86th, 2nd, 5th, 54th, 87th, 95th, and 104th Infantry Divisions and the 13th Armored Division. There was no way to know when Ed might be able to leave, or what his destination might be.

B-29s continued to devastate Japanese cities in incendiary raids, prompting General Arnold to comment that by the end of 1946 there would be nothing left to bomb. General Eisenhower returned to the United States on June 18 to cheering mobs at National Airport in Washington and a round of speeches in the nation's capital. President Truman left June 19 for the United Nations conference in San Francisco. As Japanese resistance ended on Okinawa, speculation began in the papers about possible invasion sites on the Japanese home islands. In her first voyage since V-E day, the liner *Queen Mary* arrived in New York with fourteen thousand soldiers aboard. News reached New Castle the next day of another county soldier killed, this time in the Philippines on May as fighting continued there. MacArthur announced that the Luzon operation was over on June 25, but Japanese troops holding out in the Sierra Madre to the east would be dealt with by Filipino troops.

July was frustrating at home and on duty overseas for millions of Americans. Japan could be conquered square foot by square foot if necessary, but what was the point? Even the fanatical Japanese had to be able to see that the war was over for them. People compared the radio broadcasts of the Japanese to what the Germans had said in April and found many similarities. The firebomb raids on Japanese cities continued almost day and night, leaving most to wonder how long any country could resist when another city burned to the ground every day. The Germans had decentralized their production, putting plants in hundreds of cities and towns all over the Reich, but it was known that Japanese industry was concentrated in relatively few areas. B-29s set these on fire, then went back a few days or weeks later to burn the areas which had escaped earlier. Tokyo, Yokohama, and Nagoya were practically deserted because the housing there had been almost completely incinerated. What would it take to convince these people that it was over and they had lost?

During July, the bombing continued and various task forces of the Pacific Fleet took turns raiding and shelling the Japanese mainland. From the 10th to the 18th of July, a task force of fifteen carriers, eight battleships, fifteen cruisers, and more than four dozen destroyers attacked shipping, port installations, aircraft, and industrial targets on Honshu and Hokkaido. Over a thousand planes hit Tokyo in one attack and land-based medium bombers sank fifty thousand tons of shipping.

The papers carried news of the meeting which started July 17 of the Big Three, the first since Truman had become president. This went on for more than two weeks at Potsdam, a suburb southwest of Berlin, in the Russian sector. This meeting was interrupted on July 25 for the British elections. To everyone's surprise in the United States, Churchill's Tories went down to defeat and Clement Atlee, head of the Labour Party, became prime minister. When the talks resumed at Potsdam, Churchill was gone and Stalin sat across from British and American leaders, both of whom were new at their jobs.

For Ed and Gemma, July was wasted in waiting. Ed was sitting along the Rhine signing releases for his enlisted men to go home while moving closer to the journey himself, but at the snail's pace of two points per month. By his count, as of July 15 he had fifty-five points, still thirty shy of the minimum needed. With little to do, when he heard that his old outfit, the 448th, was at Mainz, he took Milner with him to go visit them. They had moved often in the months after they had landed in France in June 1944, but had been lucky. Without knowing where they were camped, Ed drove right into their area. Ed's old friend Paul Borgman from Ft. Bliss was still with them, he discovered. They renewed acquaintances and caught up on the latest word from home.

The casualties continued to trickle into the paper now, but at least they had slowed from the awful pace of the first half of the year. Pvt. Charles Thornburg's death in the Pacific started the month, and then came an unexpected story. Ensign Julia Antic, a navy nurse, had died of illness, the third woman in service from Henry County to lose her life in the war. There was no new word about MM2/C Guy Amburgey. He had been reported missing April 27, but such reports were so common by then that there was concern, but it was tempered with hopeful anticipation. The navy asked his family not to identify his ship or where he was based. Amburgey was known all over New Castle because he was the main delivery man for the Railway Express Agency, based at the Pennsylvania Railroad station, just three blocks from the house on Plum Street. Gemma babysat for his sister and her husband when she was growing up. Guy and his wife Clemma had no children, but she waited for him at their home on 23rd Street.

As July waned and with the 788th breaking up, Ed transferred south to a camp near Schweinfurt, east of Mainz and Frankfurt, where he joined the 29th Antiaircraft Artillery Group. Schweinfurt had been the target of 8th Air Force bombers in 1943 when appalling numbers had been shot down. Here they took up more comfortable quarters in a brick building and managed to stay cleaner. Technically speaking, they were defending an airfield now, so Ed's uniform bore the patch of the 9th Air Force, which had supplied tactical aircraft, medium bombers such as B-25s and B-26s, for support missions for the campaigns in Europe.

Communication with Supreme Headquarters in Paris was difficult by telephone because of the distance, and radio range was not that great, so when there was something especially important, Ed often sent a driver. On one of these occasions the enlisted man who was going asked to take a friend along to break the monotony, and Ed agreed. On the way, the driver rounded a curve to find a flock of sheep in the road. Turning quickly to avoid them, a wheel of the top-heavy personnel carrier slipped off the edge of the road and the vehicle overturned, killing the driver's friend. Another family back home received a wire from the War Department.

There was official R and R for Ed and the other officers at Schweinfurt as well. Ed was sent to the French Riviera for a week, staying at the Hotel Martinique in Cannes. He and the other officers there lived in high style, comfortable and well fed. It was a time to get all the army grime off and be clean and comfortable without worries about duty or the weather, and to sleep in a real bed.

Ed and an officer friend from Minnesota decided to rent a boat and go out on the Mediterranean Sea one afternoon. They gave a Frenchman cigarettes to pay for renting the boat, then went out, neither of them really familiar with working a sail. When they were unable to turn it around, it capsized. As they struggled to hang on to the boat they wondered if it would all end on vacation in the Mediterranean, another foolish accident that would generate telegrams home to two more families. When the wind helped them drift close to a breakwater, they dragged the boat back to the beach and turned it in "as is," scared but safe. With this near-miss behind him, he tried to enjoy the rest and forget about the possibility of being sent to the Pacific.

After returning to Germany, Ed learned Harry Ridout was in Marseilles, ready to be shipped to the Pacific, so Ed took a train to look him up there. It was good to see an old friend again, even if neither knew what might be coming. They spent the day visiting before Ed had to take his ride back to Germany in a C-47.

Another Milestone

Gemma had her hands full with Jim, who would be a year old in August. He was progressing normally, crawling at a rapid pace and pulling himself up to chairs and other objects, and jabbering.

Work had eased up some at the Chrysler where Jess worked, but everywhere there was a sense that the war was not over by a long shot.

Wanda finished her junior year in high school in May and began dating Bill Hosea, who had graduated with Ed in the Class of 1941. Wanda was going through the usual rebellious stage, as each of her sisters had done. During hers, Gemma remained resentfully quiet, making her own future plans. Maxine and Marie had run around with a fun-loving crowd, dating and going to the area hot spots. Sometimes they got in so late they had to sneak in the house, hoping to avoid being caught. With Jess working long hours and Ethel working at the Clinic, there were more opportunities to be out on the town. Wanda had seen her three sisters marry within a year of each other and begin their lives as adults, one of them going to a distant state to do so. The other two had married in New Castle but left soon afterward. Wanda had friends as the other girls had, Geneta Kern and Judy Capshaw among them, but she liked to look nice and so had found a job at the Fashion Shop on Broad Street. This job, and later on another at Mary Woodbury's dress shop, provided some income which allowed her to stay up-to-date in the fashion world.

Wanda and Bill decided to get married so they went to Greenfield, the county seat of Hancock County, the next county to the west, and got a marriage license. It was standard practice for the county clerk to publish the names of applicants for marriage licenses in the local paper. Had they done this in New Castle, everyone in town would have known about it the next day. But no one in New Castle read the Greenfield paper, so they were able to get married secretly after finding a minister there who performed the wedding. Marie and Orville had tied the knot without telling his mother, in order to avoid her wrath, and this was pretty much the same thing. After the ceremony Bill went home and Wanda did the same. For two weeks, no one knew about the wedding. But when word leaked out at school, it didn't take long to find its way to the house on Plum Street. Wanda could not deny that she had in fact married Bill almost two weeks before. The uproar that followed faded with time so that no one seemed to remember it very well afterward.

The result was that Wanda and Bill found an apartment in a

house on North 18th Street a couple of days later and moved into it. Neither was very well prepared for such a venture, and there was little to move. There were few places available to rent in New Castle at any price, and what they found was a big step down from what they had known, and a little shabby. But it would have to do; they were on their own now. Of their four daughters' weddings, Jess and Ethel had only been able to attend Marie's. As always, Jess's anger cooled quickly. Wanda was already older than when Ethel had been a bride.

Ultimatum and Shattering Force

As the Potsdam conference wound down in July, the Allies broadcast a message to the Japanese leadership demanding that they accept unconditional surrender or face utter ruin. The Allies indicated that they did not wish to impoverish the Japanese people, urging them to lay down their arms. During the last days of July and the first week of August there was no reply.

August began quietly, but did not stay that way for long. In the paper which arrived at the Moles house on the afternoon of August 6 was a huge double headline telling of the destruction of an entire Japanese city, Hiroshima, with a single bomb carried by one plane. President Truman announced on the radio that it was an atomic bomb. The new weapon drew its power from the same process by which the sun made its energy, according to the statement. This did not mean much to most people, but in small towns and on farms across the country, it was welcome news. When Truman said there would be more to come, most hoped that the bombs would fall fast enough to convince even the Japanese that there was no hope. The Japanese set about trying to assess the damage. The next day the War Department announced that the new bomb had been tested first on July 16 in New Mexico.

On August 8, two days later, the Russians declared war on Japan. Reports told that 60 percent of Hiroshima had been destroyed in the atomic blast. The crew of the B-29 which delivered the bomb described a huge, towering column of smoke and dust from the explosion. The Japanese admitted the loss of the city. The next day the headline read SUPERBOMB HITS JAPAN AGAIN as word came that another bomb had been dropped on the city of Nagasaki while other B-29s raided Tokyo again. The Russians were invading industrial Manchuria from two directions, trying to isolate a large pocket of Japanese forces.

The next day, August 10, the radio broadcasts from Japan asked for peace terms from the Allies. One provision, that the emperor be allowed to remain in power, might be a sticking point, however. The Allies responded that they would let the emperor stay if he would take orders from the Allied commander in Japan. When no reply came for two days, B-29s resumed attacks on Tokyo. In the paper of the 14th was the news that the Japanese reply was on its way through diplomatic channels but had not arrived in Washington yet.

It arrived shortly after six o'clock that evening of August 14th and the radio carried the news to everyone that the war was finally over. Every kind of noise that could be made was heard in New Castle that night. Horns honked, factory whistles blew, firecrackers sounded, and church bells rang as the good news spread rapidly with the noise. Stores and theaters closed as most people in New Castle went downtown to join the jam of cars and people. Most factory workers on the night shift left work to join in the celebration, at least for a while. Five false alarms turned in at various fireboxes added the noise of sirens to the air. No one seemed to mind the downpour of rain that dampened the evening. Among the reasons to celebrate: OPA removed gasoline and canned food from the ration list effective the next day. Many people went to the nearest service station and told the man there to "Fill 'er up!" Governor Gates lifted the 35 m.p.h. speed limit in the state. Many churches held services to give thanks for the end of the war. It was V-J day in New Castle the next day, August 15, 1945. The best news for many became official: no more troops from Europe would be sent to the Pacific.

The Japanese insisted that it would take twelve days for the cease-fire order to reach all units, and the American fleet off Japan stayed on alert. Reports of a fighter attack and ack-ack fire against a photo reconnaissance B-29 over Tokyo brought new jitters. MacArthur ordered the Japanese to send envoys immediately to set arrangements for a formal surrender signing. Finally, on August 22, word came that American troops would begin landing in Japan on August 28 to begin the occupation. MacArthur himself arrived there on August 30. At last, on September 2, Allied brass and the Japanese signed formal documents ending the war on board the battleship USS *Missouri* anchored in the bay at Tokyo.

The War Production Board removed controls on the manufacture of automobiles on August 24, allowing Chrysler to announce that it would change over to car production as soon as possible. Some area industries continued war production. General Eisenhower announced that four hundred thousand soldiers would stay in Germany, while the other 2.5 million troops in Europe would be coming home before the end of winter. OPA reduced point values for meat, cheese, and butter at the end of August, taking the pinch out of some rationed items without ending the system. Early in September the navy reduced the release points for naval aviators to forty-four. Other officers needed forty-nine, still a considerable break. When new point requirements came out for army officers, Gemma's hopes were dashed when she read that a first lieutenant still needed eighty-five points. Still, it could be worse. All ranks above captain needed one hundred points. Uncle Sam wanted to hold on to his officers a little while longer.

Whole units returning to the East Coast from Europe now were listed in the paper so that families at home might know when to expect them. A picture in the paper showed the *Queen Mary* with all fifteen thousand men of the 35th Division aboard. Orrin could not make this trip, however, nor could nearly three thousand other members of the division who lay dead in Europe. As the troops came home, labor strikes at plants cutting back their production rose dramatically.

On September 11, Orville Hammond returned from the Philippines to report to the Naval Air Training Center at Memphis for advanced radio instruction. He had served six months on PBM patrol bombers based in the Philippines, flying convoy coverage and antisubmarine patrols. The Memphis assignment was surely temporary, Marie hoped. A week later fate proved how random the lottery of death could be. Pfc. Charles Glynn's parents of North 19th Street learned that he had been killed in a plane accident in Japan on August 29. His family members comforted each other at a requiem high mass at St. Anne's in New Castle.

At last, on September 17, General MacArthur announced that the 38th Division would be sent home soon. More than fifty-four hundred Hoosier boys went overseas with the Cyclone Division in 1944, including Clay Grubbs. Their families could look forward to their return with the expectation that a piece of the American dream might be within their grasp. The national reconversion director said in Washington that all restrictions on the construction of private homes would be lifted on October 15. There would be no price controls on homes to prolong the shortage, in spite of requests for them from OPA, but price ceilings on building materials would be continued. Other families took heart at the news that General Marshall said the point totals for discharge might be revised downward to as low as sixty by November 1.

Eager relatives scanned the paper each day for signs of their loved ones' units arriving in ports on the coasts. Nearly every day there were a dozen or more dockings with all or parts of various infantry, engineer, or support outfits debarking. On October 2, over six hundred of the 38th Division men arrived at Camp Atterbury, including the 151st Infantry Regiment of which Clay was a member. They were promised discharges by the end of the week after interviews, physicals, filling out forms, and turning in equipment. A week later, Clay was home. He could finally share the sight of their son James, born on D-Day, and begin getting used to being a civilian again. Clay stopped in at Cliff Payne's menswear store the week he returned to see about some new civvies.

The day after he returned, the army announced that it would release eighty million pounds of butter it was holding. Housewives everywhere looked forward to this event almost as much as the return of their husbands. Kenny Thompson's brother Clarence arrived back in Hagerstown October 9. George Woods from Ed's high school class returned for good on October 13 after nine months overseas as a B-17 tail gunner.

October dragged on for those whose loved ones remained far away. The newspaper was still the best source of news about units coming home and everyone in New Castle followed it religiously, hoping that the news would all be good from now on. There were many unfinished stories that began to play out in the paper. On October 4, a service for SSgt. Vaughn Bowers took place in the

Christian Church in the little Henry County town of Cadiz. The War Department had finally notified his widow Louise of their "presumptive finding of death." This meant that after checking all the prisoners in all the German camps and comparing accounts of the loss of Bowers' B-17 over Schweinfurt, the decision had been made that he must have gone down with his plane. His remains were never found.

The next day the paper announced that F2/C Paul Carter had become the latest casualty from the county, bringing the total for the war to 114. Carter's wife learned that he had died on the destroyer USS *Whitehurst* in the storm of kamikaze attacks during the Okinawa campaign. Reported missing in action like so many others because his body could not be found, a decision on Carter's fate had to await the end of the war when there was more time to sort things out. So, too, with MM2/C Guy Amburgey. The navy reviewed the information and declared him dead. He had last been seen in his gun position on his ship on April 14, 1945, during an attack. There was "no hope for his survival," the telegram to his wife read.

The Japanese had paid the price. Not until early in October did there appear the first photo of Hiroshima after the atomic attack. A dark river wound through pale rubble marked by bulldozed streets. Only telephone poles and a few shells of concrete buildings remained standing. In contrast to this grim reminder of what the war might have been for Americans, troop arrivals continued to be noted in the paper. On October 9, forty thousand arrived, including most of the 70th Division aboard *Queen Mary.* Seven to ten thousand on a given day was routine. The War Department announced that it would return 1.25 million men from the Pacific by the end of February.

In November, the war crimes tribunal opened at Nuremberg. High Nazi officials appeared in the dock, on trial for their lives for crimes against humanity. The hearings began with "not guilty" pleas by the accused, but months passed before the verdicts became final. The details of German secret plans and strategies made for interesting reading while Americans waited for the troops to come home.

On November 24 meat rationing ended, and with it ended the control of butter, margarine, and lard. Supplies were still rather skimpy, but at least the annoyance of keeping track of ration coupons and waiting in line while clerks counted the coupons and gave red points in change would end. OPA cautioned the public to hold on to the ration books, however, because sugar was still rationed and coupons would be required for its purchase. For this reason, millions of Americans kept their ration books in a safe place for years, just in case rationing came back in the readjustment period after the war. Price controls in the form of ceilings remained on most meat items as OPA tried to keep merchants from obtaining market prices they considered too high. The grocery stores responded with big ads featuring pork, mostly.

Hurry Up and Wait

With the Japanese finished, it was just a question of time before everyone but those servicemen who had been in for less than two years would be home. Ed had to await orders before he could leave, so the only thing to do was to make the best of it. He was able to write more regularly now, and he still made runs to places of interest when he had the opportunity. He did not expect ever to be able to take a ship to Europe at his own expense when the war was over. Paris was an easy destination because there was always some communication or report to be delivered there, so he went several times. It was on one of these trips that he got a glimpse of General Eisenhower at Supreme Headquarters. Only rarely was there an opportunity to see shows put on for the soldiers, but in this way Ed had the good fortune to see Bob Hope about this same time. He also looked around Koblenz, upriver where the Mosel entered the Rhine, because his father had been there on occupation duty after the Great War twenty-six years before.

More of a highlight, however, was looking up Miss Rucker, the speech and drama teacher from New Castle High School. Ed knew that she was in Paris after May 1 because there had been a note from her in a copy of the *Courier-Times* he had received in Germany. When he had finished a mission that had taken him to Paris, he looked her up at the Red Cross center in the city, and found her. This made only the second person from New Castle he had seen while overseas, and she was pleased to see him. Ed received an unexpected bonus as a result of this meeting, however. Miss Rucker had managed to secure a small supply of ice cream, and she offered some of it to Ed. After almost a year and a half of army food, the sight of real ice cream was almost miraculous. Rarely had anything tasted quite as good as ice cream in Paris that fall.

A veritable flood of babies seemed to be arriving in New Castle now. Gemma's sister Maxine delivered their first at the Clinic on November 4, and she and Kenny named her Julie. Dark-haired, round-faced, and pleasant, she was the first granddaughter born in a house of daughters and she was an instant favorite. Martha and Phil Perry had their second child, a daughter, just three days earlier. Several other young married women on Plum Street had their first babies that fall and winter, many of them just ten or eleven months after their husbands returned home after being gone to the war. Jess took a picture of Gemma with Jimmy, and cousins Mary Cowan Roland and Marguerite Cowan Bitner, both with their new babies, in front of the house on Plum Street one sunny day late in November.

Coming Home, at Last

To prepare for Ed's return, Gemma began searching in early summer for a house to rent. After two months of looking, she found one on 21st Street, a few blocks from Plum Street, and considered herself lucky. It even included a refrigerator, which was a real find, since appliances of all kinds were very scarce in every town in America. None had been made since 1941. She took little Jimmy with her and spent many days there cleaning up and painting and making everything ready. She bought a bed, dresser, and chest, and had them delivered, and gradually put together some used furniture for the living room and kitchen, and moved the baby's bed so they could begin staying there in September. She picked out a set of sturdy KitchenCraft aluminum cookware as soon as it became available that fall, putting it in the cupboards ready for use. It had already been nearly two years since they had had a home together. Now it was ready, if only he would come home.

Very good news arrived with the paper on November 27. The army announced that veterans with seventy points should be out of the ETO by December 1, and those with sixty-five to seventy points should depart during the first week of December. Even GIs with fifty-five to sixty-five points were due home by January 1. Now Gemma's hope began to rise. There might be less than a month to wait!

In mid-November the 29th AA Group finally received orders to report to Le Havre for departure November 25. They took trains farther north into Germany, then into Belgium, then through France, sleeping in the seats for what seemed like months, but was actually nine days. At the innumerable station stops they could get out and stretch their legs, but the men believed they had gone through every town in France before they finally arrived in Le Havre and took trucks to the docks.

Uncle Sam had seen fit that some of his boys would take a U.S. Navy cruiser home from the war, and the 29th Group walked up the plank onto the USS *Helena* for the trip back home. This was good news, because cruisers were fast, and better news because they were not tossed around as much as in the little destroyers. Not twenty minutes after they left France behind on the morning of November 25th, the wind and seas picked up, making for a somewhat stormy ride that November on the North Atlantic.

The navy was famed and envied for its food, and Ed learned firsthand how good it could be. The first morning out, breakfast featured real eggs! He had not eaten an egg in its recognizable form since he had left the United States, and here there were huge pans filled with eggs fried, poached, hard boiled, and scrambled. He chose the fried eggs and ate them by the platterfuls, cutting into the soft centers and mopping up with bread, washed down with coffee that had not been boiled. It made all those K rations seem worth it to have a breakfast like that, courtesy of Uncle Sam and his navy.

Ed had just loaded up on fried eggs again the second morning out when the tossing of the ship made him wonder if he was feeling as good as the day before. Just to be sure, he looked arou. for a head, and found one that some poor sailor was just about to finish mopping clean. Breakfast reversed course just as Ed wen through the door. Neither of them was very happy with the re sult. After his bout of seasickness the second day, the trip went better. At a cruiser's speed, the voyage only took five days, just like a fast liner. On the fifth morning land came in sight and they soon passed the narrows and entered New York harbor, passing in front of the Statue of Liberty. Everyone who could stand crowded the decks to get a glimpse of home. Docking and debarking seemed to take hours, but they finally reached Grand Central Station. While Ed waited there, he got a call through to Gemma in New Castle telling her that he was back in the country and guessing what day he might be home. His detachment then took a train for Camp Kilmer, New Jersey. Here the 29th AA Group said their good-byes and took separate trains for camps near their homes.

Ed's train, loaded with soldiers from every kind of unit, seemed to crawl through Pennsylvania and Ohio to Cincinnati's Union Terminal. Here there was another layover and wait. Finally they pulled out for Camp Atterbury, south of Indianapolis, arriving early in the morning of December 5. Atterbury was the discharge facility for most of Indiana, and here thousands of soldiers were impatiently enduring the process many others had already gladly suffered. The army did not want to let go of all its officers and men immediately, and an officer told Ed that he would be held in the Reserve for the time being, but could go home for now.

With that news, he turned in the equipment that belonged to the government and took his footlockers to the camp depot. A train took him to Indianapolis, where he boarded a bus to the old traction station in New Castle where his father had seen him off in 1942. There was no brass band or celebration, no crowds or excitement, but there was a taxi there which took him to the house on 22nd Street, where he arrived about 7 P.M. Wednesday, December 5, 1945. He was home at last.

Gemma welcomed him with hugs and tears, hardly believing that he was actually, really home, all for her. Like millions of other soldiers, the few people who had known and loved him had wished and prayed mightily for his return and, when it came, few others noticed. The army required him to return to Camp Atterbury after just a day and two nights for more processing and paperwork, so he put his uniform back on and went, returning

Saturday afternoon. Much of his first day home had been spent getting a look at the sixteen-month-old son he had never seen, and getting used to the wonder of it all. Jimmy already knew several words, but he did not want to have much to do with his father just at first.

For Sunday dinner the three of them went with Fred and Lillian out to the farmhouse where Lillian's sister Mabel and her husband Casher had raised their nine children. Florence, the oldest, had just married Jim Swann, freshly returned from the Philippines, and they were both there as everyone enjoyed a big dinner and then sat and visited in the afternoon. There were lots of questions for the returned heroes, and thoughts of the ones who did not come back. They had questions about people they had known, but had not heard about since school or that last notice in the paper.

It was a quiet Christmas that year, spent in trying to believe they had finally broken through to the future. Heavy snow fell a few days before Christmas, reminding Ed of the weather in Belgium. Sleet and freezing rain kept travel to a minimum on Christmas Day. The celebration of the birth of Christ that December of the last year of the war was a modest one for Gemma and Ed. It was a rebirth for them. In the tradition of both of their families, gifts were modest: little personal things for the two of them, and a toy for Jimmy.

On New Year's Eve 1945, the two of them quietly drank the champagne he had brought from France to welcome the future, which was finally theirs to share.

Epilogue

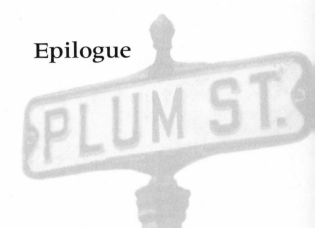

Civilian Life

Now LIFE COULD resume in the new year of 1946, and the best part of it was that there was no big hurry to find a job or do anything in particular. Gemma had carefully saved Ed's generous army pay, giving them an enviable nest egg of over $2,000. Ed chose the 52/20 plan offered by the army, giving him $20 per week for the next fifty-two weeks, a cushion large enough in itself to keep them in groceries and rent. The government did not want millions of returned GIs to all go out looking for work the day after they got home. He rested and ate and paid long visits to his mother and father so they could savor having him home again. At the house in the hollow they sat around the stove in the kitchen on winter days, just as they had done before the war. He looked up George Woods, Harry Ridout, Charlie Purvis, and other friends, talking about what they had seen and about plans for the future.

Soon after Ed returned, Gemma sent him to the Sanitary Meat Market on Broad Street for some beef, which was still in very short supply due to the government's planning mistakes. As he waited a few minutes before the market opened, a small crowd of perhaps ten or twelve, mostly women, gathered behind him. When the owner unlocked the door, a crush began which nearly knocked him to the floor inside. Using the coupons out of the ration books like any other civilian, he bought the meat he had come for, but was so disgusted by the lack of decorum he had seen that he never went back.

This time he did not have to wear his uniform to apply for work when he decided it was time, as his father had done after the last war. There were jobs about. He worked off and on at the Chrysler and at Sears and Roebuck on Broad Street, and even went into the service station business briefly with Phil Perry, pumping gas and painting cars. The money Americans had saved up when there was precious little that was legal to spend it on served as a reservoir of capital to fuel the reconversion to civilian production that was rocky at times but successful.

Like most young couples after the war, Gemma and Ed dreamed of a house of their own. Their savings offered a down payment on that dream, but with the growth of the industries in New Castle during and after the war, too many people wanted houses that the government declared would not be built while the war was still to be won. Reconversion meant plenty of jobs in the lumber industry in the Northwest as returned GIs donned hard hats and began feeding trees into sawmills. While Gemma and Ed rented, and then shared a house with Martha and Phil for a while, they looked about and found a man who would build and finish a modest house for them. They bought a lot on South Fifteenth Street, about a block from the high school, and waited for the materials to become available. For $9,000, financed in part with an FHA GI loan, they built their home and got on with the business of living.

Gemma and Ed considered going to college on the GI Bill as so many returned veterans did, but neither Jess and Ethel nor Fred and Lillian thought it was a good idea. Why would they want to do a thing like that? It would take them away from New Castle, perhaps forever, and they did not want that to happen to their children again. Gemma thought about this with Ed and discussed it many times, wondering if they ought to make the move the coming fall, or the next, but in the end, they decided not to go.

They lived the dream so many did not return to enjoy. Another son was born to them early in 1947 in their new house. They moved from 15th Street down to a house Ed built on land his father purchased after the war on Riley Road, and a third son

With the war behind them, Gemma and Ed settled down to a family
life made possible by the sacrifice of so many. By early 1947 they had a
second son, Stewart, and this time Ed could be home for it all. Jim,
born in 1944, was almost sixteen months old before his father saw him
for the first time.

was born there in 1952. Ed went into business for himself building homes along Riley Road until later in the 1950s, when he
learned the heating and cooling business and joined a firm in a
nearby town. Gemma stayed at home to raise the boys until they
reached school age, when she began to do secretarial work. They
moved away from New Castle in 1959, never to return. The three
boys grew up in the 1950s, graduated from high school in the
1960s and early 1970s, and all three graduated from college, ful-
filling the dream Gemma and Ed had pondered, then passed up.

With four daughters, Jess and Ethel eventually counted
twelve grandchildren, as each of the daughters had three children of their own. As the war ended, all four daughters lived in
New Castle or Hagerstown, but they were soon drawn to other
towns. Wanda went to Kokomo, Indiana, but ended up in Indianapolis, and Marie in Lansing, Michigan, then Phoenix. Maxine
moved with Kenny to Roanoke, Virginia, then to Omaha, and
then to Phoenix. Jess and Ethel moved to the north end of New

Castle after the war. Jess retired from the Chrysler after forty-two years, and Ethel became a licensed practical nurse and retired from Henry County Hospital. Their twelve grandchildren scattered all over the country, from Seattle to Florida and everywhere in between.

Lillian and Fred lived the rest of their lives in New Castle, too. They moved farther down Riley Road in 1950 to a bigger house with acreage where Fred farmed and raised livestock after coming home from work each day at the Chrysler, where he spent thirty-seven years, many of them as a foreman in the forge shop. It was here that they showed their grandsons how to live their dream of a quiet life spent growing much of their own food in the garden, and raising cattle, hogs, and chickens on the grain and hay produced on the farm.

*   *   *

Sometimes it seemed almost as though there had been no war, except in their memories. And there the war would play out many times, coming back in waves of remembrance and emotion recreating the sense of dread and determination they all had known. Every man and woman who came back to Plum Street, or who had spent the war there, carried a different version of it with them in their minds. They did not spend all their time thinking about it, nor was it ever completely erased from their thoughts. For many years they rarely if ever talked about it. When they did, it was usually in quiet tones, with others who had been there, or who had known the home front as Gemma and her sisters had known it.

Sometimes the war came to them in a startling way. Sarah Wright Grubbs discovered some of what had happened only years later, when she noticed pale streaks on Clay's leg that looked like scars. Clay explained to her that in a night attack by Japanese forces in the Philippines, he had been wounded by shrapnel. The friend who shared the foxhole with him that night had been killed beside him, and enemy dead littered the ground in front of his unit's position the next morning. Clay's wound was not life-

A crowd gathers at the Sanitary Meat Market on Broad Street in
New Castle in 1946. Price controls and rationing snafus throughout
the war caused scenes like this in towns all across the country, and the
disruptions did not end with the surrender of Japan.

threatening, and he didn't want to worry Sarah at home, so he
had never said anything about it.

For ten years after the war, many of those from New Castle
who died overseas came home one by one. Granite markers went
up in cemeteries across the county to commemorate their final
resting places. Glen Cowan's gravestone in South Mound Cemetery in New Castle has a B-24 etched into the granite. Billy Ridgway eventually came home to his final rest at the Mooreland
Cemetery. Elmer Pfenninger, James Capshaw, and many, many
others finally found their rest at home or in battlefield cemeteries
around the world. Some, of course, never came home. Flossie
Flannery's small picture is today preserved on a ceramic disc
atop her memorial stone in Mt. Summit Cemetery. If you visit the
U.S. Military Cemetery at Colleville in Normandy, above D-Day's
Omaha Beach, you will find Robert Pitts's name carved high on a
wall in front of thousands of white marble crosses.

There were other, more pressing things which could occupy the attention of those who returned. For most the war became a very large given, a divide separating before and after, adolescent and mature, then and now. For the most part, they let the war stay as it had been: put away in trunks and boxes, kept safe in mothballs, available for others to discover, but not offered.

The war was the defining experience of their lives, even more than the depression had been. For all the decades to follow, there would be "after the war" and "before the war." Over those years fact became legend, holding in their memories the fears and heartbreak, the yearning, and the overwhelming joy of reunion that they had known when they saved the good in the world from unspeakable darkness.

The War Comes to a New Generation

On a very warm afternoon in the summer of 1957, a little boy nearly five climbed up into the family sedan with his mother to go to the grocery store. This was the time in Jess and Ethel Moles' hometown of New Castle, Indiana, before there were super-markets as we know them today. The boy's family went each week to the Ridgway grocery store on 21st Street to do their shopping for the coming week.

The store had wood floors swept clean by Mrs. Ridgway and shelves covered with brightly patterned oilcloth. Mr. Ridgway was the meat cutter and sausage maker. He would put ham salad into a folded paper tray and wrap it with white paper and tie a string around it to keep it from coming unwrapped until it got home. If the boy's mother wanted cubed steaks she could choose the ones she liked by pointing at them in the cooler, then Mr. Ridgway would put a sheet of white paper on the scales and lay them on it as she picked them out, weigh the total and calculate the price on the scale, write the price on the package with a black grease pencil, then wrap it up with string, just like the ham salad. He had meat in the cooler and cheese and eggs and lunchmeat like the pickle-pimiento loaf that was a favorite. There was bacon, bologna, sausage, potato salad, and dill pickles. Mrs. Ridgway ran the cash register and helped keep the shelves in order. They were kindly people and seemed very old to the boy then, although they were only in their late fifties. They were his grandparents' age, so they had to be old.

It was their habit for Mr. Ridgway to come up to the middle of the store to the cash register to help Mrs. Ridgway if there were no customers that he was helping back in the meat department. This particular summer afternoon they both waited on the boy's mother at the register after she had made her selections at the meat cooler and in the rest of the store. Someone set the boy up on the counter as Mr. Ridgway put the cans and packages in the boxes and Mrs. Ridgway took the cash and gave back the change. Mrs. Ridgway asked the little boy if he was being a big helper today and if he would be in school that fall. Mr. Ridgway came around and commented what a big boy he was and asked if he knew what he wanted to be when he grew up. They asked things and acted in such a way that made a boy nearly five feel very good, and he smiled his best smile back at them and answered their questions. Mr. Ridgway helped carry the groceries to the car, shut the door, said thank you, and invited them back. They got in the front seat and as she started the car and pulled away, the boy asked her why Mr. and Mrs. Ridgway were always so nice to him and always wanted to talk and ask questions. The boy's mother, Gemma Moles Smith, answered his question, and in doing so, opened the door of history for another generation. It turns out that things had been happening right along before the little boy appeared on the scene.

Gemma, my mother, told me that there was no set number of children mothers and fathers could have. We had three children in our family and I was the youngest. Some had two. When Mr. and Mrs. Ridgway were younger they had only had one, a little boy just like me whom they named William after Mr. Ridgway, and called Billy. Mr. and Mrs. Ridgway liked me because I was well behaved and reminded them of their boy when he was little. He had grown up and gotten big and strong, but when the war began he went into the army and he had been sent away to fight. One day before the war ended he was killed, so they did not have their boy any more. My mother told me my father had been in the army in the war, too, and he had been sent off to fight like Billy Ridgway, but he had come back safely. She said that if Billy Ridgway had come home from the war, he would be in his early thirties, just a couple of years younger than my father. Mr. and Mrs. Ridgway's only child, their little boy, had been killed in the war, and they would never have any more children, nor any grandchildren.

I sat quietly the rest of the way home, thinking about this. But that sunny afternoon I learned there had been a time before the days I had known when something dark and terrible had happened, something that could take little boys away forever; something called "The War."

*   *   *

At Moles family holiday gatherings over the years, there was more and more talk about Plum Street, especially stories about how the girls had grown up in the depression and the war. Family albums began to fascinate me, and I discovered pictures of my own uncle Orville Hammond in his U.S. Navy uniform, Uncle Kenny Thompson wearing the shoulder patch and flier's cap of the 8th Air Force, my own father in his summer tans with the lieutenant's bars on his shoulders, and Wanda and Bill at our house for the holidays after the war. Pictures of my grandfather Jess in his navy whites and my other grandfather Fred in his army uniform of the Great War came out of storage and fed my curiosity enough to prompt me to ask some questions. When we visited the homes of our Smith and Moles relatives there were even more photos to see. There were pictures of my mother and aunts when they were little girls, with Toby, and with their friends, graduating from high school, as newlyweds, and with their husbands soon after the war ended. At one of the Moles family reunions nearly fifty years after the war, Maxine's daughter Julie observed that the Moles girls and their spouses experienced nearly every aspect of the depression and war years. "Someone," she remarked, "ought to collect this and write it all down."

*   *   *

This work is gratefully dedicated to Orrin Grubbs, Elmer Pfen-ninger, Billy Ridgway, James Capshaw, and all those who served in uniform and on the home front during the Second World War. So many paid with their lives and with grievous injuries so that all of us could live in freedom. Their faith and sacrifice can never be honored adequately, and the lessons of those years, purchased at such heavy cost, must never be distorted or lost.

Sources

The War Comes to Plum Street grew out of the recollections of people who lived in New Castle, Indiana, in the 1920s, 1930s, and 1940s. Oral history interviews conducted between 1990 and 1994 provided the substance of the lives around which the story was built. Those interviewed included Edward M. Smith, Gemma Moles Smith, Sarah Wright Madison, Vernie Griffin (interviewed with Julie Thompson Calhoun), Marie Moles Hammond, Walter Dugan, Judy Capshaw Van Matre, Barney Pfenninger, Orville Hammond (interviewed with Julie Thompson Calhoun), Phil and Martha Perry, Harry Ridout, Charlotte Walker, Maxine and Kenny Thompson (interviewed by Julie Thompson Calhoun), and group interviews (with Julie Thompson Calhoun) of Ethel Moles and her daughters Gemma, Maxine, Marie, and Wanda.

Much of the framework of the events of the war came out of the pages of the New Castle *Courier-Times.* I read issues of the 1920s and 1930s intermittently, and read every issue from mid-1939 through early 1946. The local paper allowed me to experience the progress of the war as those at home had done: one day at a time.

The New Castle High School yearbook *Rosennial* for 1939–1945 provided insights and a look at the faces of many of the people who were featured in this book.

Additional details on places, dates, and chronology came from the following works:

Ambrose, Stephen. *Citizen Soldiers.* New York: Simon and Schuster, 1997.

Ambrose, Stephen. *D-Day: June 6, 1944: The Climactic Battle of World War II.* New York: Simon and Schuster, 1994.

Brinkley, David. *Washington Goes to War.* New York: Alfred A. Knopf, 1988.

Esposito, Vincent. *West Point Atlas of American Wars.* Vol. II: *1900–1953.* New York: Praeger Publishers, 1959.

Fussell, Paul. *Wartime.* New York: Oxford University Press, 1989.

Jablonski, Edward. *Flying Fortress.* Garden City, N.Y.: Doubleday and Co., 1965.

Keegan, John. *The Second World War.* New York: Penguin Books USA, 1989.

Keegan, John. *Six Armies in Normandy.* New York: Penguin Books, 1983.

Middlebrook, Martin. *The Schweinfurt-Regensburg Mission.* New York: Charles Scribner's Sons, 1983.

Ryan, Cornelius. *The Longest Day.* New York: Simon and Schuster, 1959.

Shirer, William L. *20th Century Journey.* Vol. II: *The Nightmare Years 1930–1940.* Boston: Little, Brown & Co., 1984.

Sommerville, Donald. *World War II Day by Day.* Greenwich, Conn.: Dorset Press, 1989.

Stanton, Shelby. *World War II Order of Battle.* New York: Galahad Books, 1991.

Utley, Jonathan G. *An American Battleship at Peace and War: The U.S.S. Tennessee.* Lawrence: University of Kansas Press, 1991.

Whiting, Charles. *Siegfried: The Nazis' Last Stand.* New York: Stein and Day, 1982.

Index

Index

BRUCE C. SMITH is a native of New Castle, Indiana. He became involved in writing this local history of World War II while completing his Ph.D. at the University of Notre Dame.